Concepts of Programming Languages

Concepts of Programming Languages

Gracie Mckenzie

MURPHY & MOORE

www.murphy-moorepublishing.com

Murphy & Moore Publishing,
1 Rockefeller Plaza,
New York City, NY 10020, USA

ISBN: 978-1-63987-127-8

Cataloging-in-Publication Data

Concepts of programming languages / Gracie Mckenzie.
    p. cm.
Includes bibliographical references and index.
ISBN 978-1-63987-127-8
1. Programming languages (Electronic computers). 2. Languages, Artificial. 3. Electronic data processing.
4. Computer programming. I. Mckenzie, Gracie.
QA76.7 .C66 2022
005.13--dc23

For information on all Murphy & Moore Publications
visit our website at www.murphy-moorepublishing.com

Contents

Preface

Any formal language which consists of a set of instructions and is capable of producing different types of output is defined as a programming language. These are utilized in programming computers for the implementation of various algorithms. The three major components which describe a programming language are semantics, syntax and type systems. The surface of any programming language is known as syntax. It is textual in nature and makes use of sequences of words, numbers and punctuations. Semantics are divided into static semantics and dynamic semantics. Type systems are responsible for classification of different types of values and expression into types. Programming languages is an upcoming field that has undergone rapid development over the past few decades. This book is a valuable compilation of topics, ranging from the basic to the most complex theories and principles in the field of programming languages. It presents this complex subject in the most comprehensible and easy to understand language. This book will serve as a valuable source of knowledge for those interested in this field.

A short introduction to every chapter is written below to provide an overview of the content of the book:

Chapter 1 - A programming language is a set of written commands, instructions and other syntax used to create a software program for producing various forms of desired outputs. Programming languages have common principle components such as variables, control structures, data structures and syntax. This chapter aims to provide an introduction to the reader to the diverse aspects of programming languages; **Chapter 2 -** The languages that programmers use to write codes are called high-level languages. These codes can be compiled into low-level languages, which are directly recognized by the computer hardware. Programming languages have evolved over the years with the latest ones belonging to the fifth generation. The different levels and generations of programming languages are discussed at length in this chapter; **Chapter 3 -** All programming languages have particular aspects without which they would be rendered inoperative. Syntax, which refers to the set of rules determining correct statements or expressions, data type, structured programming, programming style, and control flow are certain aspects of programming languages are covered in this chapter; **Chapter 4 -** Programming paradigm refers to the style or way of programming. It is an approach to solving problems using the tools and techniques available to programming languages. Every programming language has its own unique paradigm. Object-oriented programming, aspect-oriented programming, automata-oriented programming, flow-based programming, non-structured programming, etc. are the types of programming paradigms which are examined closely in this chapter; **Chapter 5 -** Certain programming languages are extensively used worldwide by programmers due to their accessibility, availability or ease-of-usage. This chapter sheds light on some prominent programming languages like C++, Java, Python and the C programming language for a thorough understanding of the subject matter.

Finally, I would like to thank my fellow scholars who gave constructive feedback and my family members who supported me at every step.

Gracie Mckenzie

Introduction to Programming Language

A programming language is a set of written commands, instructions and other syntax used to create a software program for producing various forms of desired outputs. Programming languages have common principle components such as variables, control structures, data structures and syntax. This chapter aims to provide an introduction to the reader to the diverse aspects of programming languages.

Language has been our primary means of communication and human interaction for thousands of years. For a community, the language contained the words that the people need to communicate, words themselves are abstract, but they indicate the meaning, they point to objects or actions, etc.

When you look at your computer, you'll find it's not so much different. There are many pieces of hardware and software that need to communicate with each other. Your application is reacting to the mouse and keyboard or even the mic; it can read files from your disk storage and so on. But at the end of the day, the machine understands nothing but bits, 1s, and 0s, the combination of which creates meaning.

The very earliest computers were actually programmed by changing ones and zeros manually, alternating the circuit and the wiring. Of course, it was not easy to create many programs as most were used for specific applications only, and they were gigantic in size so they were quite limited. That's why the creation of programming languages was a revolutionary step that took the field to another level. Unlike normal languages, keywords in programming languages are limited, and by combining these keywords, developers are able to create different types of programs. There are special pieces of software that turn the code you write into machine language that the machine understands. So what is programming language? In short, a programming language is the set of instructions through which humans interact with computers.

The code is pretty much like writing a paragraph of instruction or creating a to-do list to computers. Unlike us humans, the to-do list and instructions you write for the computer has to be extremely detailed and written in some logic.

With code and programming, you can get the computer to draw complex shapes and create rich computer graphics, and then create programs that understand game mechanics and help you build games that feel real with gravity and particle collision, with these programs you can create the most intense and immersive games of all sorts.

With code and programming, you can create and send content all over the world with your blog and personal website and style your blog to meet your style. You can build tech-driven business solutions and reach a wider range of customer and cater to a wider range of needs.

Furthermore, with code and programming, you can create smart home applications, like an automated pet feeder, a smart mirror or even create a robot that can help around with household tasks and be your virtual assistant to talk to and understand you. Unlike what many people think, there's a lot of art involved in computer engineering and computer science.

Here is the code to write "Hello World!" in C programming language.

```
1 #include
2 int main()
3 {
4 printf("Hello, World!");
5 return 0;
6 }
```

Uses of Programming Languages

Web Development

If you're interested in building websites there are two intertwining parts to look into.

First, there's front-end development, which is the part of web development that creates the application that runs on your browser and adjusts the styling, the colors, the interactions. It's basically concerned with what the user of a website sees. You are reading this blog on some screen which is shown to you by front-end code. Front-end basics start with HTML and CSS with use of JavaScript. Javascript has become one of the most dominant languages in the last few years for front-end work.

The other part for creating websites is back-end development, which is related to the server, the computer that runs the website software and serves it to the world. It's mostly concerned with routing, which pages to deliver to the user when they visit a certain URL, it also communicates with the database that stores the website's information and sends this data over to the user. Back-end development is where the magic happens and there are many options to choose from when it comes to a programming language, you can stick to Javascript just like in front-end development, or go with PHP, Ruby, C#, Elixir, Python, Erlang.

Game Development

Game development is one of the most interesting tracks there is, many developers enjoy it and there are developers who develop games just for having fun. Creating games requires what's called a game engine, which is software that is used as the infrastructure for building the game and defines what the game has and what it can do. If you're familiar with Epic Games and Fortnight, Epic Games is, in fact, a game engine and Fortnight is built upon it. The languages used in game development are mostly C++, C# since it requires a lot of memory optimization and fast performance to create rich graphics. It's not limited to C++ and C#, however, and it kind of is about which engine you're using and which platform you're targeting, Lua and Java are also very famous candidates in this industry.

Mobile Development

Creating mobile applications is a little tricky, as there is more than one operating system for mobiles and the different operating system would require different languages for these applications. An operating system is the piece of software on your device that is responsible for dealing with the hardware of this device, it's the layer that sits between the application you create and the hardware, whether it's a mic or a touchscreen or GPS. The most two common operating systems are Android and IOS. Android is most commonly used in Samsung while IOS is used in Apple. To create Android apps, you'd need either Java or Kotlin, and for creating IOS applications you'd need Objective-C or Swift. Recently, it became possible to create mobile applications for both Android and IOS using Javascript or Dart.

What are the Most Popular Programming Languages?

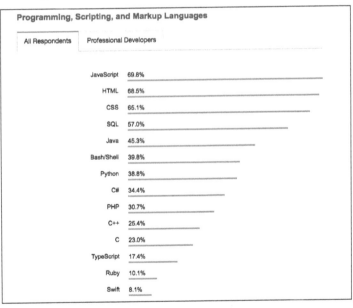

According to the Stack Overflow Developer Survey of 2018 where more than 100,000 developers are surveyed about their development career. The most popular industry field was found to be web development with more than 57% of developers working as back-end developers, and 37% working as front-end developers. This earns JavaScript the first place as the most popular programming language of all, followed by Java, then Python. Github's 2017 Octoverse showed similar results with JavaScript being the most popular language, followed by Python, Java, and then Ruby.

Generic Programming

Generic programming is a programming method that is based in finding the most abstract representations of efficient algorithms. That is, you start with an algorithm and find the most general set of requirements that allows it to perform and to perform efficiently. The amazing thing is that many different algorithms need the same set of requirements and there are multiple implementations of these requirements.

Generic programming arose out of Stepanov's work with Ada Language, and was then moved over to C++ to form the Standard Template Library. It's also been argued that Lisp supported generic programming well before Stepanov's work, in the form of macros. Lisp Macros (combined with Dynamic Typing) allow one to express any code fragment in terms of its barest parameters, allowing a level of abstraction that Template Meta programming is only beginning to match.

In some ways, generic programming is simply Well Factored Code. The process of breaking a system into reusable chunks will naturally lead to more abstract and generalized routines. One possible difference is that generic programming seeks to determine the most general representation in isolation, while Refactoring only generalizes code as the client system requires.

There is some confusion in C++ circles over the definition of Generic Programming, as the most common use for the STL is to provide parameterized container types. This is an instance of generic programming (it seeks to make code more general), but is more properly termed Parametric Polymorphism. Generic programming also covers parameterization over behavior (Higher Order Functions) and the use of interfaces or Type Classes to specify algorithm requirements.

Concept Cpp introduces Generic Programming into C++ in a more rigorous way and can be used, for example, to enforce requirements when using the STL.

Once And Only Once requires generalizing code via Re Factoring in order to simplify the implementation. By this method, many abstractions precipitate out of the code, abstractions that we wouldn't even see otherwise. There's the rub. How do you know what abstractions are useful? And how do you know your abstractions are usefully implemented? Yes, there are standard data structures and algorithms. But anything from a specific problem domain we probably won't understand enough to abstract until we write a few systems, as per the Rule of Three. Usually, writing the abstraction up-front is Premature Abstraction.

At the very least, you need to leave the abstraction in flux, even if you know up-front that you'll need an abstraction and know the problem domain. This is true even if that planning involved analyzing other implementations. Most of the tweaked library code ends up being refactored from the applications themselves.

Example of Generic Programming

To demonstrate the facilities and opportunities of the described methods a short example calculating the value of a determinant of a matrix is presented. While relatively simple in terms of mathematical sophistication, it provides the opportunity to show the procedures and methods of generic programming in the C++ programming language, which differ quite significantly from those usually prevalent in C++ run time expressions.

The selection of the C++ programming language for use in examples starting with the fact that

C++ is a multi-paradigmatic programming language, since it supports the following programming paradigms:

- Structured imperative – as a direct derivative of the C language.

- Object-oriented – it has direct support for inheritance and virtual functions.

- Functional programming – using libraries such as Boost Phoenix.

- Generic programming – using the Meta programming facilities.

The currently unique combination of features present in C++, makes it highly suitable for deployment in the field of scientific computing. Furthermore, not only is a mature tool chain for C++ available, but generic programming has been a part of the C++ programming language in the form of the STL form the initial standardization. The underlying design patterns have since been examined and elaborated. Additionally, the mechanisms directly supporting generic programming in C++ has been the subject of investigation as well as the performance penalties encountered due to abstractions in generic programming. With the advent of multi-core CPUs, the issue of parallelization has increased in importance and has been shown to be compatible with generic programming in C++. Finally, generic programming in C++ has already been successfully applied to scientific computing.

Concepts for scientific computing have already been impressively demonstrated as applicable for topological frameworks especially for the use in numerical schemes to solve partial differential equations due to physical problems. Building on such a firm base and since examples are already broadly available, this thesis attempts to investigate the interaction and interrelation of the realm of topology and geometry. A particular contribution of this work deals with the physical phenomena between both classical and quantum descriptions using integral descriptions, which are connected to the geometric aspects found in theory. While this work shares fundamental components of topology and their implementation, it is the abstract geometrical requirements which are a driving force for the investigation and application of programming concepts. As source code is much more easily constructed than ideas and thought patterns, it is the attitude with which to approach and solve problems which is of primary concern and which has been further developed.

Since the implementation makes use of both, run time and compile time structures, special consideration of elements crossing the border between these two worlds is required. To make efficient use of the facilities provided by meta programming, generic programming methods necessarily need to cross this border, as every of these points of evaluation embosses their respective advantages and disadvantages on the executable. Only their compound use can converge to optimal use.

Mathematical Description

Determinants have several applications from orientation tests to eigenvalue problems. A very simple algorithm to calculate the value of a determinant is to apply Laplace expansion to the determinant. While it is not the most efficient algorithm, it is well suited to demonstrate the use of a generic C++ program incorporating template Meta programming techniques, due to its recursive nature. For completeness the algorithm is outlined shortly before showing an implementation.

Given a matrix,

$$A = \begin{pmatrix} a_{11} & \cdots & a_{1n} \\ \vdots & \ddots & \vdots \\ a_{n1} & \cdots & a_{nn} \end{pmatrix}$$

Its determinant `det(A )` can be calculated by breaking it down into a series of smaller determinants. To this end a column `j` is `chosen` to arrive at the formula,

$$\det(A) = \sum_{1}^{n} (-1)^{i+j} a_{ij} \det(A_{ij})$$

The matrices A_{ij} are minors to the original matrix A , meaning that the rows and columns indicated by the indices are omitted to obtain A_{ij}. This procedure can be performed recursively until the determinant expressions are already known, such as is the case for 3×3 or 2×2 matrices or even the trivial case of a single value. The final expression is then of a form,

$$\det(A) = \sum_{\sigma} \left(sign(o) \prod_{i} a_{ij(i)} \right)$$

where σ is a permutation and sign (σ) the sign of the permutation. The recursive nature of the construction of this sum of products makes this algorithm well suited for implementation using the functional style required by template Meta programming.

It favours the implementation of an algorithm, how the correct access patterns into the data are to be constructed and how to combine this data. Thus while patterns of access will be completely available at compile time, the actual values, which will be manipulated may be supplied at run time. This distinction offers the compiler the complete set of information of memory accesses and it can therefore do its best to optimize them. However it should not go unnoted that the optimizer may be overwhelmed by the amount of data connected to the calculation as the size of matrices increases. While the consequences depend on the particular optimizer in use by the compiler, a sub optimal solution is the most likely result, with an abnormal termination being an extreme, but not impossible case.

The structural, purely compile time parts shall be given first. It constructs sequences of types, which encode the required operations. These operations are then carried out using a run time adaptor. These results in a clear and complete separation of the algorithmic structure created at compile time and the data structure used to store actual values. The compile time structure in this case is thus equivalent to a computer program written by a programmer by hand, only that it is constructed algorithmically from the structural rules provided by the mathematical description. The use of the algorithm requires the binding of the compile time prescription to run time values. Since only when combining a run time matrix accessor with the compile time structure an algorithm for the calculation of the value of the determinant is obtained. Otherwise the compile time structure merely implements a means of determining permutations as is evident from Equation $\det(A)=\sum_{\sigma}\left(sign(o)\prod_{i}a_{ij(i)}\right)$. This fact is also an indication that the description here is for demonstration purposes of a venue for generic programing, instead of considering it for high performance determinant calculations. In this regard it would be much more fitting to use an implementation following Gaussian elimination, LU or QR factorization, which, while still costly, have far less computational complexity than the number of permutations.

Compile Time Structure

It should be recalled that C++ meta programs are completely stateless, making recursion the only option to express repetitions. In the following the mpl name space indicator shall be short for `boost::mpl` which indicates the Boost MPL library.

Examining the terms involved in Equation $\det(A)=\sum_{1}^{n}(-1)^{i+j}a_{ij}\det(A_{ij})$ and Equation provides $\det(A)=\sum_{\sigma}\left(sign(o)\prod_{i}a_{ij(i)}\right)$ the guidelines for the definition of the compile time structure. The recursion to sub determinants is a means of construction all the required permutations required for the calculation of the determinant. Thus the necessary tasks may be broken down into the following steps:

- Determine a mechanism to encode a single element A_{ij}.

- Choose a representation for the multiplication of elements.

- Incorporate the sign associated with a permutation.

- Set an encoding for the sequence of additions.

A short outline of each of these steps is provided before the meta programs for the generation and manipulation are detailed. Access to any of the elements of the matrix data set is determined by the pair of indices. To encode this in a compile time structure, the indices are encoded into integral types such as `mpl::long_` and encapsulated into a `mpl::pair`. Thus, a matrix element A_{ij} shall be represented by:

Listing: A pair of indices encoded into an `mpl::pair`.

```
typedef mpl::long_<i> pos_i;

typedef mpl::long_<j> pos_j;


typedef mpl::pair<pos_i,pos_j>::type matrix_element_type;
```

This encoding concerns itself purely with the position ij, not with the value stored at the indicated position.

The multiplication of thusly encoded elements is accomplished utilizing a simple type sequence, the `mpl::vector`.

Listing: A sequence of pairs representing elements for multiplications.

```
typedef mpl::pair<pos_i1,pos_j1>::type matrix_element_type_1;

typedef mpl::pair<pos_i2,pos_j2>::type matrix_element_type_2;

typedef mpl::vector<matrix_element_type_1,

    matrix_element_type_2>::type mult_sequence;
```

In order to bond a sign, which is encoded as a integral constant, to the multiplication sequence an `mpl::pair` is used:

Listing: A sequence of pairs representing elements for multiplications.

```
typedef mpl::pair<sign_type,

    mult_sequence>::type mult_signed_sequence;
```

The resulting sequences are then collected within an `mpl::vector` which encodes all the necessary operations.

Listing: A sequence of pairs representing elements for multiplications.

```
typedef mpl::vector<mult_signed_sequence_1,

    mult_signed_sequence_2

    >::type determinant_structure_type;
```

Having outlined the means of representation, the means with which to generate these representations is still missing and is provided in the following.

Compile Time Meta Program

The top level of the compile time program takes the form of a simple struct containing the invocation of the recursive meta program components with the natural order of the indices. It accepts a sole input parameter indicating the size of the data set.

Listing: Top level of the determinant meta program.

```
template<long size>

struct determinant_struct_sequence

{

  typedef typename mpl::range_c<long,0,size>::type initial_map;

  typedef typename recursive_determinant<initial_map, initial_map,
```

```
        size>::type type;
```

```
};
```

The recursive part is given in the next piece of code. Particularly it is the specialization for two-dimensional data sets, which ends the recursion. It uses the well-known prescription to calculate the determinant in this case. To this end the correct mappings are extracted into the types x0, x1, y0 and y1. The obtained indices are then paired into an mpl::pair which specifies the access to a single point within the data set.

The pairs are enclosed into compile time containers, mpl::vectors, which encodes the multiplication of the pairs it contains. This has the benefit of making the multiplications extensible in a simple fashion. The two possible configurations of the two-dimensional case are represented by the types first and second for the term corresponding to the main diagonal and the off diagonal terms respectively.

Finally the two types corresponding to multiplication are packaged into another pair, which now links the sign with which the expression is to be evaluated to the multiplications, and assembled into another compile time container which is used to store the additive terms. It is this compile time container which is returned by the meta function.

Listing: A two-dimensional determinant serves as the end of the recursion of the determinant meta program.

```
template<typename MappingTypeX, typename MappingTypeY>

struct recursive_determinant<MappingTypeX, MappingTypeY, 2>

{

  typedef typename mpl::at_c<MappingTypeX,0>::type x0;

  typedef typename mpl::at_c<MappingTypeX,1>::type x1;


  typedef typename mpl::at_c<MappingTypeY,0>::type y0;

  typedef typename mpl::at_c<MappingTypeY,1>::type y1;


  typedef typename mpl::vector<typename mpl::pair<x0,y0>::type,
        typename mpl::pair<x1,y1>::type
        >::type first;


  typedef typename mpl::vector<typename mpl::pair<x1,y0>::type,
        typename mpl::pair<x0,y1>::type
```

```
            >::type second;


  typedef typename mpl::vector<

    typename mpl::pair<typename mpl::long_<1>::type,

        first>::type,

    typename mpl::pair<typename mpl::long_<-1>::type,

        second>::type>::type type;

};
```

The parameters are the same as in the two-dimensional case, with the exception of leaving the size unspecialized. The implementation then proceeds by omitting an element from one of the index sequences. The return type is constructed by folding a parameterized functor over the sequence of indices, whose consecutive results are gathered within a compile time container. The types generated by the repeated functor invocations encode the terms which need to be summed for the calculation of the value of the determinant.

Listing: Main recursion meta algorithm.

```
template<typename MappingTypeX, typename MappingTypeY,

    long matrix_size>

struct recursive_determinant

{

  typedef typename omit_view_c<MappingTypeY,

        0>::type remappedY;


  typedef typename mpl::range_c<long,

        0, matrix_size>::type steps;


  typedef typename mpl::fold<

    steps,

    mpl::vector<>,

    recurse<MappingTypeX, remappedY,

      typename mpl::at_c<MappingTypeY,0>::type>

  >::type type;
```

```
};
```

The functor follows Boost MPL semantics for functors by containing a nested struct named `apply`. The additional information of the outside mappings along with the currently discarded index are supplied directly to the recurse template, while the nested apply is fed with arguments accumulating previous evaluations as well as the current evaluation item during the fold.

It is the functor's task to construct determinants for the minors within the apply struct. To this end it omits an element from the so far unaltered index sequence, thus creating an expression corresponding to a minor of the given matrix, which in turn is passed to the recursive determinant meta function `recursive_determinant`. The element corresponding to the omitted row and column for the construction of the minor is again encoded in a pair along with the appropriate sign, which is also fully determined at compile time using a utility meta function sign. This element is multiplied with the result from the evaluation of the minor's determinant, as indicated in Equation $\det(A) = \sum_{1}^{n} (-1)^{i+j} a_{ij} \det(A_{ij})$. This multiplication is accomplished by appropriately inserting the signed local element into the compile time container generated for the sub determinant. The final result is obtained by concatenating the current result with the results obtained from previous calls using the `mpl::joint_view` construct.

Listing: Functor used to obtain the return type of the recursive determinant meta function.

```
template<typename MappingTypeX, typename MappingTypeY,

    typename LostType>

struct recurse

{

  template<typename StateType, typename c>

  struct apply

  {

  static const size_t length =

        mpl::size<MappingTypeX>::type::value;


  typedef typename omit_view<MappingTypeX,c>::type

            reduced_mapping;

  typedef typename recursive_determinant<reduced_mapping,

          MappingTypeY,

          length-1>::type

          sub_determinant_type;
```

```
typedef typename mpl::at<MappingTypeX,c>::type current_index;


typedef typename mpl::pair<current_index,
        LostType>::type
            local_element_type;
typedef typename mpl::pair<
    typename mpl::long_<sign<c::value>::value>::type,
    local_element_type>::type signed_local_element_type;


typedef typename append_to_subsequences<sub_determinant_type,
        signed_local_element_type>::type
        sub_multiplied_type;


typedef typename mpl::joint_view<StateType,
            sub_multiplied_type>::type
            type;
    };
};
```

The next snippet of code shows a simple calculation at compile time, as used to determine the sign. Note that only simple operators and static const integer types are available.

Listing: Utility meta function for sign calculation.

```
template<long exponent>

struct sign

{

 static const long value = (exponent % 2) ? -1 : 1;

};
```

The next piece of code shows how intermediate results are concatenated to appropriately encode the desired mathematical operations. The procedure is again split into two components. The top level meta function being.

Listing: Utility meta function used to correctly combine intermediate result.

```
template<typename SequenceType, typename ItemType>

struct append_to_subsequences

{

 typedef typename mpl::fold<

  SequenceType,

  mpl::vector<>,

  push_back<mpl::_1,

    signed_inserter<mpl::_2,ItemType> >

    >::type type;

};
```

It should not go unnoted that the `push_back` here is a meta function working on the compile time container `mpl::vector` in the same fashion as the run time equivalent would on a `std::vector`. However, where the run time function simply modifies an existing container, the compile time version `generates` a completely new sequence, due to the immutable nature of C++ meta programming. The `mpl::_1 and mpl::_2` are named to resemble their run time lambda expressions.

A further utility meta function `signed_inserter` is employed to transform the elements of the input sequence before pushing them into the result sequence, in order to match the chosen logical encoding.

Listing: Generic algorithm for calculating determinants compile time meta program.

```
template<typename SignedSequType, typename ItemType>

struct signed_inserter

{

 typedef typename SignedSequType::first initial_sign_type;

 typedef typename SignedSequType::second coefficients_type;


 typedef typename ItemType::first additional_sign_type;

 typedef typename ItemType::second item_type;


 typedef typename mpl::times<initial_sign_type,
```

```
        additional_sign_type>::type

        sign_type;


  typedef typename mpl::push_back<coefficients_type,

        item_type>::type

        extended_sequence_type;

  typedef typename mpl::pair<sign_type,

        extended_sequence_type>::type type;

};
```

First the input elements, which are expected to be pairs, are unpacked. Then the resulting sign is calculated by using the `mpl::times` meta function, which works on integral constant types such as `mpl::int_`, on the extracted individual signs. The element to be added is pushed into the co-effcient sequence. It should again be noted that this does not mutate the original sequence in any way, but rather results in a completely new sequence, which contains the original types along with the pushed type. The extended sequence is then repacked together with the calculated sign type to resulting type of this meta function.

All the meta functions so far are suffcient to generate a structure of types, which encodes all the operations associated with a determinant, by providing all the required permutations at compile time. This structural part is in fact completely independent from the task of computing determinants and can be freely reused beyond the field of matrices and matrix data types. Since this part of the algorithm is not tied to the domain of matrices, this implementation, which follows the mathematical description very closely, is consequently completely independent of the matrix data type for which a determinant is to be calculated. It therefore surpasses any plain attempt to arrive at data type independence using a simpler template approach, which attempts to simply make a generic implementation from a procedural implementation by converting it to template functions, since that will implicitly introduce the matrix data type. It is this implicit nature which degrades the level of generality.

The components shown this far solely belong to the compile time regime. In order to enable the evaluation of determinants whose values are determined at run time, additional facilities are required which bridge the run time / compile time border.

Run Time Adaption

The first component of the run time adaption deals with the evaluation of multiplications. The following unary function object is a key component of this endeavor:

Listing: Function object for the evaluation of the multiplicative sequences.

```
template<typename MatrixAccessorType, typename NumericType>
```

```
struct multiplication_sequence_eval

{

  const MatrixAccessorType& matrix;

  NumericType& return_value;

  multiplication_sequence_eval(const MatrixAccessorType& matrix,

        NumericType& return_value) :

   matrix(matrix), return_value(return_value) {};


  template< typename U >

  inline void operator()(U x)

  {

    typedef typename U::first first;

    typedef typename U::second second;


    return_value *= matrix(first::value, second::value);

  }

};
```

It is parametrized on the access mechanism to the data contained within the matrix as well as the numeric type indicating the type of the result of the computations. Matrix access is held by constant reference within the object, thus being able to access the data in place in a safe manner. The return value is also used by reference and hence also has to be supplied at construction time.

Evaluation of the result of the multiplicative sequence takes place in the templated `operator ()`. The parameter it formally takes is merely a dummy whose value is never actually used. It is used solely for type deduction. The indices for access to the matrix are extracted from the supplied type and fed into the matrix access mechanism. In this fashion consecutive evaluations of the `operator` along a type sequence enable to evaluation of the multiplication of the matrix elements indicated by the indices. A fact which might escape attention due to the compactness of the specification using the template mechanism is that each individual type within the type sequence will spawn its own implementation of `operator ()` specialized to appropriately.

Another unary function object `determinant_structure_eval` is used to not only initiate the iteration required by the `multiplication_sequence_eval` function object, but also to aggregate the individual results of multiplication.

Listing: Function object for the aggregation of multiplicative terms.

```cpp
template<typename MatrixAccessorType, typename NumericType>
struct determinant_structure_eval
{
 const MatrixAccessorType& matrix;
 NumericType& result;

 determinant_structure_eval(const MatrixAccessorType& matrix,
        NumericType& result) :
  matrix(matrix), result(result) {};

 template<typename SignedSequenceType>
 inline void operator()(SignedSequenceType X)
 {
 typedef typename SignedSequenceType::first sign_type;
 typedef typename SignedSequenceType::second sequence_type;

 NumericType local_result(1);

 mpl::for_each<sequence_type>
  (multiplication_sequence_eval<MatrixAccessorType,
        NumericType>(matrix,
            local_result));

 result += sign_type::value * local_result;


 }
};
```

The structure of the function object follows exactly the same pattern as in the previous case. The difference lies solely in the computations within `operator()`. The sequence of multiplications is extracted and evaluated using the MPL's sole run time algorithm, `mpl::for_each`, which traverses the type sequence and invokes a supplied unary function object. By using the `multiplication_sequence_eval` function object, the terms indicated in the type sequence are multiplied. Finally, the sign of the current term, which has been extracted from the input data type, is applied in the final addition.

Now that the components have been defined it is possible to define a top level interface for the calculation of a determinant. Casting it into the form of a function object:

Listing: Top level interface.

```cpp
template<typename DeterminantStructure>

struct determinant_interface

{

  template<typename MatrixAccessorType, typename NumericT>

  inline void operator()(const MatrixAccessorType& matrix_access,

       NumericT& result)

  {

  result = NumericT(0);

  mpl::for_each<DeterminantStructure>(

  determinant_structure_eval<MatrixAccessorType,

       NumericT>(matrix_access,result) );

  }

};
```

Here the determinant structure has to be specified explicitly during type creation, while the `MatrixAccessorType` and `NumericType` can be derived automatically from the arguments of the `operator()`. This allows for the reuse of the function object for matrices of the same size, and hence of the same structure, but different matrix types or different numerical requirements.

Re-examining the provided run time implementations allows to assess the requirements placed on the matrix and numeric data types. The matrix data type's requirement is determined by its use in Listing. It is required that an operator() is available with which to access the data within the matrix, when supplied with two integer type arguments. No further restrictions, such as memory layout, apply in the given implementation for matrices. In fact anything complying with the required interface will be considered a valid matrix with respect to evaluation.

The requirements enforced on the numeric data type, besides being capable of the basic numeric operations of addition and multiplication, are on the one hand connected to a convertibility/assignability of the result of accessing the matrix to the numeric type, as seen in Listing. Additionally the numeric type needs to be construct able as done in Listing.

To complete the given example, the application of the compile time determinant structure and the given run time evaluations is presented using a simple matrix constructed from `std::vector`. Since this representation does not provide the required access mechanism, a thin wrapper is required. It is presented in Listing and shows how access is remapped to the inherent mechanisms.

```
template<typename MatrixT>

struct vector_vector_like_matrix

{

  const MatrixT& matrix;

  vector_vector_like_matrix(const MatrixT& mx):matrix(mx){};



  double operator()(long x, long y) const

  {

  return matrix[x][y];

  }

};
```

Equipped with the wrapper, the final deployment is illustrated in Listing. First, the compile time program is evoked, resulting in a data type encoding the instructions to be processed. It requires no information about the run time values of the matrix but takes only the size of the matrix as input. Next, the matrix type is defined and instantiated and this instance bound to the wrapper shown in Listing. Omitting the insertion of values into the matrix the snippet of code proceeds to provide a variable to contain the result and finally applies the compile time algorithm to the matrix via the `matrix_access` wrapper, thus completing the demonstration of how to calculate the determinant using compile time meta-programming methods.

Listing: Application of the compile time determinant.

```
typedef determinant_struct_sequence<3>::type det_struct;

typedef std::vector<std::vector<double> > matrix_type;

matrix_type matrix(3, std::vector<double>(3,0));

vector_vector_like_matrix<matrix_type> matrix_access(matrix);



double result(0);

determinant_interface<det_struct>()(matrix_access, result);
```

It has to be stressed at this point that the purpose is to illustrate the procedures and idioms encountered in meta-programming, not to arrive at the optimal solution in terms of run-time, as there are more advanced methods of obtaining the value of a determinant than the presented algorithm. The recursive nature, which might be detrimental in a run time implementation eases implementation and is eliminated for run time evaluation, since the recursive construction of the prescription has already been completed at compile time.

Furthermore the presented implementation is versatile with respect to acceptable data types. The structure itself is indeed completely agnostic to the employed numeric data type. In contrast to more effcient algorithms `this` brute force implementation also does not require division operations, thus making it viable to a wider range of data types from a theoretical as well as practical point of view.

Finally, the generated compile time structure is not limited to be used for the evaluation of determinants. The structure encountered in the calculation of the determinant may be applied to other fields, such as geometric products in the field of geometric algebra.

So far a short outline of the basic settings of digital computers has been sketched into which all further considerations must be mappable. Several different strategies, so called programming paradigms, for describing such a mapping have been presented, which have also been related to different programming languages. After noting several key differences between pure mathematical structures and their realizations within machines, the mathematically simple example of calculating determinants illustrating the procedure of using a compile time program to fully determine the memory accesses and computational steps while leaving the freedom for the values, on which is to be acted on to be supplied at run time. The implemented algorithm was chosen for its relative simplicity which allows demonstrating what may hide behind relatively simple use of generic implementations. It should therefore be reiterated that for a performance sensitive calculation of determinants different algorithms should be considered. On the other hand it demonstrates how the calculation of permutations can be extracted from the task and made available as an algorithm for reuse.

Basic Components of Programming Languages

Variables

Variables are used to store information to be referenced and manipulated in a computer program. They also provide a way of labeling data with a descriptive name, so our programs can be understood more clearly by the `reader` and ourselves. It is helpful to think of variables as containers that hold information. Their sole purpose is to label and store data in memory. This data can then be used throughout your program.

Assigning Value to Variables

Naming variables is known as one of the most difficult tasks in computer programming. When you are naming variables, think hard about the names. Try your best to make sure that the name you assign your variable is accurately descriptive and understandable to another reader. Sometimes that other reader is yourself when you revisit a program that you wrote months or even years earlier.

When you assign a variable, you use the = symbol. The name of the variable goes on the left and the value you want to store in the variable goes on the right.

```
1   irb :001 > first_name = 'Joe'
2   => "Joe"
```

Here we've assigned the value 'Joe', which is a string, to the variable first_name. Now if we want to reference that variable, we can.

```
1   irb :002 > first_name
2   => "Joe"
```

As you can see, we've now stored the string 'Joe' in memory for use throughout the program.

Note: Make sure you don't confuse the assignment operator (=) with the equality operator (==). The individual = symbol assigns value while the == symbol checks if two things are equal. Let's try a little something. Look at the following irb session.

```
1   irb :001 > a = 4
2   => 4
3   irb :002 > b = a
4   => 4
5   irb :003 > a = 7
6   => 7
```

What is the value of b at this point? Take your best guess and then type this session into irb to find out. You'll notice that the value of b remains 4, while a was re-assigned to 7. This shows that variables point to values in memory, and are not deeply linked to each other.

Getting Data from a User

Up until now, you've only been able to assign data to variables from within the program. However, in the wild, you'll want other people to be able to interact with your programs in interesting ways. In order to do that, we have to allow the user to store information in variables as well. Then, we can decide what we'd like to do with that data.

One way to get information from the user is to call the gets method. Gets stands for "get string", and is a lot of fun. When you use it, the program waits for the user to 1) type in information and 2) press the enter key. Let's try it out. Type these examples in `irb` to get the feel and play around with them for a bit if you'd like to.

```
1   irb :001 > name = gets
2   Bob
3   => "Bob\n"
```

After the code, `name = gets`, the computer waited for us to type in some information. We typed "Bob" and then pressed enter and the program returned "`Bob\n`". The \n at the end is the "new-line" character and represents the enter key. But we don't want that as part of our string. We'll use chomp chained to gets to get rid of that - you `can put.chomp` after any string to remove the carriage return characters at the end.

```
1   irb :001 > name = gets.chomp
2   Bob
3   => "Bob"
```

Now we can use the name variable as we so please.

```
1   irb :001 > name = gets.chomp
2   Bob
3   => "Bob"
4   irb :002 > name + ' is super great!'
5   => "Bob is super great!"
```

Variable Scope

A variable's scope determines where in a program a variable is available for use. A variable's scope is defined by where the variable is initialized or created. In Ruby, variable scope is defined by a block. A block is a piece of code following a method invocation, usually delimited by either curly braces `{}` or `do/end`. Be aware that not all do/end pairs imply a block. Now that you have an idea of what constitutes a variable's scope, one rule that we want you to remember is this.

Inner Scope can Access Variables Initialized in an Outer Scope, but not Vice Versa

Looking at some code will make this clearer. Let's say we have a file called `scope.rb`.

```
1   # scope.rb
2
3   a = 5
4
5   3.times do |n|      # method invocation with a block
6       a = 3
7       b = 5           # b is initialized in the inner scope
8   end
9
10  puts a
11  puts b              # is b accessible here, in the outer scope?
```

What is the value of a when it is printed to the screen? Try it out.

The value of a is 3. This is because a is available to the inner scope created by 3.times do... end, which allowed the code to re-assign the value of a. In fact, it re-assigned it three times to 3. Let's try something else. We'll modify the same piece of code.

```
1   # scope.rb
2
3   a = 5
4
5   3.times do |n|      # method invocation with a block
6       a = 3
7       b = 5           # b is initialized in the inner scope
8   end
9
10  puts a
11  puts b              # is b accessible here, in the outer scope?
```

What result did you get when running that program? You should have gotten an error to the tune of:

```
1   scope.rb:11:in `<main>': undefined local variable or method `b' for main:Object
2   (NameError)
```

This is because the variable b is not available outside of the method invocation with a block where it is initialized. When we call `puts  b` it is not available within that outer scope.

Note: the key distinguishing factor for deciding whether code delimited by { } or do/end is considered a block (and thereby creates a new scope for variables), is seeing if the { } or do/end immediately follows a method invocation. For example:

```
1   arr = [1, 2, 3]
2
3   for i in arr do
4     a = 5         # a is initialized here
5   end
6
7   puts a          # is it accessible here?
```

The answer is yes. The reason is because the for...do/end code did not create a new inner scope, since for is part of Ruby language and not a method invocation. When we use each, times and other method invocations, followed by {} or do/end, that's when a new block is created.

Types of Variables

Before we move on, you should be aware that there are five types of variables. Constants, global variables, class variables, instance variables, and local variables. While you should not worry too much about these topics in depth yet, here is a brief description of each.

Constants are declared by capitalizing every letter in the variable's name, per Ruby convention. They are used for storing data that never needs to change. While most programming languages do not allow you to change the value assigned to a constant, Ruby does. It will however throw a warning letting you know that there was a previous definition for that variable. Just because you can, doesn't mean you should change the value. In fact, you should not. Constants cannot be declared in method definitions, and are available throughout your application's scopes.

Example of a Constant Declaration

```
1   MY_CONSTANT = 'I am available throughout your app.'
```

Global variables are declared by starting the variable name with the dollar sign ($). These variables are available throughout your entire app, overriding all scope boundaries. Rubyists tend to stay away from global variables as there can be unexpected complications when using them.

Example of a global variable declaration:

```
1   $var = 'I am also available throughout your app.'
```

Class variables are declared by starting the variable name with two @ signs. These variables are accessible by instances of your class, as well as the class itself. When you need to declare a variable that is related to a class, but each instance of that class does not need its own value for this variable, you use a class variable. Class variables must be initialized at the class level, outside of any method definitions. They can then be altered using class or instance method definitions.

Example of a class variable declaration:

```
1   @@instances = 0
```

Instance variables are declared by starting the variable name with one @ sign. These variables are available throughout the current instance of the parent class. Instance variables can cross some scope boundaries, but not all of them. You will learn more about this when you get to OOP topics, and should not use instance variables until you know more about them.

Example of an instance variable declaration:

```
1   @var = 'I am available throughout the current instance of this class.'
```

Local variables are the most common variables you will come across and obey all scope boundaries. These variables are declared by starting the variable name with neither $ nor @, as well as not capitalizing the entire variable name.

Example of a local variable declaration:

```
1   var = 'I must be passed around to cross scope boundaries.'
```

Control Structures

A program is usually not limited to a linear sequence of instructions. During its process it may bifurcate, repeat code or take decisions. For that purpose, C++ provides control structures that serve to specify what has to be done by our program, when and under which circumstances.

With the introduction of control structures we are going to have to introduce a new concept: the compound-statement or block. A block is a group of statements which are separated by semicolons (;) like all C++ statements, but grouped together in a block enclosed in braces: { }:

```
{ statement1; statement2; statement3; }
```

Most of the control structures that we will see in this section require a generic statement as part of its syntax. A statement can be either a simple statement (a simple instruction ending with a semicolon) or a compound statement (several instructions grouped in a block). In the case that we want the statement to be a simple statement, we do not need to enclose it in braces ({}). But in the case that we want the statement to be a compound statement it must be enclosed between braces ({}), forming a block.

Conditional Structure: if and Else

The `if` keyword is used to execute a statement or block only if a condition is fulfilled. Its form is:

```
if (condition) statement
```

Where `condition` is the expression that is being evaluated. If this condition is true, statement is executed. If it is false, statement is ignored (not executed) and the program continues right after this conditional structure. For example, the following code fragment prints x is 100 only if the value stored in the x variable is indeed 100:

```
if (x == 100)

  cout << "x is 100";
```

If we want more than a single statement to be executed in case that the condition is true we can specify a block using braces { }:

```
if (x == 100)

{

  cout << "x is ";

  cout << x;

}
```

We can additionally specify what we want to happen if the condition is not fulfilled by using the keyword else. Its form used in conjunction with if is:

```
if (condition) statement1 else statement2
```

For example:

```
if (x == 100)

  cout << "x is 100";

else

  cout << "x is not 100";
```

prints on the screen x is 100 if indeed x has a value of 100, but if it has not -and only if not- it prints out x is not 100. The if + else structures can be concatenated with the intention of verifying a range of values. The following example shows its use telling if the value currently stored in x is positive, negative or none of them (i.e. zero):

```
if (x > 0)

  cout << "x is positive";
```

```
else if (x < 0)

  cout << "x is negative";

else

  cout << "x is 0";
```

Remember that in case that we want more than a single statement to be executed, we must group them in a block by enclosing them in braces { }.

Iteration Structures (Loops)

Loops have as purpose to repeat a statement a certain number of times or while a condition is fulfilled.

The While Loop

Its format is:

```
while (expression) statement
```

and its functionality is simply to repeat statement while the condition set in expression is true. For example, we are going to make a program to countdown using a while-loop:

```
// custom countdown using while

#include <iostream>

using namespace std;

int main ()

{

  int n;

  cout << "Enter the starting
number > ";

  cin >> n;

  while (n>0) {

  cout << n << ", ";

  --n;

  }

  cout << "FIRE!\n";

  return 0;
```

```
}
```

```
Enter the starting number > 8
```

```
8, 7, 6, 5, 4, 3, 2, 1, FIRE!
```

When the program starts the user is prompted to insert a starting number for the countdown. Then the while loop begins, if the value entered by the user fulfills the condition n>0 (that n is greater than zero) the block that follows the condition will be executed and repeated while the condition (n>0) remains being true.

The whole process of the previous program can be interpreted according to the following script (beginning in main):

- User assigns a value to n.

- The while condition is checked (n>0). At this point there are two posibilities:

  ◦ Condition is true: statement is executed (to step 3).

  ◦ Condition is false: ignore statement and continue after it (to step 5).

- Execute statement:

  ```
  cout << n << ", ";
  ```

  ```
  --n;
  ```

  (Prints the value of n on the screen and decreases n by 1)

- End of block. Return automatically to step 2

- Continue the program right after the block: print FIRE! and end program.

When creating a while-loop, we must always consider that it has to end at some point, therefore we must provide within the block some method to force the condition to become false at some point, otherwise the loop will continue looping forever. In this case we have included --n; that decreases the value of the variable that is being evaluated in the condition (n) by one - this will eventually make the condition (n>0) to become false after a certain number of loop iterations: to be more specific, when n becomes 0, that is where our while-loop and our countdown end.

Of course this is such a simple action for our computer that the whole countdown is performed instantly without any practical delay between numbers.

The do-while Loop

Its format is:

```
        do statement while (condition);
```

Its functionality is exactly the same as the while loop, except that condition in the do-while loop is evaluated after the execution of statement instead of before, granting at least one execution of statement even if `condition` is never fulfilled. For example, the following example program echoes any number you enter until you enter 0.

```
// number echoer
#include <iostream>
using namespace std;
int main ()
{
 unsigned long n;
 do {
 cout << "Enter number (0 to
end): ";
 cin >> n;
 cout << "You entered: " << n
<< "\n";
 } while (n != 0);
 return 0;
}
Enter number (0 to end): 12345
You entered: 12345
Enter number (0 to end): 160277
You entered: 160277
Enter number (0 to end): 0
You entered: 0
```

The do-while loop is usually used when the condition that has to determine the end of the loop is determined within the loop statement itself, like in the previous case, where the user input within the block is what is used to determine if the loop has to end. In fact if you never enter the value 0 in the previous example you can be prompted for more numbers forever.

The for Loop

Its format is:

```
for (initialization; condition; increase)
```

```
  statement;
```

and its main function is to repeat statement while condition remains true, like the while loop. But in addition, the for loop provides specific locations to contain an initialization statement and an increase statement. So this loop is specially designed to perform a repetitive action with a counter which is initialized and increased on each iteration. It works in the following way:

- Initialization is executed. Generally it is an initial value setting for a counter variable. This is executed only once.

- Condition is checked. If it is true the loop continues, otherwise the loop ends and statement is skipped (not executed).

- Statement is executed. As usual, it can be either a single statement or a block enclosed in braces { }.

- Finally, whatever is specified in the increase field is executed and the loop gets back to step 2.

Here is an example of countdown using a for loop:

```
// countdown using a for loop

#include <iostream>

using namespace std;

int main ()

{

  for (int n=10; n>0; n--) {

  cout << n << ", ";

  }

  cout << "FIRE!\n";

  return 0;

}

10, 9, 8, 7, 6, 5, 4, 3, 2, 1,

FIRE!
```

The initialization and increase fields are optional. They can remain empty, but in all cases the semicolon signs between them must be written. For example we could write: for (;n< 10;) if we wanted to specify no initialization and no increase; or for (;n< 10;n++) if we wanted to include an increase field but no initialization (maybe because the variable was already initialized before). Optionally, using the comma operator (,) we can specify more than one expression in any of the fields included in a for loop, like in `initialization,` for example.

The comma operator (,) is an expression separator, it serves to separate more than one expression where only one is generally expected. For example, suppose that we wanted to initialize more than one variable in our loop:

```
for ( n=0, i=100 ; n!=i ; n++, i-- )

{

  // whatever here...

}
```

This loop will execute for 50 times if neither n or i are modified within the loop:

n starts with a value of 0, and i with `100`, the condition is `n!=i` (that n is not equal to i). Because n is increased by one and i decreased by one, the loop's condition will become false after the 50th loop, when both `n` and `i` will be equal to `50`.

Jump Statements

The Break Statement

Using `break` we can leave a loop even if the condition for its end is not fulfilled. It can be used to end an infinite loop, or to force it to end before its natural end. For example, we are going to stop the count down before its natural end (maybe because of an engine check failure?):

```
// break loop example

#include <iostream>

using namespace std;

int main ()

{

  int n;

  for (n=10; n>0; n--)

  {

  cout << n << ", ";
```

```
 if (n==3)

 {

 cout << "countdown

aborted!";

 break;

 }

 }

 return 0;

}
```

10, 9, 8, 7, 6, 5, 4, 3,

countdown aborted!

The continue statement The continue statement causes the program to skip the rest of the loop in the current iteration as if the end of the statement block had been reached, causing it to jump to the start of the following iteration. For example, we are going to skip the number 5 in our countdown:

```
// continue loop example

#include <iostream>

using namespace std;

int main ()

{

 for (int n=10; n>0; n--) {

 if (n==5) continue;

 cout << n << ", ";

 }

 cout << "FIRE!\n";

 return 0;

}
```

10, 9, 8, 7, 6, 4, 3, 2, 1,

FIRE!

The Goto Statement

goto allows to make an absolute jump to another point in the program. You should use this feature with caution since its execution causes an unconditional jump ignoring any type of nesting limitations. The destination point is identified by a label, which is then used as an argument for the goto statement. A label is made of a valid identifier followed by a colon (:).

Generally speaking, this instruction has no concrete use in structured or object oriented programming aside from those that low-level programming fans may find for it. For example, here is our countdown loop using goto:

```cpp
// goto loop example

#include <iostream>

using namespace std;

int main ()
{
  int n=10;
  loop:
  cout << n << ", ";
  n--;
  if (n>0) goto loop;
  cout << "FIRE!\n";
  return 0;
}
```

```
10, 9, 8, 7, 6, 5, 4, 3, 2, 1,
FIRE!
```

The Exit Function

exit is a function defined in the cstdlib library.

The purpose of exit is to terminate the current program with a specific exit code. Its prototype is:

```cpp
void exit (int exitcode);
```

The exitcode is used by some operating systems and may be used by calling programs. By convention, an exit code of 0 means that the program finished normally and any other value means that some error or unexpected results happened.

The Selective Structure: Switch

The syntax of the `switch` statement is a bit peculiar. Its objective is to check several possible constant values for an expression. Something similar to what we did at the beginning of this section with the concatenation of several `if` and `else if` instructions. Its form is the following:

```
switch (expression)

{

  case constant1:

  group of statements 1;

  break;

  case constant2:

  group of statements 2;

  break;

  .

  .

  .

  default:

  default group of statements

}
```

It works in the following way: switch evaluates `expression` and checks if it is equivalent to `constant1`, if it is, it executes `group of statements 1` until it finds the break statement. When it finds this break statement the program jumps to the end of the `switch` selective structure.

If expression was not equal to constant1 it will be checked against `constant2`. If it is equal to this, it will execute `group of statements 2` until a break keyword is found, and then will jump to the end of the `switch` selective structure.

Finally, if the value of expression did not match any of the previously specified constants (you can include as many case labels as values you want to check), the program will execute the statements included after the `default:` label, if it exists (since it is optional). Both of the following code fragments have the same behavior:

switch example	if-else equivalent
```switch (x) { case 1: cout << "x is 1"; break; case 2: cout << "x is 2"; break; default: cout << "value of x unknown"; }```	```if (x == 1) { cout << "x is 1"; } else if (x == 2) { cout << "x is 2"; } else { cout << "value of x unknown"; }```

The `switch` statement is a bit peculiar within the C++ language because it uses labels instead of blocks. This forces us to put `break` statements after the group of statements that we want to be executed for a specific condition. Otherwise the remainder statements -including those corresponding to other labels- will also be executed until the end of the `switch` selective block or a break statement is reached.

For example, if we did not include a `break` statement after the first group for case one, the program will not automatically jump to the end of the `switch` selective block and it would continue executing the rest of statements until it reaches either a `break` instruction or the end of the `switch` selective block. This makes unnecessary to include braces { } surrounding the statements for each of the cases, and it can also be useful to execute the same block of instructions for different possible values for the expression being evaluated. For example:

```
switch (x) {

  case 1:

  case 2:

  case 3:

  cout << "x is 1, 2 or 3";

  break;

  default:

  cout << "x is not 1, 2 nor 3";

}
```

Notice that switch can only be used to compare an expression against constants. Therefore we cannot put variables as labels (for example `case  n:` where n is a variable) or ranges (`case (1..3):`) because they are not valid C++ constants.

Data Structures

The data structure name indicates itself that organizing the data in memory. There are many ways of organizing the data in the memory as we have already seen one of the data structures, i.e., array in C language. Array is a collection of memory elements in which data is stored sequentially, i.e., one after another. In other words, we can say that array stores the elements in a continuous manner. This organization of data is done with the help of an array of data structures. There are also other ways to organize the data in memory. Let's see the different types of data structures.

The data structure is not any programming language like C, C++, java, etc. It is a set of algorithms that we can use in any programming language to structure the data in the memory. To structure the data in memory, 'n' number of algorithms were proposed, and all these algorithms are known as Abstract data types. These abstract data types are the set of rules.

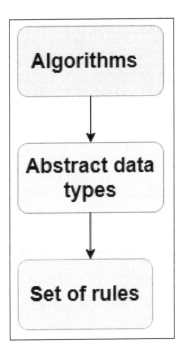

Types of Data Structures

There are two types of data structures:

- Primitive data structure.

- Non-primitive data structure.

Primitive Data Structure

The primitive data structures are primitive data types. The int, char, float, double, and pointer are the primitive data structures that can hold a single value.

Non-Primitive Data structure

The non-primitive data structure is divided into two types:

- Linear data structure.

- Non-linear data structure.

Linear Data Structure

The arrangement of data in a sequential manner is known as a linear data structure. The data structures used for this purpose are Arrays, Linked list, Stacks, and Queues. In these data structures, one element is connected to only one another element in a linear form.

When one element is connected to the 'n' number of elements known as a non-linear data structure. The best example is trees and graphs. In this case, the elements are arranged in a random manner.

Data structures can also be classified as:

- Static data structure: It is a type of data structure where the size is allocated at the compile time. Therefore, the maximum size is fixed.

- Dynamic data structure: It is a type of data structure where the size is allocated at the run time. Therefore, the maximum size is flexible.

Major Operations

The major or the common operations that can be performed on the data structures are:

- Searching: We can search for any element in a data structure.

- Sorting: We can sort the elements of a data structure either in an ascending or descending order.

- Insertion: We can also insert the new element in a data structure.

- Updation: We can also update the element, i.e., we can replace the element with another element.

- Deletion: We can also perform the delete operation to remove the element from the data structure.

What is Data Structure?

A data structure is a way of organizing the data so that it can be used efficiently. Here, we have used the word efficiently, which in terms of both the space and time. For example, a stack is an ADT (Abstract data type) which uses either arrays or linked list data structure for the implementation. Therefore, we conclude that we require some data structure to implement a particular ADT.

An ADT tells what is to be done and data structure tells how it is to be done. In other words, we can say that ADT gives us the blueprint while data structure provides the implementation part. Now the question arises: how can one get to know which data structure to be used for a particular ADT?

As the different data structures can be implemented in a particular ADT, but the different implementations are compared for time and space. For example, the Stack ADT can be implemented by both Arrays and linked list. Suppose the array is providing time efficiency while the linked list is providing space efficiency, so the one which is the best suited for the current user's requirements will be selected.

Advantages of Data Structures

The following are the advantages of a data structure:

- Efficiency: If the choice of a data structure for implementing a particular ADT is proper, it makes the program very efficient in terms of time and space.

- Reusability: he data structures provide reusability means that multiple client programs can use the data structure.

- Abstraction: The data structure specified by an ADT also provides the level of abstraction. The client cannot see the internal working of the data structure, so it does not have to worry about the implementation part. The client can only see the interface.

Programming Tool

Software or a programming tool is a set of computer programs that are used by the developers to create, maintain, debug, or support other applications and programs. Software development tools are simply tools (generally software themselves) that programmers practice to create other software. For Example – language libraries, code editors, debuggers, etc. Any software deploy tool that enables a programmer to build stable software matching the needs or goals of a customer is placed into this category.

Agile development tools can be of different types like linkers, compilers, code editors, GUI designers, assemblers, debuggers, performance analysis tools, and many others. There are some factors that need to consider while selecting the corresponding development tool, based on the type of design.

Few of such factors are:

- Company criteria.

- Usefulness of tool.

- Integration of one tool with another.

- Choosing an appropriate environment.

- Learning curve.

Why do Software Development Tools Matter?

All professionals need software designing tools in order to do their jobs. A carpenter needs an assortment of hammers, saws, planes, tape measures and the like. An auto mechanic needs wrenches and sockets, ratchets and impact tools. A plumber needs pipe wrenches, brazing tools, saws, etc. Same ways, software developers need the right software planning tools for accomplishing their respective assignments. Software development tools play a very important role in the IT field, although they are less substantial than the tools used by other professionals.

Software development tools can be things like interpreters that work directly with code, but they can also be tools that help to make the lives of developers simpler and easier. For instance, while a user panel assigned to answering the questions of programmers and sharing knowledge might not have a direct influence on the development of a particular piece of software, but it does provide relevant solutions for developers who necessitate answers to vital questions.

So, you can find a very wide variety of other options in the category of software development tools. Anything that might help to boost the efficiency and accuracy can be conceivably be added to this category, including communication tools like Slack, libraries like Stack Overflow, and repositories like GitHub.

In other words, the selection of software engineering tools to be used in its development process can completely shape or break a project. Once the targeted ecosystem and programming language(s) are chosen, and the requirements and end goals are also well-enough understood, the next task is starting the work of a software development project is to choose the tools that will be utilized throughout the process. It's also important to be knowledgeable of the types of tools that are available for employment, their benefits, and the implications for using them.

Where are Development Tools Found?

You can find software development tools in many different places, and in numerous different configurations. For instance, APIs comprises of tools that enable software developers to achieve a specific goal, such as programming language libraries. SDKs include a very wide range of programming tools that allow programmers to create software for specific platforms and systems. Integrated development environments provide entire toolbars for programmers, allowing them to create programs in a single environment, test them in the same environment and even deploy them at the opportune time.

The Evolution of Software Development Tools

Many changes in IT happen as an indirect result of the development or induction of some other technological innovation. Some changes in the development of IT systems come and go faster as compared to fashion in clothing. IT trends are less like a straight timeline of incremental advances, and more like a churning cycle of twirling ideas that gain fame and then fall out of service as people strive to see what works and what doesn't, what's more effective, and vice versa.

Originally, software development tools hold only of those tools that are used during the actual design and testing phases of software development. However, today, there are software management tools that can be used throughout the software development life cycle. The original software development toolbox might have contained a basic text editor, as well as a linking loader, a compiler, and a tool for debugging software.

Today, things are much more complicated, with tools that can be used during quality assurance, all phases of testing, and even during the design and deployment phases. Some examples of project management solution that helps developers organize and stay productive during projects are Microsoft Project, Wrike, etc.

Software development tools continue to evolve and change, as the needs of programmers grow. In the near future, we may be using more of our development efforts in developing systems that can emerge and acquire by themselves (machine learning), but someone still has to process those systems. Human power is still like to be needed to operate the tools.

Semantics

Semantics for a programming language models the computational meaning of each program. There are several levels of semantics: static semantics, dynamic semantics, and equivalences.

- Static semantics models compile-time checks: When (abstract) syntax is restricted to be context-free, checking whether programs satisfy well-formedness constraints necessarily becomes part of semantics. It is called static semantics, since it concerns only those checks that can be performed before running the program, e.g. checking that all parts of the program are type-correct. The only relevant feature of the static semantics of a program is whether the program has passed the checks or not (although error reports issued by compilers could be modelled when these are implementation-independent).

- Dynamic semantics models run-time behavior: Dynamic semantics concerns the observable behaviour when programs are run. Here, we may assume that well-formedness of the programs has already been checked by the static semantics: we do not need to consider the dynamic semantics of ill-formed programs.

- Equivalences between programs may abstract from details of models: A formal semantics should give, for each program, an abstract model that represents just the relevant features of all possible executions of that program. Then two programs are regarded as semantically equivalent when their models are the same (up to isomorphism). An alternative approach is to give less abstract models, and then define a semantic equivalence relation for each model.

- Complete descriptions include static semantics, dynamic semantics, and semantic equivalence: Given a program accepted by a context-free concrete syntax, a static semantics is needed in order to determine whether the program is well-formed, and thus executable. The dynamic semantics then provides a model of program executions. The semantic equivalence relation abstracts from those features that are irrelevant to implementation correctness. All together this provides the complete semantics of the given program.

- These notes focus on dynamic semantics, based on context-free abstract syntax.

There are several main approaches to dynamic semantics:

- Operational semantics, where computations are modelled explicitly.

- Denotational semantics, where only the contribution of each construct to the computational meaning of the enclosing program is modeled.

- Axiomatic semantics, which (in effect) models the relationship between pre and post-conditions on program variables.

The operational framework known as Structural Operational Semantics (SOS) is a good compromise between simplicity and practical applicability, and it has been widely taught at the undergraduate level. A modular variant of SOS called MSOS has some significant pragmatic advantages over the original SOS framework, but otherwise remains conceptually very close to it. The hybrid framework called Action Semantics —not to be confused with the UML Action Semantics—combines features of denotational and operational semantics.

Structural Operational Semantics

The Structural Operational Semantics (SOS) framework was proposed by Plotkin in 1981. The main aim was to provide a simple and direct approach, allowing concise and comprehensible semantic descriptions based on elementary mathematics. The basic SOS framework has since been presented in various textbooks (e.g.), and exploited in numerous papers on concurrency. The big-step form of SOS (also known as Natural Semantics) was used during the design of Standard ML, as well as to give the official definition of that language.

SOS uses Rules to Specify Transition Relations

SOS uses rules to give inductive specifications of transition relations on states that involve both abstract syntax trees and computed values. When describing a purely functional programming language (or a pure process calculus such as CCS), SOS rules look very simple. For instance:

$$\frac{E_1 \rightarrow E_1'}{\mathrm{cond}\left(E_1,\ E_2,\ E_3\right) \rightarrow \mathrm{cond}(E_1', E_2,\ E_3)}$$
$$\mathrm{cond}\left(\mathrm{true}, E_2, E_3\right) \rightarrow E_2$$

$$\mathrm{cond}\left(\mathit{false}, E_2, E_3\right) \rightarrow E_3$$

Notice that there are no labels on the transitions in the above SOS rules: labels are normally used in SOS only in connection with communication and synchronization between concurrent processes, and don't occur at all with transitions for sequential programming constructs. In the next section, we shall see that labels are more widely exploited in the modular variant of the SOS framework, MSOS.

States are not Restricted to Syntax Trees

In the original SOS framework, syntax is not clearly separated from auxiliary semantic entities: both syntactic and semantic entities are allowed as components of states, as illustrated in connection with bindings and stores below. In contrast, MSOS insists that states remain purely syntactic.

Bindings

Declarations (and some other constructs) bind identifiers to particular values. A bindings map or environment gives the current association between identifiers and their bound values, and generally has a restricted scope. Bindings are usually represented by explicit components of states.

In fact the treatment of bindings in SOS is somewhat awkward. Suppose that the states for expression evaluation include bindings: State = Exp × Env. This requires the specification of transitions (E, ρ) → (E , ρ) where the environment ρ remains unchanged. Clearly, it would be tedious to have to write (and read) ρ twice each time a transition is specified, and it is usual practice to introduce the notation $\rho \vdash E \rightarrow E$ as an abbreviation for (E, ρ) → (E, ρ). Thus when the functional language being described involves bindings, the SOS rules given above would be reformulated as follows:

$$\frac{\rho \vdash E_1 \longrightarrow E_1'}{\rho \vdash \mathit{cond}\left(E_1, E_2, E_3\right) \longrightarrow \mathit{cond}\left(E_1', E_2, E_3\right)}$$
$$\rho \vdash \mathit{cond}\left(\mathit{true}, E_2, E_3\right) \longrightarrow E_3$$

$$\rho \vdash cond(false, E_2, E_3) \longrightarrow E_2$$

Alternatively, bindings can be eliminated as soon as they have been computed by substituting the bound values for the identifiers throughout the scope of the bindings. However, an explicit definition of the result [ρ] T of substitution of ρ throughout T requires the tedious specification of a defining equation for each non-binding construct T, for instance:

$$[\rho]cond(E_1,\ E_2,\ E_3) = cond([\rho]E_1, [\rho]E_2, [\rho]E_3)$$

as well as some rather more intricate equations for the binding constructs.

Stores

Assignments involve (irreversible) changes to particular locations in a store. Variable identifiers are generally bound to locations, and assignments affects the values stored at locations, but not the current bindings.

- The separate modelling of binding and assignment allows a simple treatment of aliasing: It is best not to confuse binding with assignment: Abstractly, a variable declaration has the effect of allocating part of the store to hold the value of the variable, and binds the identifier to some entity, traditionally called a location, that refers to that part of the store; it may also initialize the value of the variable. Assignment of a value to the variable affects only the store, not the binding of the variable identifier. The usefulness of this distinction can be seen most clearly in languages that allow so-called aliasing, where variable identifiers are bound to the same location: assigning a new value to one of them causes the value of the other(s) to change as well.

- Effects on storage are represented by explicit store components of states: When the described language isn't purely functional, and expression evaluation can have side-effects, the states for expression evaluation include the current store as well as the environment: State = Exp × Env × Store. Transitions between such states are written $\rho \vdash E, \sigma \rightarrow E', \sigma'$, so the rules given above would be reformulated as follows:

$$\frac{\rho \vdash E_1, \sigma \rightarrow E_1', \sigma'}{\rho \vdash cond(E_1, E_2, E_3), \sigma \rightarrow cond(E_1', E_2, E_3),\ \sigma'}$$

$$\rho \vdash cond(true, E_2, E_3), \sigma \rightarrow E_2, \sigma$$

$$\rho \vdash cond(false, E_2, E_3), \sigma \rightarrow E_3, \sigma$$

$$\frac{\rho \vdash E_1, \sigma \rightarrow E_1', \sigma'}{\rho \vdash assign(E_1, E_2), \sigma \rightarrow assign(E_1', E_2), \sigma'}$$

$$\frac{\rho \vdash E_2, \sigma \rightarrow E_2', \sigma'}{\rho \vdash assign(E_1, E_2), \sigma \rightarrow assign(E_1, E_2'), \sigma'}$$

$$\rho \vdash assign(L, V), \sigma \rightarrow (\ ), \sigma[L \rightarrow V]$$

Communications

- Communication between concurrent processes is represented by labels on transitions: Finally, suppose that expression evaluation can involve process creation and communication. The conventional technique in SOS is here to add labels to transitions. The SOS rules given above would be reformulated thus:

$$\frac{\rho \vdash E_1, \sigma \xrightarrow{L} E_1', \sigma'}{\rho \vdash cond(E_1, E_2, E_3), \sigma \xrightarrow{L} cond(E_1', E_2, E_3), \sigma'}$$

$$\rho \vdash cond(true, E_2, E_3), \sigma \xrightarrow{\tau} E_2, \sigma$$

$$\rho \vdash cond(false, E_2, E_3), \sigma \xrightarrow{\tau} E_3, \sigma$$

(τ is some fixed label that indicates a silent, uncommunicative step.)

- Rules require reformulation when components of states or labels on transitions are added, changed, or removed: As illustrated above, the formulation of rules in conventional SOS has to change whenever the components of the model involved in transitions (i.e. states and labels) are changed. This is in marked contrast to the situation with MSOS, where the formulation of transitions in rules is stable, allowing the rules for each programming construct to be given definitively, once-and-for-all.

Small-Step and Big-Step Styles

- In conventional SOS, the small-step and big-step styles are commonly regarded as alternatives: Formally, the big-step style can be regarded as a special case of the small-step style: computations in the big-step style simply don't involve any intermediate states, only initial and final states. Note also that if one has defined a small-step SOS, the transitive closure of the small-step relation provides the corresponding big-step relation. In practice, authors of SOS descriptions usually choose one style or the other—and then stick to it, since changing styles involves major reformulation. In general, however, it seems better to mix the small-step and big-step styles, choosing the more appropriate style for each kind of construct by consideration of the nature of its computations:

  ○ Big-step SOS is better for constructs whose computations are pure evaluation, with no side-effects, no exceptions, and always terminating—e.g., for evaluating decimal numerals to numbers, for matching patterns against values, and for types.

  ○ Small-step SOS is better for all other constructs, since it makes explicit the order in which the steps of their computations are made, which is usually significant. Moreover, small-step SOS copes more easily with specifying interleaving, exception handling, and concurrency than big-step SOS does.

- Big-step SOS can be applicable to modelling languages: Sometimes, modelling languages are used to specify declarative aspects of software, such as relationships between classes of objects. The focus is on the static structure of the model, not on any behavioural interpretation. Although small-step SOS is inappropriate for specifying static structure, big-step SOS can be used here to give a formal description of the intended semantics, provided that the abstract syntax is tree-structured. For instance, the big-step transition relation between a construct and its computed value may represent that the value satisfies the construct; an object may be regarded as satisfying any class to which it belongs. The satisfaction relationship between algebraic specifications and algebras in Casl is defined using big-step SOS.

- Small-step SOS can be applicable to behavioral semantics of modelling languages: For example, the behavioral semantics of the visual modeling language State Flow has been specified by transforming diagrams to abstract syntax trees, and then defining their small-step SOS in a conventional style.

Informal Conventions

The official Definition of Standard ML is not entirely formal: A major example of an SOS in the pure big-step style is the Definition of Standard ML. The description covers the static and dynamic semantics of the entire language (both the core and module levels), and has been carefully written by a group of highly qualified authors. Nevertheless, its degree of formality still leaves something to be desired—especially in connection with two "conventions" that were adopted:

- The "store convention" allows the store to be left implicit in rules where it is not being extended, updated, or inspected.

- The "exception convention" allows the omission of rules that merely let unhandled exceptions preempt further sub-expression evaluation.

For instance, consider the following rule for the evaluation of conditional expressions:

$$\frac{\rho \vdash E_1 \to true \quad \rho \vdash E_2 \to V}{\rho \vdash cond\left(E_1, E_2, E_3\right) \to V}$$

By the above conventions, this rule abbreviates the following three rules:

$$\frac{\rho \vdash E_1, \sigma \to true, \sigma' \quad \rho \vdash E_2, \sigma' \to V, \sigma''}{\rho \vdash cond\left(E_1, E_2, E_3\right), \sigma \to V, \sigma''}$$

$$\frac{\rho \vdash E_1, \sigma \to raised\left(EX\right), \sigma'}{\rho \vdash cond\left(E_1, E_2, E_3\right), \sigma \to raised\left(EX\right), \sigma'}$$

$$\frac{\rho \vdash E_1, \sigma \to true, \sigma' \quad \rho \vdash E_2, \sigma' \to raised(EX), \sigma''}{\rho \vdash cond\left(E_1, E_2, E_3\right), \sigma \to raised(EX), \sigma''}$$

where raised(EX) indicates that the evaluation of a sub-expression has raised an exception with value EX. Such conventions are completely unnecessary when using the MSOS approach.

Modular SOS

- Modular SOS allows individual constructs to be described once and for all: As the name suggests, Modular SOS (MSOS) is a variant of SOS that ensures a high degree of modularity: the rules specifying the MSOS of individual language constructs can be given once and for all, since their formulation is completely independent of the presence or absence of other constructs in the described language. When extending a pure functional language with concurrency primitives and/or references, the MSOS rules for the functional constructs don't need even the slightest reformulation. In denotational semantics, the problem of obtaining good modularity has received much attention, and has to a large extent been solved by introducing so-called monad transformers. MSOS provides an analogous (but significantly simpler) solution for the structural approach to operational semantics.

- States are purely syntactic in MSOS, and labels are exploited more than in SOS: The crucial feature of MSOS is to insist that states are merely abstract syntax and computed values, omitting the usual auxiliary information (such as environment and stores) that they include in SOS. The only place left for auxiliary information is in the labels on transitions. This seemingly minor notational change—coupled with the use of symbolic indices to access the auxiliary information—is surprisingly beneficial. MSOS rules for many language constructs can be specified independently of whatever components labels might have; rules that require particular components can access and set those components without mentioning other components at all.

- Rules for constructs for control flow are particularly simple: For instance, the MSOS rules for conditional expressions do not require labels to have any particular components, and their formulation remains valid regardless of whether expressions are purely functional, have side-effects, raise exceptions, or interact with concurrent processes:

$$\frac{E_1 \xrightarrow{X} E_1'}{cond\left(E_1, E_2, E_3\right) \xrightarrow{X} cond\left(E_1', E_2, E_3\right)}$$

$$cond\left(true, E_2, E_3\right) \rightarrow E_2$$

$$cond\left(false, E_2, E_3\right) \rightarrow E_3$$

The label X in the first rule above could include the current environment, the initial and final stores, and any emitted communication signals. When labels are omitted, as in the second and third rule, the transitions are required to be unobservable, with no change to the store, and no emitted communication signals. Labels on adjacent transitions in a computation are required to be composable: bindings must remain fixed, and the final store of the label on a transition must be the same as the initial store of the label on the following transition.

- Rules involving auxiliary information in labels refer only to the required components:

$$\frac{E_1 \xrightarrow{X} E_1'}{assign\left(E_1, E_2\right) \xrightarrow{X} assign\left(E_1', E_2\right)}$$

$$\frac{E_1 \xrightarrow{X} E_2'}{assign(E_1, E_2) \xrightarrow{X} assign(E_1', E_2')}$$

$$\frac{\sigma' = \sigma[L \mapsto V], \quad U \in Unobs}{assign(L,V) \xrightarrow{\{\sigma,\sigma',U\}} E_2}$$

In the first two rules above, the label X is arbitrary. In the last rule, however, the relationship between the store σ at the start of the transition and the store σ at the end of the transition is determined, and any other components are required to be unobservable.

Reduction Semantics

This framework was developed by Felleisen and his colleagues towards the end of the 1980's. It has been used primarily in theoretical studies, where it is sometimes preferred to SOS; for instance, Reppy used Reduction Semantics to define (parts of) Concurrent ML.

- States are abstract syntax trees, corresponding to well-formed terms: States don't involve abstract mathematical values (numbers, sets, maps, etc.) at all: they are purely syntactic. For example, numerical expressions compute decimal numerals rather than abstract mathematical numbers. If needed, however, auxiliary constructs may be added to the abstract syntax (as in SOS).

- Transitions are term rewriting steps, called reductions: Term Rewriting is an interesting and well-developed topic in its own right. A rewriting step is called a reduction (regardless of whether the resulting term is actually smaller than the previous one or not). The sub-term that gets rewritten in a reduction is called a redex, and the resulting sub-term is called a reduct. Reductions may normally be made in any sub-term, and continue until no more are possible—perhaps never terminating.

- Redexes are restricted to occurrences in evaluation contexts: When the term being reduced corresponds to the abstract syntax of a program, the location of the redexes of the reductions should be restricted to follow the flow of control of the computation (otherwise reductions could be prematurely made in parts of the program that were not even supposed to be executed, leading to unintended results).

An evaluation context C: Ctx is a term with a single hole. If t is a term, C[t] is the result of replacing the hole in C by t. A reduction in a context C is written C[t] –→ C [t'] (written with a longer arrow), and can be made whenever there is an ordinary reduction t → t' (written with a shorter arrow). In fact C[t] here is generally the entire program context of t, assuming that there are no further rules that would allow a reduction in a context to be regarded as an ordinary reduction.

Rules may be given also for rewriting the context as well as the term in that context: C[t] –→ C [t']; in this case it is not required that t → t' should be an ordinary reduction. The evaluation contexts for use in reduction semantics are specified by a context-free grammar.

- Simple SOS rules correspond to reductions: Comparing SOS with Reduction Semantics, the simple rules of an SOS generally correspond directly to rules for ordinary reductions. For example, consider the following reduction rules for continuing with the evaluation of a conditional expression after its condition has been evaluated:

$$cond\left(true, E_2, E_3\right) \to E_2$$

$$cond\left(false, E_2, E_3\right) \to E_3$$

- Conditional SOS rules correspond to productions for evaluation contexts: Many conditional SOS rules simply express the flow of control of the computation, such as indicating which sub-expression is to be evaluated first. These SOS rules correspond not to reduction rules, but rather to productions in the grammar for evaluation contexts. For example, the rules for evaluating the condition of a conditional expression and the two sides of an assignment expression correspond to the following productions for contexts:

$$Ctx ::= cond\left(Ctx, Exp, Exp\right) \middle| assign\left(Ctx, Exp\right) \middle| assign\left(Exp, Ctx\right)$$

  The absence of further contexts for conditional expressions prevents the premature reduction of the branches. The order of evaluation of the sub expressions in an assignment expression is left open above, allowing interleaving; sequential evaluation would be specified by using assign(Val, Ctx) instead of assign(Exp, Ctx).

- Reductions that replace the evaluation context do not correspond directly to SOS rules: A significant advantage of Reduction Semantics is that it is straightforward to specify rules that affect the entire context of the sub-expression being evaluated. For example, the following rule specifies clearly that when 'exit' is evaluated, the remaining evaluation of the entire program is terminated.

$$C\left[exit\right] \to null$$

  Exceptions can be specified in a similar way, although to restrict exception handling to the innermost matching handler requires the introduction of many new evaluation contexts.

- Computed values are simply canonical terms in normal form: The computed values in a Reduction Semantics for a language like ML would include not only numerals and Booleans, but also tuples, lists, and records with values as components. The syntax of values is specified by a context free grammar—for example, by taking some of the productions for expressions Exp from the grammar for the full abstract syntax, and replacing Exp by Val (except within abstractions).

- Bindings are represented by substitution, which is it tedious to specify: Substitution replaces identifiers by the values to which they are bound, and can be specified by reduction rules (or defined educationally). In Reduction Semantics, there is unfortunately no alternative to the use of substitution to deal with the bindings that arise in the semantics of local declarations.

- Effects on storage are represented by rewriting a store term: A term representing a store is a sequence of canonical assignments, i.e. assignments where the location and the value have already been evaluated. There is only one level of store—in contrast to the situation with local bindings—so it can be kept as a separate component of the entire program context:

$$ProgCtx ::= prog - ctx(Ctx, Store)$$

$$Store ::= skip \mid seq(Store, update(Loc, Val))$$

When the left- and right-hand sides of an assignment expression (or statement) have been evaluated, the effect of the assignment is simply added to the store, by giving a reduction that replaces the entire context:

$$prog - ctx(C[assign(L, V)], \sigma) \rightarrow$$

$$prog - ctx(C[null], seq(\sigma, update(L, V)))$$

Inspecting the value stored at a particular location also involves the context, but does not change it:

$$\frac{\sigma = seq(\sigma', update(L, V))}{prog - ctx(C[stored(L)], \sigma) \rightarrow prog - ctx(C[V], \sigma)}$$

$$\sigma = seq(\sigma', update(L', V)), \qquad L' \neq L',$$

$$\frac{prog - ctx(C[stored(L)], \sigma') \rightarrow prog - ctx(C[V], \sigma')}{prog - ctx(C[stored(L)], \sigma) \rightarrow prog - ctx(C[V], \sigma)}$$

- Reduction rules for communication involve separate evaluation contexts for the concurrent processes involved: For example, suppose that a system of concurrent processes is represented as a map from thread identifiers to states of threads, then synchronous communication can be specified thus:

$$\{I_1 = C_1[send(K, V)]\} + \{I_2 = C_2[receive(K)]\} + TM \rightarrow$$

$$\{I1 = C1[null]\} + \{I_2 = C_2[V]\} + TM$$

Abstract State Machine Semantics

Abstract State Machines (ASM) is an operational semantics framework that was proposed by Gurevich in the late 1980's. The main aim was to specify the individual steps of computations at the proper level of abstraction; issues such as control flow and scopes of bindings were regarded as of secondary importance. The framework has been applied to several major languages, including ML and Java. However, the details and general style of ASM specifications vary considerably between different publications; here, we shall follow, which appears to be competitive with SOS in its accessibility.

- States interpret static and dynamic function symbols: The interpretation of a function symbol is a map from arguments to results. The function is called static when the map doesn't change during a computation. In contrast, the values of dynamic functions on particular arguments can be initialized, changed, or made undefined. Static functions of no arguments correspond to ordinary constants, whereas dynamic functions of no arguments correspond to simple updatable variables.

- Functions corresponding to arithmetic operations are static, and so is the no-argument function body that gives the abstract syntax of the initial program. In contrast, the dynamic no-argument function pos gives the position of the phrase currently being executed in the tree representing what remains to be executed, which is itself represented by the 1-argument dynamic function rest body: Pos → Phrase, where the set Phrase contains not only all possible abstract syntax trees, but also computed values, and trees where some nodes have been replaced by their computed values.

- Transitions assign values to functions for particular arguments: A transition may simultaneously assign values for several functions on various arguments. Each assignment may be conditional, depending on the values of terms formed from the function symbols. All the terms involved in a simultaneous set of assignments are evaluated before any of the assignments are actually made, so the testing of the conditions and the resulting state are independent of the order of the assignments. The values of functions on particular arguments only change due to explicit assignment: their values on other arguments remain stable.

ASM semantics of conditional expressions.

$$execJavaExp_I = case\ context(pos)of$$

$$...$$

$$cond(^{\alpha}E_1,^{\beta}E_1,^{\gamma}E_1) \rightarrow pos := \alpha$$

$$cond(\blacktriangleright V_1,^{\beta}E_2,^{\gamma}E_3) \rightarrow ifV_1\ then\ pos := \beta\ else\ pos := \gamma$$

$$cond(^{\alpha}true,\blacktriangleright V_2,^{\gamma}E_3) \rightarrow yieldUp(V_2)$$

$$cond(^{\alpha}false,\ ^{\beta}E_2,\blacktriangleright V_3) \rightarrow yieldUp(V_3)$$

$$...$$

- ASM specifications often introduce auxiliary notation: The introduction of appropriate auxiliary notation allows transition rules to be specified rather concisely. However, ASM specifications of different languages tend to introduce different auxiliary notation, which leads to quite varied specifications of the same construct, and makes it difficult to reuse a transition rule from one ASM directly in another ASM. For example, the auxiliary notation introduced in the ASM specification of Java includes:

  ○ context(pos), returning either restbody(pos) or restbody(up(pos)).

○ yieldUp(V), abbreviating the transition restbody := restbody[V/up(pos)] performed simultaneously with pos := up(pos), thus combining the replacement of a phrase by its computed result V with the adjustment of pos.

To "streamline the notation", positions are indicated directly in patterns for phrases, the current value of pos being written ▶ . After these preliminaries, transition rules for evaluating Java's conditional expressions can be specified.

Note that transitions are specified by assignments written with ':=', and the '→'s above are merely part of the 'case' notation for pattern-matching (which is not itself provided by the ASM framework, but introduced ad hoc) in.

- Bindings are modelled by stacks of frames in ASM: The dynamic no-argument function locals: (Id, Val) Map gives maps from local variable identifiers directly to the values that they are storing. To cope with redeclaration of local variables and with recursive procedural activation (both of which may require different values for the same variable identifier to coexist), a stack of frames is maintained, each frame storing the relevant locals. Thus the transition for an assignment expression assign (I, ▶ V), where the new value V has already been computed, can be specified by locals: = locals [I → V], without overwriting the value of other active local variables having the same identifier I (the notation used for maps in is actually slightly different).

  It might seem more natural to treat locals as a unary dynamic function from variable identifiers to values, but the ASM framework is first-order, and doesn't allow functions themselves to be used as values.

- Exceptions are modelled by propagation: In the Definition of Standard ML, an informal "exception convention" was introduced, so that a lot of tedious transition rules could be left implicit. In the ASM specification of Java, the propagation of raised exceptions is specified explicitly by introducing a predicate propagates Abr on phrases, then using a special pattern phrase (▶ A) which matches arbitrary phrases that have a raised exception A as any immediate component.

- Multiple threads can be modelled in various ways: Separate ASM agents can be set up to execute threads independently, with access to the same storage. Synchronization between threads can be achieved using dynamic functions which indicate that particular threads have locked particular storage areas (since a lock can be both tested and conditionally set in a single transition).

In the cited ASM for Java, however, a different approach is used—motivated mainly by the requirement that the model should be executable using a recently-developed prototyping system called Asm-Gofer. The idea is that at every transition during a computation for a multi-threaded Java program, an active thread is selected arbitrarily, using a so-called choice function, which is itself left unspecified. In contrast to the situation with Distributed ASMs, this modelling of threads on a single ASM allows computations that perpetually switch between threads, without making any actual progress.

Denotational Semantics

The framework of Denotational Semantics was developed by Scott and Strachey at Oxford in the late 1960's. One of the main aims was to provide a proper mathematical foundation for reasoning about programs and for understanding the fundamental concepts of programming languages. Denotational Semantics has since been used in teaching as well as in research. It has also been used to define the functional programming language Scheme; attempts to give denotational semantics for larger programming languages have generally been less successful, although several major descriptions have been given using a notational variant of denotational semantics called VDM.

Denotations

- The denotation of a part of a program represents its contribution to overall behavior: The denotation of a construct is typically a function of arguments that represent the information available before its execution, and the result represents the information available afterwards. The intermediate states during the execution of the construct are generally of no relevance (except when interleaving is allowed) and are thus not represented, cf. big-step SOS (Natural Semantics). Usually, no termination is represented by a special value written $\perp$ (the bottom element in a partial ordering based on information content).

- Denotations are defined inductively: Semantic functions map constructs to their denotations. For example, let Exp be the abstract syntax of expressions, and let Den be the set of all (potential) denotations of expressions. A semantic function for expressions:

$$\mathcal{E} : Exp \rightarrow Den$$

  is defined inductively by semantic equations such as:

$$\varepsilon \left[\!\left[\, cond\left(E_1, E_2, E_3\right) \right]\!\right] = F \left[\!\left[\, \varepsilon[[E_1]], \, \varepsilon[[E_2]], \, \varepsilon\left[[E_3]\right] \right]\!\right]$$

- λ-notation is used to specify how the denotations of components are to be combined: F : Den³ → Den above is defined using so-called λ-notation, which is a mathematical notation for function abstraction (a function with argument xis written λx.t), application, and composition, extended with a case construct and a few other useful features. Note that both E and F above are higher-order functions, assuming that Den is a set of functions.

- Denotations of loops and recursive procedures are least fixed-points of continuous functions on Scott-domains: To define the denotation d of a loop, for instance, we need to be able to provide a well-defined solution to d = F (d), where F (d) is a particular composition of d with the denotations of the loop condition and body. It turns out that such an equation always has a solution, and in particular it has a least solution— provided only that F : Den → Den is continuous in a certain sense on Den, which has to be a Scott-domain: a cpo (complete partially-ordered set). In fact F is always continuous when defined using λ-notation, so in practice, familiarity with the mathematical foundations of Denotational Semantics is not required.

Direct and Continuation-Passing Styles

The denotational semantics of a purely functional language may be in direct or in continuation-passing style. Using the direct style let Den = Val⊥; then the denotations of conditional expressions can be defined as follow:

$$\varepsilon[\![cond(E_1, E_2, E_3)]\!] =$$
$$case\ \varepsilon\|E_1\|\ of\ true \Rightarrow \varepsilon[\![E_2]\!] |$$
$$flase \Rightarrow \varepsilon[\![E_3]\!]$$

Note that if the denotation of E_1 is ⊥, then so is that of the whole conditional expression; this reflects that if the evaluation of E_1 never terminates, then neither does that of the enclosing expression. If the evaluation of E_1 does terminate, it should give either tt or ff, which are here the denotations of the corresponding Boolean constants:

$$\varepsilon[\![true]\!] = tt \qquad \varepsilon[\![flase]\!] = f$$

(In Denotational Semantics, one generally avoids use of syntactic phrases such as true and false in the set of denotations.) The so-called continuation style of denotational semantics looks rather different. Here one would take Den = K → A, where K = Val → A and A is some set of values representing the possible results of executing complete programs (e.g. for ML, A would be Val together with some values representing unhandled exceptions). The idea is that the continuation given as argument to $\mathcal{E}$ [[E_1]] is supposed to be applied to the value computed by E_1; if E_1 never terminates, or terminates exceptionally, the continuation is simply ignored. The continuation for E_1 involves the denotations of E_2 and E_3, which are both given the continuation k provided for the entire conditional expression.

$$\mathcal{E}[\![cond(E_1, E_2, E_3)]\!] =$$
$$\lambda k.\mathcal{E}[\![E_1]\!](\lambda t.case\ t\ of\ tt \Rightarrow \mathcal{E}[\![E_2]\!]k\ |\ ff \Rightarrow \mathcal{E}[\![E_3]\!]k)$$

If E_1 is simply true, its denotation applies the continuation k to the corresponding value:

$$\mathcal{E}[\![true]\!] = \lambda k.k(tt) \qquad etc.$$

Bindings are represented by explicit arguments of denotations: Regardless of whether denotations are in the direct style or using continuations, the dependency of the values of identifiers on the bindings provided by their context is represented by letting denotations be functions of environments. For instance, let Den = Env → Val⊥; then the direct semantics for conditional expressions would be formulated as follows:

$$\mathcal{E}[\![cond(E_1, E_2, E_3)]\!] =$$
$$\lambda\rho.case\ \mathcal{E}[\![E_1]\!]\rho\ of\ tt \Rightarrow \mathcal{E}[\![E_2]\!]\rho\ |$$
$$ff \Rightarrow \mathcal{E}[\![E_3]\!]\rho$$

The denotation of an identifier simply applies the environment to the identifier itself:

$$\mathcal{E}\big[\![I]\!\big] = \lambda\rho.\rho(I)$$

Effects on storage are represented by letting denotations be functions from stores to stores: It might seem that the easiest would be to add stores as arguments and results to the direct-style denotations given above, taking Den = Env → (Store → (Val × Store) $_{\perp}$). However, that would lead to the following semantic equation for conditional expressions, which is not as perspicuous as one might wish:

$$\mathcal{E}\big[\![cond(E_1, E_2, E_3)]\!\big] =$$
$$\lambda\rho.\lambda\sigma.\big(\lambda(t,\sigma').case\ t\ of\ tt \Rightarrow \mathcal{E}\big[\![E_2]\!\big]\rho\ \sigma'\,|\,ff \Rightarrow \mathcal{E}\big[\![E_3]\!\big]\rho\sigma'\big)$$
$$\big(\mathcal{E}\big[\![E_1]\!\big]\rho\sigma\big)$$

So let us instead try adding stores to the denotations used with the continuation style semantics. The appropriate set of denotations is then Den = Env → K → C, where K = Val → C, and C = Store → A and we may give a relatively straightforward-looking semantic equation—not even mentioning the stores, which automatically follow the flow of control in continuation semantics:

$$\varepsilon\big[\![cond(E_1, E_2, E_3)]\!\big] =$$
$$\lambda\rho.\lambda\rho.\,\varepsilon\big[\![E_1]\!\big]\rho\big(\lambda\rho.case\ t\ of\ tt\big) \Rightarrow \varepsilon\big[\![E_2]\!\big]\rho k\,|$$
$$ff \Rightarrow \big(\big[\,\varepsilon\big[\![E_3]\!\big]\rho k\big)$$

No determinism and interleaving can be represented by letting denotations be set-valued functions: In operational frameworks based on transition relations, the possibility of nondeterministic computations doesn't make any difference to how rules are formulated. In denotational semantics, however, the use of functions as denotations means that the ranges of the functions have to be changed to allow them to return sets of possible results; moreover, other functions that are to be composed with these set-valued functions have to be extended to functions that take sets as arguments. As one may imagine, the extra notation required leads to further complication of the specifications of denotations.

Since interleaving generally entails no determinism, its denotational description obviously requires the use of set-valued functions. However, a further problem arises: it simply isn't possible to compose functions that map initial states to (sets of) final states so as to obtain a function corresponding to their interleaving at intermediate states. So-called resumptions are needed: these are functions representing the points at which interleaving can take place, and correspond closely to the computations used in operational semantics.

Denotational semantics is applicable to modelling languages: The denotation of a model can be taken to be the set of entities that the model specifies. As with big-step SOS, the abstract syntax of the modelling language has to be tree-structured.

Denotational semantics is applicable to modelling languages: The denotation of a model can be taken to be the set of entities that the model specifies. As with big-step SOS, the abstract syntax of the modelling language has to be tree-structured.

Monadic Semantics

Use of monadic notation gives good modularity: The straightforward use of λ-notation to specify how denotations are combined requires awareness of the exact structure of the denotations: whether they are functions of environments, stores, continuations, etc. When new constructs are added to a language, it may be necessary to change the structure of the denotations, and reformulate all the semantic equations that involve those denotations. Thus it appears that use of λ-notation is a major hindrance to obtaining modularity in denotational descriptions.

However, suppose that we define some auxiliary notation for combining denotations, corresponding to fundamental concepts such as sequencing. We may then be able to specify denotations using the auxiliary notation, without any dependence on the structure of denotations. If we later change that structure, we shall also have to change the definition of the auxiliary notation—but the use of that notation in the semantic equations may remain the same.

Monadic Semantics provides a particular auxiliary notation for use in Denotational Semantics. It was developed by Moggi at the end of the 1980's, and inspired by category-theoretic concepts. The basic idea is that denotations compute values of particular types; when two such denotations are sequenced, the value computed by the first one is made available to the second one, written 'let x = d_1 in d_2' (where d_2 usually depends on x). The only other bit of essential notation is for forming a denotation that simply computes a particular value v, which is written '[v]'. A set of denotations equipped with this notation may be regarded as a mathematical structure called a monad. Here is how the semantic equation for conditional expressions looks in the monadic variant of Denotational Semantics:

$$\mathcal{E}\left[\left[cond\left(E_1, E_2, E_3\right)\right]\right] =$$
$$let\ t = \mathcal{E}\left[\left[E_1\right]\right]\ in$$
$$case\ t\ of\ tt \Rightarrow \mathcal{E}\left[\left[E_2\right]\right] | ff \Rightarrow \mathcal{E}\left[\left[E_3\right]\right]$$

Note that as well as being independent of the structure of denotations, the monadic semantic equation is also more perspicuous and suggestive of the intended semantics than our previous semantic equations were.

Monad transformers add support for further features: How about further ways of combining denotations that might be needed, but which are not based on sequencing? Some monad transformers are available: fundamental ways of adding features to denotations (bindings, effects on storage, exceptions, nondeterministic choice, interleaving, etc.), together with appropriate notation. Unfortunately, it isn't always so straightforward to combine different monad transformers, and difficulties can arise when trying to redefine auxiliary notation in connection with applying a monad transformer.

Axiomatic Semantics

Axiomatic Semantics was developed primarily by Hoare in the late 1960's. The main aim was initially to provide a formal basis for the verification of abstract algorithms; later, the framework was applied to the definition of programming languages, and consideration of Axiomatic Semantics influenced the design of Pascal.

- A Hoare Logic gives rules for the relation between assertions about values of variables before and after execution of each construct: Usually, the constructs concerned are only statements S. Suppose that P and Q are assertions about the values of particular variables; then the so-called partial correctness formula P{S} Q states that if P holds at the beginning of an execution of S and the execution terminates, Q will always hold at the end of that execution. Notice that P{S} Q does not require S to terminate, nor does it require Q to hold after an execution of S when P didn't hold at the beginning of the execution. A Hoare Logic specifies the relation P{S} Q inductively by rules, in the same way that as an SOS specifies a transition relation.

- Expressions are assumed to have no side-effects: Expressions are used in assertions, so their interpretation has to be purely mathematical, without effects on storage, exceptions, non-terminating function calls, etc. For example, consider conditional statements with the following abstract syntax, where the conditions are restricted to pure boolean-valued expressions:

$$Stm ::= cond(Exp, Stm, Stm)$$

A typical rule given for this construct is:

$$\frac{(P \wedge E)\{S_1\} R, \qquad (P \wedge \neg E)\{S_2\} R}{P\{cond(E, S_1, S_2)\} R}$$

Notice the use of E as a sub-formula in the assertions, holding when the expression evaluates to true. Similarly, the usual rule for assignment is:

$$P[E / I]\{update(I, E)\} P$$

This involves the substitution P [E/I] of an expression E for an identifier I in an assertion P.

- Bindings can be represented by explicit environments: In many presentations of Hoare Logic, bindings are left implicit: the relation P{S} Q is defined on the basis of a fixed set of bindings. To reflect local declarations, it is necessary to use more elaborate formulae such as ρ | P{S} Q, where the current bindings ρ are made explicit.

- Hoare Logic for concurrent processes involves rules for interleaving: Hoare Logic is exploited in connection with the development and verification of concurrent processes. The rules can get rather complicated.

- Predicate transformer semantics is essentially denotational: In connection with a methodology for developing programs from specifications, Dijkstra defined, for each statement S and post condition Q, the weakest precondition P guaranteeing total correctness: if P holds at the beginning of the execution of S, then S always terminates, and Q holds at the end of the execution. Although the assertions used here are similar to those in Hoare Logic, the definition of the weakest precondition P is actually inductive in the structure of the statement S, and Dijkstra's semantics is better considered as denotational (with the denotations being predicate transformers, i.e. functions on the interpretation of assertions) rather than axiomatic.

Action Semantics

The Action Semantics framework was developed by the present author, in collaboration with Watt, in the second half of the 1980's. (The UML Action Semantics is to some extent similar in spirit to the original Action Semantics framework, although there are major technical differences.)

- Action Semantics is a hybrid of denotational and operational semantics. As in denotational semantics, inductively-defined semantic functions map phrases to their denotations, only here, the denotations are so-called actions. The notation for actions is itself defined operationally.

- Action Semantics avoids the use of higher-order functions expressed in λ-notation: The universe of pure mathematical functions is so distant from that of (most) programming languages that the representation of programming concepts in it is often excessively complex. The foundations of reflexive Scott-domains and higher-order functions are unfamiliar and inaccessible to many programmers (although the idea of functions that takes other functions as arguments, and perhaps also return functions as results, is not difficult in it).

- Action semantics provides a rich action notation with a direct operational interpretation: The universe of actions involves not only control and data flow, but also scopes of bindings, effects on storage, and interactive processes, allowing a simple and direct representation of many programming concepts.

Computed values are given by actions, and the action combination 'A1 then A2' passes all the values given by A1 to A2. For example, assuming evaluate: Exp → Action, the value computed by evaluate E1 is the one tested by the action 'given true' below:

$$evaluate\ cond\left(E_1, E_2, E_3\right)$$
$$= evaluate\ E_1\ then$$
$$\left(given\ true\ then\ evaluate\ E_2\ otherwise\ evaluate\ E_3\right)$$

Bindings are implicitly propagated to the sub-actions of most actions, and can always be referred to, as illustrated below:

$$evaluate\ I = give\ the\ val\ bound\ to\ I$$

Effects on storage implicitly follow the flow of control:

$$evaluate\ assign(E_1, E_2) =$$
$$evaluate\ E_1\ and\ evaluate\ E_2$$
$$then\ update(the\ loc\#1, the\ val\#2)$$

Concurrent processes are represented by agents that perform separate actions, with asynchronous message-passing.

Semantic Domains

Semantic Domains are Semantic Fields that are characterized by set of domain words which often occur in texts about corresponding domain.

- Words belonging to the same lexical field are called "domain words".

- Usually large potion of the language terminology is characterized by domain words.

Lexical Coherence Assumption

Basic hypothesis:

- A great percentage of the concepts expressed in the same text belongs to the same domain.

- It's a basic property of any natural language: domain-specific words co-occur with each other in the same text; this property is called "lexical coherence".

- There are common areas of human knowledge such as Economics, Politics, Law, Science, etc. All these areas demonstrate lexical coherence.

So, what about Semantic Fields?

- Semantic Fields are lexically coherent: words in one SF tend to co-occur in texts.

- We call these fields "Semantic Domains": they are Semantic Fields characterized by lexically coherent words.

Lexical coherence assumption:

- We assume that real-world documents are lexically coherent.

- This guarantees the existence of Semantic Domains.

- It's also proven by experiments: in real texts if you count the percentage of words that belong to the same domain, you'll see that the most belong to one domain.

There are 3 types of words:

- Text-Related Domain words: words that have at least one sense that contributes to determining the domain of the whore text. e.g. word "bank" in a text about economy.

- Text-Unrelated Domain words: words that are from some non-generic domain, but don't contribute to the domain of the text. e.g. word "church" in a text about economy.

- Text-Unrelated Generic words: don't bring any relevant domain information. e.g. "to be".

Let's put the lexical coherence assumption more formally:

- "One domain per discourse" ($\approx$ text, document) assumption.

- If a word is used in one sense in some discourse.

- Then other occurrences of this word should also have the same sense.

- Smart way of putting it: "multiple occurrences of a word in coherent portions of texts tend to share the same domain".

The lexical coherence assumption allows us to represent Semantic Domains by the set of domain-specific texts.

Role of Semantic Domains

Characterizing word senses (i.e. lexical concepts)

- Typically by assigning domain labels to words in a lexicon.

- E.g. Crane has senses in Zoology and Construction.

- WordNet Domains - extension of WordNet that adds the information about domain.

Characterizing Texts

- Can use Semantic Domains for text categorization.

- At the textual level, semantic domains are clusters of texts on similar topics.

- So can see Semantic Domains as a collection of domain-specific texts.

Practical points of view: Semantic Domains are lists of related terms that describe a particular subject/area.

Representation

Domain Sets

- Domain relations: two words are domain-related if they belong to the same domain.

- Domain set is used to describe semantic classes of texts.

- Semantic classes of strongly related lexical concepts are domain concepts.

- So a domain set should relate each word to one or more domain sets.

Requirements of an "ideal" domain set:

- Completeness: all possible texts should be assigned to at least one domain.

- Balancement: number of texts belonging to each domain should be uniform.

- Separability: the same text/concept can't be assigned to more than one domain.

Usually not achievable:

- It's quite difficult to define a complete domain set, general enough to represent all possible aspects of human knowledge.

- And it's also not possible to collect a corpus that contains all the human knowledge.

- A certain degree of overlapping is unavoidable (e.g. math/physics).

Domain Model

We can easily obtain term-based representation of documents e.g. by using Vector Space Models

- But VSMs have lexical ambiguity problem.

- Domain terms are typically highly correlated within texts: they tend to co-occur inside the same types of text.

- This is justified by the lexical coherence property of natural languages (Leacock96).

Domain model is a computational model for Semantic Domains to represent domain information:

- It describes relations at the term level.

- It does that by defining a set of term clusters (see also Term Clustering).

- Each cluster represent a semantic domain: set of terms that often co-occur in texts with similar topics.

- It's a way to represent domain information at the textual level.

Domain Model:

- Is a matrix that describes the degree of association between terms in the vocabulary and Semantic Domains?

- Rows are indexed by words.

- Columns are the corresponding domains.

Domain Model is a shallow model for lexical semantics, but it capture ambiguity and variability.

DM is represented by an n×k rectangular matrix D.

- D contains the domain relevance for each term w.r.t each domain.
  E.g.

	Medicine	CS
HIV	1	0
AIDS	1	0
virus	0.5	0.5
laptop	0	1

Formally,

- Let D= {D1, Dk} be a set of domains.

- We have n words V= {w1, wn} (n - vocabulary size).

- Then D is an n×k matrix, where Diz is domain relevance of term wi w.r.t. domain Dz.

- Let R (Dz,o) denote domain relevance of domain Dz w.r.t. some linguistic object o (text, term, concept).

- It gives a measure of association between Dz and o.

- Typically higher values indicate higher association and often the value ranges from 0 to 1.

DMs can describe ambiguity and variability:

- Ambiguity: by associating one term to several domains.

- Variability: by associating different terms to the same domain.

A domain Model defines a Domain Space.

Obtaining Domain Models

- Domain Models can be obtained from unsupervised learning or manual annotation.

- Can use WordNet Domain.

- By performing Term Clustering.

Domain relations among terms can be detected by analyzing co-occurrence in the corpus:

- Motivated by the lexical coherence assumption.

- Co-occurring terms have a good chance to show domain relations.

WordNet Based Domain Model

WordNet Domains is an extension of WordNet:

- Each synset here is annotated with one or more domain labels.

- It has ~ 200 domain labels.

Using WordNet Domain for building a domain model:

- If D= {D1, Dk} are domains of the word net domains.

- C= {c1, cs} are concepts (synsets) from WordNet.

- Then let senses (w) be a set of all synsets that contain w: senses (w) = {c|c∈C,c is a sense of w}.

- Let Rs:D×C→R be a domain relevance function for concepts.

- dom(c) is a domain assignment function, dom(c)⊆D: returns a set of domains associated with a synset c.

- $R\_s (D, c) = \backslash begin \{cases\}.$

$1 / |\text{dom}(c)| \& \text{ if } D \in \text{dom}(c) \backslash\backslash 1 / k \& \text{ if } \text{dom}(c) \equiv \backslash\{ \backslash text\{Factotum\} \backslash\} \backslash\backslash 0 \& \text{ otherwise } \backslash\backslash \backslash end\{cases\}$.

- Factotum = generic concept for all non-domain words.

- k - Cardinality of D.

- Rs(D,c)≈ estimated prior probability of the domain given the concept.

This is for synsets, not words,

- Now let V= {w1, wn} the vocabulary.

- Then domain relevance of a word is a function R: D×V→R.

- Define $R\, as\, R\left(D_z, w_i\right) = \dfrac{1}{\left|senses\left(w_i\right)\right|} \sum_{c \in senses(w_i)} R\left(D_z, c\right)$

- So it's average relevance of all wi's senses.

- If w has only one sense, then R (Dz,w)=Rs(Dz,c).

- A word with several senses ("polysemous") will be less relevant than a word with few senses.

- Words with just one sense are ("monosemic") - they will be the most relevant: they provide more information about the domain.

This is consistent with the phenomenon that less frequent words are more informative: because they have fewer senses:

The domain model D is defined as Dij=R (Dj,wi).

Limitations:

- D is fixed because WordNet Domains is fixed.

- WordNet Domains is limited: not complete.

- Lexicon in WordNet Domains is also limited.

Corpus-Based Acquisition of Domain Models

We want automatically extract domain models from corpus:

- To avoid subjectivity.

- To find more flexible models.

Term Clustering techniques are usually used for this:

- Usually need soft clustering techniques for this: want one term to be in several clusters.

- There are several ways.

- Fuzzy C-Means, Information bottleneck method, etc.

LSA is done by projecting TermVSM and TextVSM to a common LSA space using some linear transformations:

- First-order (shallow) relations between terms: their co-occurrence in texts.

- It takes into account both second-order relations: their semantics, established by co-occurrence.

DO SVD:

- $T=W\Sigma P^T$.

- W (for Words) is orthogonal eigenvectors of TT^T: word vectors.

- P (for Passages) is orthogonal eigenvectors of TT^T: document vectors.

- Truncated SVD: use Σ_k: first k singular values and the rest set to 0.

- $T_k=W_\Sigma kP^T \approx T$ the best approximation.

Now let's define the domain matrix,

- $D=I^N \sqrt{\sum}$.

- I^N is a diagonal matrix s.t. $I_{ii}^N = \dfrac{1}{\|w_i\|}$.

- w_i is ith column of $W\sqrt{\sum}$ - principal components ($W\sqrt{\sum}$ are loadings for words).

Domain Space

Domain Models define the Domain Space. Once a DM is determined, we can define a Domain Space,

- It's a geometric space where terms and documents can be represented as vectors.

- It's a Vector Space Model.

There are some problems of VSMs:

- TextVSM can't deal with lexical ambiguity and variability.

- E.g.: "he's affected by AIDS" and "HIV is a virus" don't have any words in common.

- So in the TextVSM the similarity is 0: these vectors are orthogonal even though the concepts are related.

- On the other hand, similarity between "the laptop has a virus" and "HIV is a virus" is not 0: due to the ambiguity of "virus".

Term VSM:

- Feature sparseness.

- If we want to model domain relations, we're mostly interested in domain-specific words.

- Such words are quite infrequent compared to non-domain words, so vectors for these words are very sparse, esp in large corpus.

- So similarity between domain words would tend to 0.

- The results overall will not be very meaningful and interesting.

Domain Spaces ftw. So a Domain Space is a cluster-based representation for estimating term and text meaning:

- It's a vector space where both terms and texts can be compared.

- Once a domain space is defined by a matrix D, can represent both terms and texts by domain vectors.

- Domain vectors - vectors that represent relevance among linguistic objects and each domain.

- Domain space is:

- It's an instance of Generalized Vector Space Model.

- For text t_i in the Text VSM.

- $t'_i = t_i(I_{idf}D)$ (TODO: why left multiplication?).

- Where I_{idf} is a diagonal matrix s.t. $I^{idf}_{ii} = idf(w_i)$ - it's inverse document frequency of word w_i.

- So we define a mapping function and thus have a generalized VSM.

In the domain space the vector representation of terms and documents is "augmented" by domain relations represented by the domain model.

Geometrically:

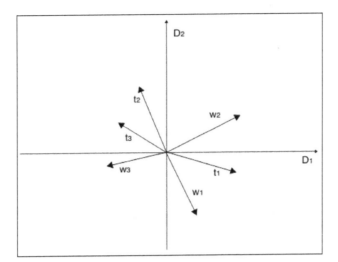

- Source: Semantic Domains in Computational Linguistics (book).
- Both terms and texts are represented in common vector space.
- So comparison between terms and texts are possible.
- Also, the dimensionality of Domain Space is generally lower.

Domain Space allows to reduce the impact of ambiguity and variability: by introducing non-sparse space.

So advantages of DS:

- Lower dimensionality.
- Sparseness is avoided.
- Duality: allows direct and uniform similarity between texts and terms.

Domain Kernel

Domain Kernel is a similarity function for terms and documents in the domain space. Domain Kernel is a Mercer Kernel, so it can be used in any kernel-based algorithm.

This kernel is represented by a DOmain Model matrix D.

- $K: R^n \cup V \rightarrow R^k$.
- Maps texts $t \in R^n$ and terms $w_i \in V$ into Domain Space: $t' \in R^k$ and $w' \in R^k$.

K is defined as:

- $K(w)=w'_i$ if $w=w_i \in V$.
- $K(w)=w'_i$ if $w_i \varepsilon V$.

- $K(w) = \dfrac{\sum t \in_T tf(w,t) \cdot t'}{\left\| \sum t \in_T tf(w,t) \cdot t' \right\|}$ *if* $w \notin V.$

- $K(t)=t(I^{\text{textidf}}D)=t'$ for documents.

- tf(w,t) is a term frequency of w in text t.

- I^{idf} is a diagonal matrix with $I_{ii}^{idf} = \dfrac{1}{\left| \{ t \in T \,|\, tf(w_i,t) > 0 \} \right|}.$

Can compute the similarity using cosine

K is defined for any term and text: K is a mercer kernel by construction: it's a dot product, but unlike many other kernels, it reduces the dimensionality instead of increasing it.

Usage

- After that we can use Domain Models for many NLP task.

- Can use domain model to estimate topic similarity.

Domain Kernels can be used for any instance-based algorithm in many NLP applications:

- Document Classification.

- Document Clustering.

- Term Clustering.

- Can use any Machine Learning algorithm with this kernel, e.g. SVM.

Static and Dynamic Semantics

The static and dynamic semantics are properties of the abstract syntax (terms) rather than the concrete syntax (strings). Therefore we will deal exclusively with abstract syntax here.

The static semantics can further be decomposed into two parts: variable scope and rules of typing. They determine how to interpret variables, and discern the meaningful expressions.

Variable scope is encoded directly into the terms representing the abstract syntax. The second step will be to give the rules of typing in the form of an inductively defined judgment. This is not very interesting for arithmetic expressions, comprising only a single type, but it serve to illustrate the ideas.

The dynamic semantics varies more greatly between different languages and different levels of abstraction. The basic principle of variable binding called `lexical scoping` is that the name of a bound variable should not matter. In other words, consistently renaming a variable in a program should not affect its meaning. Everything below will follow from this principle.

We now make this idea of "consistent renaming of variables" more precise. The development in takes simultaneous substitution as a primitive; we avoid the rather heavy notation by only dealing with a single substitution at a time. This goes hand in hand with the decision that binding prefixes such as `x.t` only ever bind a single variable, and not multiple ones. We use the notation `{y/x/t}` to denote the result of substituting y for x in t, yet to be defined. With that we will define renaming of x to y with the equation,

```
x.t ≡ y.{y/x}t
```

which can be applied multiple times, anywhere in a term. For this to preserve the meaning, y most not already occur free in x.t, because otherwise the free occurrence of y would be captured by the new binder. As an example, consider the term,

```
let(num(1), x.let(plus(x, num(1)), y.plus(y, x)))
```

which should evaluate to num(3). It should be clear that renaming y to x should be disallowed. The resulting term,

```
let(num(1), x.let(plus(x, num(1)), x.plus(x, x)))
```

means something entirely different and would evaluate to num(4). To make this side condition more formal, we define the set of free variables in a term.

$$FV(x) = \{x\}$$
$$FV(o(t_1, \ldots, t_n)) = \bigcup_{1 \le i \le n} FV(t_i)$$
$$FV(x.t) = FV(t) \setminus \{x\}$$

So before defining the substitution {y/x}t we restate the rule defining variable renaming, also called α-conversion, with the proper side condition:

$$x.t \equiv y.\{y/x\}t \quad provided \ y/ \in FV(t)$$

Now back to the definition of substitution of one variable y for another variable x in a term t, {y/x}t. The definition recurses over the structure of a term.

$$\{y/x\}x = y$$
$$\{y/x\}z = z \qquad provided \ x \neq z$$
$$\{y/x\}o(t_1, \ldots, t_n) = o(\{y/x\}t_1, \ldots, \{y/x\}t_n)$$

$$\{y/x\}x.t = x.t$$
$$\{y/x\}z.t = x.\{y/x\}t \quad provided \ x \neq z \ and \ y \neq z$$
$$\{y/x\}y.t \quad undefined \ provided \ x \neq z$$

Note that substitution is a partial operation. The reason the last case must be undefined is because any occurrence of x in t would be replaced by y and thereby captured. As an example while this must be ruled out, reconsider,

```
let(num(1), x.let(plus(x, num(1)), y.plus(y, x)))
```

which evaluates to num(3). If we were allowed to rename x to y we would obtain,

```
let(num(1), y.let(plus(y, num(1)), y.plus(y, y)))
```

which once again means something entirely different and would evaluate.

In the operational semantics we need a more general substitution, because we need to substitute one term for a variable in another term. We generalize the definition above, taking care to rewrite the side condition on substitution in a slightly more general, but consistent form, in order to prohibit variable capture.

$$\{u/x\}x = u$$

$$\{u/x\}z = z \qquad provided \ x \neq z$$

$$\{u/x\}o(t_1, \ldots, t_n) = o(\{u/x\}t_1, \ldots, \{u/x\}t_n)$$

$$\{u/x\}x.t = x.t$$

$$\{y/x\}z.t = x.\{u/x\}t \ \ provided \ x \neq z \ and \ y/ \in FV(u)$$

$$\{u/x\}z.t \ \ undefined \ provided \ x \neq z \ and \ y \in FV(u)$$

In practice we would like to treat substitution as a total operation. This cannot be justified on terms, but, surprisingly, it works on α-equivalence classes of terms! Since we want to identify terms that only differ in the names of their bound variables, this is sufficient for all purposes in the theory of programming languages. More formally, the following theorem (which we will not prove) justifies treating substitution as a total operation.

Theorem 1 (Substitution and α-Conversion)

- *If $u \equiv u'$, $t \equiv t'$ and $\{u/x\}t$ and $\{u'/x\}t'$ are both defined, then $\{u/x\}t \equiv \{u'/x\}t'$.*
- Given `u`, `x`, and `t`, then there always exists a `t'` $\equiv$ `t` such that $\{u/x\}t'$ is defined.

We sketch the proof of part (ii), which proceeds by induction on the size of t. If $\{u/x\}t$ is defined we choose `t'` to be `t`. Otherwise, then somewhere the last clause in the definition of substitution applies and there is a binder `z.t1` in t such that z ∈ FV(u). Then we can rename z to a new variable z 0 which occurs neither in free in u nor free in `z.t1` to obtain z'.t' 1. Now we can continue with z 0.{u/x}t'1. by an appeal to the induction hypothesis.

The algorithm described in this proof is in fact the definition of `capture avoiding substitution` which makes sense whenever we are working modulo α-equivalence classes of terms.

With the variable binding, renaming, and substitution understood, we can now formulate a first version of the typing rules for this language. Because there is only one type, `tnat`, the rules are somewhat trivialized. Their only purpose for this small language is to verify that an expression e is closed, that is, `FV (e) = { }`. In order to specify this inductively, we use a new judgment form a so-called hypothetical judgment. We write it as,

$$J_1, \ldots, J_n \vdash J$$

which means that J follows from assumptions `J1, ... , Jn`. Its most basic property is that,

$$J_1, \ldots, J_i, \ldots J_n \vdash J_i$$

always holds, which should be obvious: if an assumption is identical to the judgment we are trying to derive, we are done. We will nonetheless restate instances of this general principle for each case. The particular form of hypothetical judgment we consider is,

```
x1:nat,... , xn:nat ⊢ e : nat
```

which should be read:

Under the assumption that variables x1, ... , xn stand for natural numbers, e has the type of natural number.

We usually abbreviate a whole sequence of assumptions with the letter Γ. 2 We write '·' for an empty collection of assumptions, and we abbreviate ·, x:nat by x:nat.

$$\frac{x : nat \in \Gamma}{\Gamma \vdash x : nat} \qquad \frac{}{\Gamma \vdash num(k) : nat}$$

$$\frac{\Gamma \vdash e_1 : nat \quad \Gamma \vdash e_2 : nat}{\Gamma \vdash plus(e_1, e_2) : nat} \qquad \frac{\Gamma \vdash e_1 : nat \quad \Gamma \vdash e_2 : nat}{\Gamma \vdash times(e_1, e_2) : nat}$$

$$\frac{\Gamma \vdash e_1 : nat \quad \Gamma, x : nat \vdash e_2 : nat}{\Gamma \vdash let(e_1, x.e_2) : nat}$$

The point of being interested in typing for this small language is only to guarantee that there are no free variables in a term to the evaluation will not get stuck. This property can easily be verified.

Theorem

```
If  ·  `  e : nat then FV(e) = { }.
```

Proof: We cannot prove this directly by rule induction, since the second premise of the rule for let introduces an assumption. So we generalizing to,

```
If x1:nat,... , xn:nat ⊢e : nat then FV(e) ⊆ {x1,... , xn}.
```

This generalized statement can be proved easily by rule rule induction. Next we would like to give the operational semantics, specifying the value of an expression. We represent values also as expressions, although they are restricted to have the form num(k). There are multiple ways to specify the operational semantics, for example as a structured operational semantics or as evaluation semantics. We give two forms of evaluation semantics here, which directly relate an expression to its value although they do not specify how to compute the value precisely. The first way3 employs a hypothetical judgment in which we make assumptions about the values of variables. It is written as,

$$x1 \Downarrow v_1, \ldots, x_n \Downarrow v_n \vdash e \Downarrow v.$$

We call $x1 \Downarrow v_1, \ldots, x_n \Downarrow v_n \vdash e \Downarrow v.$ an environment and denote an environment by η. It is important that all variables xi in an environment are distinct so that, the value of a variable is uniquely determined.

$$\frac{x \Downarrow v \in \eta}{\eta \vdash x \Downarrow v} \qquad\qquad \frac{}{\eta \vdash num(k) \Downarrow num(k)}$$

$$\frac{\eta \vdash e1 \Downarrow num(k_1) \quad \eta \vdash e_2 \Downarrow num(k_2)}{\eta \vdash plus(e_1,e_2) \Downarrow num(k_1 + k_2)} \quad \frac{\eta \vdash e_1 \Downarrow num(k_1) \quad \eta \vdash e_2 \Downarrow num(k_2)}{\eta \vdash times(e_1,e_2) \Downarrow num(k_1 \times k_2)}$$

$$\frac{\eta \vdash e1 \Downarrow v_1 \quad \eta, x \Downarrow v_1 \vdash e_2 \Downarrow v_2}{\eta \vdash let(e_1,x.e_2) \Downarrow v_2} \quad (x \text{ not declared in } \eta)$$

In the rule for let we make the assumption that the value of x is v1 while evaluating e2. One may be concerned that this operational semantics is partial, in case bound variables with the same name occur nested in a term. However, since us working with α-equivalences classes of terms we can always rename the inner bound variable to that the rule for let applies. We will henceforth not make such a side condition explicit, using the general convention that we rename bound variables as necessary so that contexts or environment declare only distinct variables.

An alternative semantics uses substitution instead of environments. For this judgment we evaluate only closed terms, so no hypothetical judgment is needed.

$$\textit{No rule for variables x} \qquad\qquad \frac{}{num(k) \Downarrow num(k)}$$

$$\frac{e_1 \Downarrow num(k_1) \quad e_2 \Downarrow num(k_2)}{plus(e_1,e_2) \Downarrow num(k_1 + k_2)} \quad \frac{e_1 \Downarrow num(k_1) \quad e_2 \Downarrow num(k_2)}{times(e_1,e_2) \Downarrow num(k_1 \times k_2)}$$

$$\frac{e_1 \Downarrow v_1 \quad \{v_1 / x\} e_2 \Downarrow v_2}{let(e_1,x.e_2) \Downarrow v_2}$$

Denotational Semantics

Denotational semantics is based on the recognition that programs and the objects they manipulate are symbolic realizations of abstract mathematical objects, for example,

- Strings of digits realize numbers.

- Function subprograms realize (approximate) mathematical functions.

The idea of denotational semantics is to associate an appropriate mathematical object, such as a number, a tuple, or a function, with each phrase of the language. The phrase is said to denote the mathematical object, and the object is called the denotation of the phrase.

Syntactically, a phrase in a programming language is defined in terms of its constituent parts by its BNF specification. The decomposition of language phrases into their sub phrases is reflected in the abstract syntax of the programming language as well. A fundamental principle of denotational semantics is that the definition be compositional. That means the denotation of a language construct is defined in terms of the denotations of its sub phrases. Later we discuss reasons for having compositional definitions.

Traditionally, denotational definitions use special brackets, the emphatic brackets⟦ ⟧, to separate the syntactic world from the semantic world. If p is a syntactic phrase in a programming language, then a denotational specification of the language will define a mapping meaning, so that meaning [[p]] is the denotation of p—namely, an abstract mathematical entity that models the semantics of p.

For example, the expressions "2*4", "(5+3)", "008", and "8" are syntactic phrases that all denote the same abstract object, namely the integer 8. Therefore with a denotational definition of expressions we should be able to show that,

$$\text{meaning } [[2*4]] = \text{meaning } [[(5+3)]] = \text{meaning } [[008]] = \text{meaning } [[8]] = 8.$$

Functions play a prominent role in denotational semantics, modeling the bindings in stores and environments as well as control abstractions in programming languages. For example, the "program".

$$\text{fact}(n) = \text{if } n=0 \text{ then } 1 \text{ else } n*\text{fact}(n-1)$$

denotes the factorial function, a mathematical object that can be viewed as the set of ordered pairs,

$$\{<0,1>,<1,1>,<2,2>,<3,6>,<4,24>,<5,120>,<6,720>, ...\}$$

and a denotational semantics should confirm this relationship. A denotational specification of a programming language consists of five components, two specifying the syntactic world, one describing the semantic domains, and two defining the functions that map the syntactic objects to the semantic objects.

The Syntactic World

Syntactic categories or syntactic domains name collections of syntactic objects that may occur in phrases in the definition of the syntax of the language—for example,

Numeral, Command, and Expression.

Commonly, each syntactic domain has a special metavariable associated with it to stand for elements in the domain—for example,

C: Command,

E: Expression,

N: Numeral,

I: Identifier.

With this traditional notation, the colon means "element of". Subscripts will be used to provide additional instances of the metavariables. Abstract production rules describe the ways that objects from the syntactic categories may be combined in accordance with the BNF definition of the language. They provide the possible patterns that the abstract syntax trees of language phrases may take. These abstract production rules can be defined using the syntactic categories or using the metavariables for elements of the categories as an abbreviation mechanism.

Command ::= while Expression do Command+

E ::= N | I | E O E | – E

They do not fully specify the details of syntax with respect to parsing items in the language but simply portray the possible forms of syntactic constructs that have been verified as correct by some other means.

The Semantic World

Semantic domains are "sets" of mathematical objects of a particular form. The sets serving as domains have a lattice-like structure. For now we view these semantic domains as normal mathematical sets and structures—for example,

Boolean = { true, false } is the set of truth values,

Integer = { ... , -2, -1, 0, 1, 2, 3, 4, ... } is the set of integers, and

Store = (Variable → Integer) consists of sets of bindings (functions mapping variable names to values).

We use the notation A → B to denote the set of functions with domain A and codomain B.

The Connection between Syntax and Semantics

Semantic functions map objects of the syntactic world into objects in the semantic world. Constructs of the subject language—namely elements of the syntactic domains—are mapped into the semantic domains. These functions are specified by giving their syntax (domain and codomain), called their signatures—for example,

meaning : Program → Store

evaluate : Expression → (Store → Value)

and by using semantic equations to specify how the functions act on each pattern in the syntactic definition of the language phrases. For example,

evaluate $[\![E_1 + E_2]\!]$ sto = plus(evaluate $[\![E_1]\!]$ sto, evaluate $[\![E_2]\!]$ sto)

states that the value of an expression "E1 + E2" is the mathematical sum of the values of its component subexpressions. Note that the value of an expression will depend on the current bindings in the store, here represented by the variable "sto". The function evaluate maps syntactic expressions to semantic values—namely, integers—using mathematical operations such as plus. We refer to these operations as auxiliary functions in the denotational definition.

Figure: Contains a complete denotational specification of a simple language of nonnegative integer numerals. This definition requires two auxiliary functions defined in the semantic world, where Number x Number denotes the Cartesian product.

plus : Number x Number → Number

times : Number x Number → Number

Syntactic Domains
N : Numeral   -- nonnegative numerals
D : Digit   -- decimal digits
Abstract Production Rules
Numeral ::= Digit | Numeral Digit
Digit ::= 0 | 1 | 2 | 3 | 4 | 5 | 6 | 7 | 8 | 9
Semantic Domain
Number = { 0, 1, 2, 3, 4, ... }   -- natural numbers
Semantic Functions
value : Numeral → Number
digit : Digit → Number
Semantic Equations
value [[N D]] = plus (times(10, value [[N]]), digit [[D]])
value [[D]] = digit [[D]]
digit [[0]] = 0   digit [[3]] = 3   digit [[6]] = 6   digit [[8]] = 8
digit [[1]] = 1   digit [[4]] = 4   digit [[7]] = 7   digit [[9]] = 9
digit [[2]] = 2   digit [[5]] = 5

Figure: A Language of Numerals.

We need two syntactic domains for the language of numerals. Phrases in this language are mapped into the mathematical domain of natural numbers. Generally we have one semantic function for each syntactic domain and one semantic equation for each production in the abstract syntax. To distinguish numerals (syntax) from numbers (semantics), different typefaces are employed. Note the compositionality of the definition in that the value of a phrase "N D" is defined in terms of the value of N and the value of D. As an example of evaluating a numeral according to this denotational definition, we find the value of the numeral 65:

value [] = plus(times(10, value [[6]]), digit [[5]])

= plus(times(10, digit [[6]]), 5)

= plus(times(10, 6), 5)

= plus(60, 5) = 65

Solely using the specification of the semantics of numerals, we can easily prove that value [[008]] = value [[8]]:

value [[008]] = plus(times(10, value []), digit [[8]])

= plus(times(10, plus(times(10, value [[0]]), digit [[0]])), 8)

= plus(times(10, plus(times(10, digit [[0]]), 0)), 8)

= plus(times(10, plus(times(10, 0), 0)), 8)

= 8 = digit [[8]] = value [[8]]

Although the syntactic expression "008" inside the emphatic brackets is written in linear form, it actually represents the abstract syntax tree shown in Figure that reflects its derivation,

<numerals>⇒< numerals ><digit>⇒< numerals ><digit><digit>⇒

<digit>< digit >< digit >⇒0 < digit >< digit >⇒0 0 <digit>⇒0 0 8.

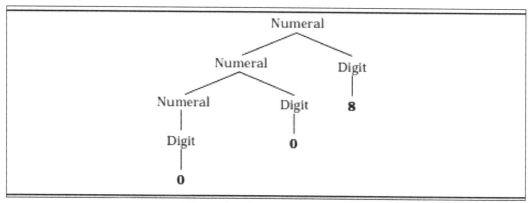

Figure: An Abstract Syntax Tree.

The elements of the syntactic world inside of the emphatic brackets are always abstract syntax trees. We write them in a linear form only for convenience. The abstract production rules will be used to describe the abstract syntax trees and the concrete syntax to disambiguate them.

Compositionality

The principle of compositionality has a long history in mathematics and the specification of languages. In his book on the semantics of programming languages, Tennent suggests three reasons for using compositional definitions:

- In a denotational definition, each phrase of a language is given a meaning that describes its contribution to the meaning of a complete program that contains it. Furthermore, the meaning of each phrase is formulated as a function of the denotations of its immediate sub phrases. As a result, whenever two phrases have the same denotation, one can be replaced by the other without changing the meaning of the program. Therefore a denotational semantics supports the substitution of semantically equivalent phrases.

- Since a denotational definition parallels the syntactic structure of its BNF specification, properties of constructs in the language can be verified by structural induction, the version of mathematical induction introduced in Chapter that follows the syntactic structure of phrases in the language.

- Compositionality lends certain elegance to denotational definitions, since the semantic equations are structured by the syntax of the language. Moreover, this structure allows the individual language constructs to be analyzed and evaluated in relative isolation from other features in the language.

As a consequence of compositionality, the semantic function value is a homomorphism, which means that the function respects operations. As an illustration, consider a function H: A → B where A has a binary operation f: AxA → A and B has a binary operation g: BxB → B. The function H is a homomorphism if H (f(x,y)) = g(H(x),H(y)) for all x,y∈A. For the example in Figure, the operation f is concatenation and g (m,n) = plus(times (10, m), n). Therefore value (f(x,y)) = g(value(x),value(y)), which thus demonstrates that value is a homomorphism.

Programming Language Specification

Formal specifications and supporting tools have shown to be very effective to improve the quality and correctness of a software system. A compiler is large and complex software; it takes as input a program written in some language and generates as output a program in another language. One of the main characteristics of any compiler is to preserve the semantics of the program being compiled. Therefore, developing correct compilers that can generate target code without introducing any errors is critically important.

Let's consider the language of infix integer arithmetic expressions with optional parentheses, the operators plus, minus, times, divide, and unary negation, and with spaces and tabs allowed between numbers and operators. We'll call the language Ael, for Arithmetic Expression Language.

When designing a language, it's a good idea to start by sketching forms that you want to appear in your language as well as forms you do not want to appear.

Examples	Non-Examples
432	43 2
24* (31/899 +3-0)/(54 /2+ 4+2*3)	24*(31/// /)/(5+---+))
(2)	[fwe]23re 3 1 124efr$#%^@
8*(((3-6)))	--2--

Concrete Syntax

Next, we look at the legal forms, and create a grammar for the concrete syntax.

```
exp = space* exp space* op space* exp space*

 | space* numlit space*

 | space* "-" space* exp space*

 | space* "(" space* exp space* ")" space*

op = "+" | "-" | "*" | "/"
```

```
numlit = digit+

digit = "0".."9"

space = " " | "\t"
```

All those "space*" occurrences make the description hard to read. But we're using so, so let's use the fact that if a rule name begins with a capital letter, it will be as if space* appears between all of the expressions on the right hand side. This gives us:

```
Exp = Exp op Exp

  | numlit

  | "-" Exp

  | "(" Exp ")"

op = "+" | "-" | "*" | "/"

numlit = digit+

digit = "0".."9"

space = " " | "\t"
```

This simple but very powerful idea leads to some useful terminology: Lexical categories start with lowercase letters. Phrase categories start with capital letters. The lexical definitions show us how to combine characters into words and punctuation (called tokens), and the phrase definitions show us how to combine words and symbols into phrases (where the words and symbols can, if you wish, be surrounded by spacing). But we still have problems. This grammar can parse the string 9-3*7 in two ways.

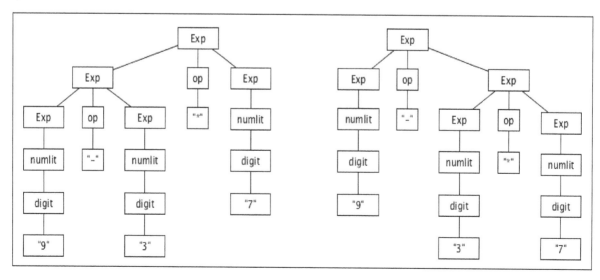

This means our syntax description is ambiguous. One way to get rid of the ambiguity is to add extra rules to build in operator precedence:

```
Exp = Term (("+" | "-") Term)*

Term = Factor (("*" | "/") Factor)*

Factor = "-"? Primary

Primary = "(" Exp ")" | numlit

numlit = digit+

digit = "0".."9"

space = " " | "\t"
```

This takes care of precedence concerns, but what if we wanted our grammar to specify associativity? We can do that too. Here is a way to make our binary operators left-associative:

```
Exp = Term | Exp ("+" | "-") Term

Term = Factor | Term ("*" | "/") Factor

Factor = Primary | "-" Primary

Primary = numlit | "(" Exp ")"

digit = "0".."9"

numlit = digit+

space = " " | "\t"
```

Abstract Syntax

We had to do a lot of specification work to define expressions as strings of characters. For example, we needed extra tokens (parentheses) and extra categories (Term, Factor, Primary) in order to capture precedence, and use other tricks to capture associativity. None of this crap matters if our languages were just trees! So let's define function A to turn a phrase into an abstract syntax tree. We write trees in the form {ABC...} where A is the root and B, C... are the children.

$$\mathcal{A}(E + T) = \{\text{Plus } \mathcal{A}(E) \, \mathcal{A}(T)\}$$
$$\mathcal{A}(E - T) = \{\text{Minus } \mathcal{A}(E) \, \mathcal{A}(T)\}$$
$$\mathcal{A}(T * F) = \{\text{Times } \mathcal{A}(T) \, \mathcal{A}(F)\}$$
$$\mathcal{A}(T / F) = \{\text{Divide} \mathcal{A}(T) \mathcal{A}(F)\}$$
$$\mathcal{A}(-P) = \{\text{Negate } \mathcal{A}(P)\}$$

$$\mathcal{A}(n) = \{\text{Numlit}n\}$$

$$\mathcal{A}((E)) = A(E)$$

Static Semantics

Think of how in a language like Java, an expression like x+5 looks beautifully well-formed and well-structured. But if x hasn't been declared, or has a type other than a number or string, the expression doesn't mean anything. So while it is syntactically correct, it can be determined meaningless without ever running a program containing it.

Ael doesn't have any semantic rules that can be checked statically. Perhaps we could imagine some.... If we had, say, limited all integer literals to 64 bits, we would probably put that requirement in the static semantics (even though in theory it is checkable in the syntax).

Dynamic Semantics

A dynamic semantics computes the meaning of an abstract syntax tree. In Ael, the meaning of expressions will be integer numeric values. Assuming the existence of a function valueof for turning number tokens into numeric values, we'll define function $\mathcal{E}$, mapping abstract syntax trees to value, as follows:

$$\mathcal{E}\{\text{Plus } e_1 \; e_2\} = \mathcal{E}e_1 + \mathcal{E}e_2$$

$$\mathcal{E}\{\textit{Minus } e_1 \; e_2\} = \mathcal{E}e_1 - \mathcal{E}e_2$$

$$\mathcal{E}\{\textit{Times } e_1 \; e_2\} = \mathcal{E}e_1 \div \mathcal{E}e_2$$

$$\mathcal{E}\{\text{Divide } e_1 \; e_2\} = \mathcal{E}e_1 \div \mathcal{E}e_2$$

$$\mathcal{E}\{\text{Negate } e\} = -\mathcal{E}e$$

$$\mathcal{E}\{\text{Numlit } n\} = \textit{valueof}(n)$$

Applying the Specification

Let's determine the meaning of this string:

-8 * (22- 7)

The Character String

SPACE	HYPHEN	DIGIT EIGHT	SPACE	TAB	ASTERISK	SPACE	LEFTPAREN
DIGIT TWO	DIGIT TWO	HYPHEN	SPACE	SPACE	DIGIT SEVEN	RIGH TPAREN	

Let's apply the lexical rules to tokenize the string:

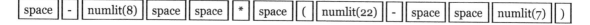

| space | - | numlit(8) | space | space | * | space | (| numlit(22) | - | space | space | numlit(7) |) |

The spaces will be skipped eventually, so we can just as well view the token stream like this:

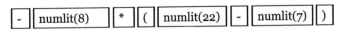

Parsing uncovers the derivation tree, also known as the concrete syntax tree:

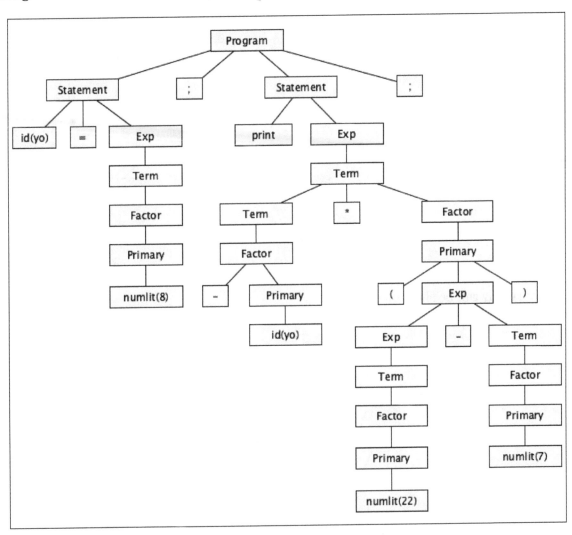

The static semantics is applied to the concrete syntax tree to produce the abstract syntax tree, namely:

{Times{Negate{Numlit8}}{Minus{Numlit22}{Numlit7}}}

which might be a little easier to read like this:

{Times

{Negate{Numlit8}}

{Minus{Numlit22}{Numlit7}}}

or even easier to read in tree form like this:

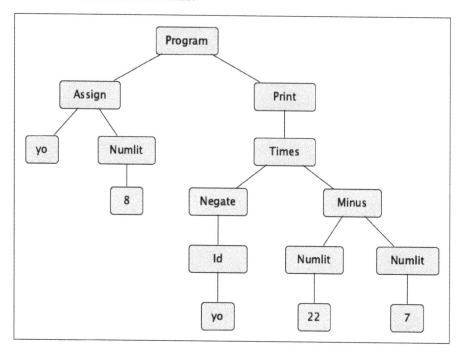

which, informally can be shortened to:

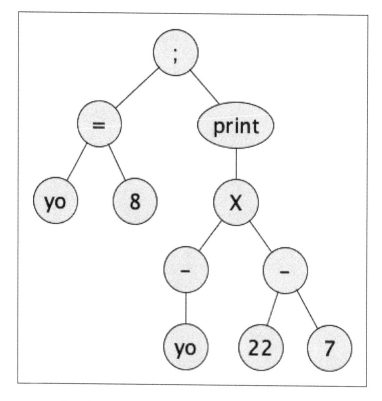

Notice how ASTs are way simpler than concrete trees. In fact in real compilers, unless the language is extraordinarily simple, you never see a concrete tree! Parsers generally go straight to the abstract syntax tree (though there are exceptions).

Finally, we apply the dynamic semantics to the AST to compute the meaning:

$$\mathcal{E}\{Times\{Negate\{Numlit8\}\}\{Minus\{Numlit22\}\{Numlit7\}\}\}$$
$$= \mathcal{E}\{Negate\{Numlit8\}\} \times \mathcal{E}\{Minus\{Numlit22\}\{Numlit7\}\}\}$$
$$= -\mathcal{E}Numlit8\} \times (\mathcal{E}\{Numlit22\} - \mathcal{E}\{Numlit7\})$$
$$= -8 \times (22 - 7)$$
$$= -8 \times 15$$
$$= -120$$

References

- What-is-programming-language: hackr.io, Retrieved 18, June 2020
- Generic-Programming: wiki.c2.com, Retrieved 21, March 2020
- Data-structure-tutorial: javatpoint.com, Retrieved 02, August 2020
- Software-tools, glossary: goodfirms.co, Retrieved 11, April 2020
- Semantic-Domains: mlwiki.org, Retrieved 29, January 2020

Levels and Generations of Programming Languages

The languages that programmers use to write codes are called high-level languages. These codes can be compiled into low-level languages, which are directly recognized by the computer hardware. Programming languages have evolved over the years with the latest ones belonging to the fifth generation. The different levels and generations of programming languages are discussed at length in this chapter.

Levels

Machine Languages

A machine language can be viewed as an agreed-upon formalism, designed to manipulate a memory using a processor and a set of registers.

Memory: The term "memory" refers loosely to the collection of hardware devices designed to store data and instructions. Some computer platforms store data and instructions in the same memory device, while others employ different data and instruction memories, each featuring a separate address space. Conceptually speaking, all memories have the same structure: a continuous array of cells of some fixed width, also called words or locations, each having a unique address. Hence, an individual word (representing either a data item or an instruction) is specified by supplying its address. We will refer to such individual words using the notations `Memory[address], RAM[address], or M[address] for brevity`.

Processor: The processor, normally called Central Processing Unit or CPU, is a device capable of performing a fixed set of operations. These typically include arithmetic and logic operations, memory access operations, and control (also called branching) operations. The operands of these operations are the current values of registers and selected memory locations. Likewise, the results of the operations can be stored either in registers or in selected memory locations.

Registers: Memory access is a relatively slow operation requiring long instruction formats (an address may require 32 bits). For this reason, most processors are equipped with several registers, each capable of holding a single value. Located in the processor's immediate proximity, the registers serve as a high-speed local memory, allowing the processor to quickly store and retrieve data. This setting enables the programmer to minimize the use of memory access commands, thus speeding up the program's execution. We will refer to the registers as `R0, R1, R2,` etc.

Languages: A machine language program is a series of coded instructions. For example, a typical instruction in a 16-bit computer may be "`1010001100011001`". In order to figure out what this instruction means, we have to know the rules of the game, i.e. the instruction set of the underlying hardware platform. For example, the language may be such that each instruction consists of four 4-bit fields: the left-most field codes a CPU operation, and the remaining fields represent the operation's operands. Thus the above command may code the operation "set R3 to R1+R9", depending of course on the hardware specification and the machine language syntax.

Since binary codes are rather cryptic, machine languages are normally specified using both binary codes and symbolic mnemonics (a mnemonics is a symbolic label that "stands for" something -- in our case binary codes). For example, the language designer can decide that the operation code "1010" will be represented by the mnemonic "add", and that the registers of the machine will be symbolically referred to using the symbols R0, R1, R2, …. Using these conventions, one can specify machine language instructions either directly, as "1010001100011001", or symbolically, as, say, "ADD R3,R1,R9".

Taking this symbolic abstraction one step further, we can allow ourselves to not only read symbolic notation, but to actually write programs using symbolic commands rather than binary instructions. Next, we can use a text processing program to parse the symbolic commands into their underlying fields (mnemonics and operands), translate each field into its equivalent binary representation, and assemble the resulting codes into binary machine instructions. The symbolic notation is called assembly language, or simply assembly, and the program that translates from assembly to binary is called assembler.

Since different computers vary in terms of CPU operations, number and type of registers, and assembly syntax rules, the result is a tower of Babel of machine languages, each with its own obscure syntax. Yet irrespective of this variety, all machine languages support similar sets of generic commands.

Commands: Arithmetic and logic commands: Every computer is required to perform basic arithmetic operations like addition and subtraction as well as basic Boolean operations like bit-wise negation, bit shifting, etc. Different machines feature different sets and versions of such operations, and different ways to apply them to combinations of registers and selected memory locations. Here are some typical possibilities that can be found in various machines:

```
// In all the examples, x is a user-defined label referring to a certain
memory location.

ADD R2,R3 // R2ÅR2+R3 where R2 and R3 are registers

ADD R2,x // R2ÅR2+x

AND R4,R5,R2 // R4Åbit wise "And" of R5 and R2

SUBD x // DÅ(D-x) where D is a register

ADD x // add the value of x to a special register called "accumulator"
```

Memory Access commands: Memory access commands fall into two categories. First, as we have just seen, in some cases arithmetic and logical commands are allowed to operate on selected memory locations. Second, all computers feature explicit load and store commands, designed to move data between the registers and the memory.

Memory access commands may use several types of addressing modes -- ways of specifying the address of the required memory word. As usual, different computers offer different possibilities and different notations, but three memory access modes are almost always supported:

Direct addressing: The most common way to address the memory is to express a specific address or use a symbol that refers to a specific address:

```
LOAD R1,67 // R1ÅMemory

// Assume that sum refers to memory address 67

LOAD R1,sum // R1ÅMemory
```

Immediate addressing: This form of addressing is used to load constants – i.e. load values that appear in the instruction proper: instead of treating the field that appears in the "load" command as an address, we simply load the value of the field itself into the register.

```
LOADI R1,67 // R1Å67
```

Indirect addressing: In this addressing mode the address of the required memory location is not hard-coded into the instruction; instead, the instruction specifies a memory location that holds the required memory address. This addressing mode is used to manage pointers in highlevel programming languages. For example, consider the high-level command "x=arr[j]" where arr is an array and x and j are variables. How can we translate this command into machine language? Well, when the array arr is declared and initialized in the high-level program, a memory segment of the correct length is allocated to hold the array data. Second, another memory location, referred to by the symbol arr, is allocated to hold the base address of the array's segment.

Now, when the compiler is asked to translate a reference to cell arr[j], it goes through the following process. First, note that the j'th entry of the array should be physically stored in a memory location that is at a displacement j from the array's base address (assuming, for simplicity, that each array element uses a single word). Hence the address corresponding to the expression arr[j] can be easily calculated by adding the value of j to the value of arr. Thus in the C programming language, for example, a command like x=arr[j] can be also expressed as x=*(arr+j), where the notation "*n" stands for "the value of Memory[n]". When translated into machine language, such commands typically yield the following code (depending on the assembly language syntax):

```
// translation of x=arr[j] or x=*(arr+j):

ADD R2,arr,j // R2Åarr+j

LOAD* R1,R2 // R1Åmemory[R2]

STR R1,x // xÅR1
```

Flow of control commands: While programs normally execute in a linear fashion, one command after the other, they also include occasional branches to locations other than the next command. Branching serves several purposes including repetition (jump backward to the beginning of a loop), conditional execution (if a Boolean condition is false, jump forward to the location after the "if-then" clause), and subroutine calling (jump to the first command of some other code segment).

In order to support these programming constructs, every machine language features means to jump to various locations in the program, both conditionally and unconditionally. In assembly languages, locations in the program can also be given symbolic names, using some syntax for specifying labels. Program 1 illustrates a typical example.

```
High level                    Low level

// a while loop               // typical translation
while (R1>=0) {               beginWhile:
    code segment 1                JNG R1,endWhile // if R1<0 goto endWhile
}                                 here comes the translation of code segment 1
code segment 2                    JMP beginWhile    // goto beginWhile
                              endWhile:
                                  here comes the translation of code segment 2
```

Figure: Program, High- and low-level branching logic. The syntax of goto commands varies from one language to another, but the basic idea is the same.

Unconditional jump commands like "JMP beginWhile" specify only the address of the target location. Conditional jump commands like "JNG R1,endWhile" must also specify a condition, expressed in some way. In some languages the condition is an explicit part of the command, while in others it is a by-product of a previous command. Here are some possible examples (noting again that the commands' syntax is less important than their general spirit):

```
// Assume that the foo label is defined elsewhere in the program (not shown
here).

JGE R1,foo // if R1>=0 then goto foo

SUB R1,R2;JEQ foo // R1ÅR1-R2; if (result=0) then goto foo

JZR foo // if (result of the previous command = 0) then goto foo

JMP foo // goto foo (unconditionally)
```

This ends our general and informal introduction of machine languages, and the generic commands that can typically found in various hardware platforms.

Hack Machine Language Specification

Hack is a typical Von Neumann platform: a 16-bit machine, consisting of a CPU, two separate memory modules serving as instruction memory and data memory, and two memory-mapped I/O devices: a screen and a keyboard.

Memory Address Spaces: The Hack programmer is aware of two distinct memory address spaces: an instruction memory and a data memory. Both memories are 16-bit wide and have a 15-bit address space, meaning that the maximum size of each memory is 32K 16-bit words.

The CPU can only execute programs that reside in the instruction memory. The instruction memory is a read-only device, and thus programs are loaded into it using some exogenous means. For example, the instruction memory can be implemented in a ROM chip which is pre-burned with the required program. Loading a new program can be done by replacing the entire ROM chip (similar to replacing a cartridge in a game computer). In order to simulate this operation, hardware simulators of the Hack platform must provide means to load the instruction memory from a text file containing a machine language program.

Registers: The Hack programmer is aware of two registers called D and A. These generalpurpose 16-bit registers can be manipulated explicitly by arithmetic and logical instructions, e.g. `A=D-1` or `D=!A` (where "!" means 16-bit "not"). While D is used solely to store data values, A doubles as both a data register and an address register. That is to say, depending on the instruction context, the contents of A can be interpreted either as a data value, or as an address in the data memory, or as an address in the instruction memory.

First, the A register can be used to facilitate direct access to the data memory (which, from now on, will be often referred to as "memory"). As the next section will describe, the syntax of the Hack language is such that memory access instructions do not specify an explicit address. Instead, they operate on an implicit memory location labeled "M", e.g. `D=M+1`. In order to resolve this address, the contract is such that M always refers to the memory word whose address is the current value of A. For example, if we want to effect the operation `D=Memory[516]-1`, we have to set the A register to 516, and then issue the instruction `D=M-1`.

Second, in addition to doubling as a general-purpose register and as an address register for the data memory, the hard working A register is also used to facilitate direct access to the instruction memory. As we will see shortly, the syntax of the Hack language is such that jump instructions do not specify a particular address. Instead, the contract is such that any jump operation always affects a jump to the instruction memory word addressed by A. For example, if we want to affect the operation "goto 35", we set A to 35 and issue a "goto" command. This will cause the computer to fetch the instruction located in InstructionMemory in the next clock cycle.

Example: Since the Hack language is quite self-explanatory, we start with an example. The only non-obvious command in the language is "`@address`", where address is either a number or a symbol representing a number. This command simply stores the specified value into the A register. For example, if sum refers to memory location 17, then both "`@17`" and "`@sum`" will have the same effect: $A \leftarrow 17$.

And now to the example: Suppose we have to add all the numbers between 1 and 100, using repetitive addition. Program 2 gives a C language solution and a possible compilation into the Hack language.

C language	Hack machine language
```// sum the numbers 1...100```	```// sum the numbers 1...100```

```
// sum the numbers 1...100         // sum the numbers 1...100
int i=1;                                @i      // i refers to some mem. loc.
int sum=0;                              M=1     // i=1
while (i<=100){                         @sum    // sum refers to some mem. loc.
    sum+=I;                             M=0     // sum=0
    i++;                            (loop)
}                                       @i
                                        D=M     // D=i
                                        @100
                                        D=D-A   // D=i-100
                                        @end
                                        D;jgt   // if (i-100)>0 goto end
                                        @i
                                        D=M     // D=i
                                        @sum
                                        M=D+M   // sum=sum+i
                                        @i
                                        M=M+1   // i=i+1
                                        @loop
                                        0;jmp   // goto loop
                                    (end)
```

Figure: Program, C and assembly versions of the same program.

Although the Hack syntax is more accessible than that of typical machine languages, it may still look rather obscure for readers who are not used to low-level programming. In particular, note that every operation involving a memory location requires two Hack commands: one for selecting the address on which we want to operate, and one for specifying the desired operation. Indeed, the Hack language consists of two generic instructions: an address instruction, also called Ainstruction, and a compute instruction, also called C-instruction. Each instruction has a binary representation, a symbolic representation, and an effect on the computer, as we now turn to specify.

The A-Instruction

The A-instruction is used to set the A register to a 15-bit value:

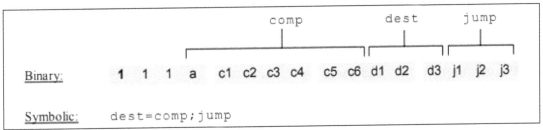

Figure: A-Instruction syntax.

This instruction causes the computer to store a constant in the A register. For example, the instruction @5, which is equivalent to 0000000000000101, causes the computer to store the binary representation of 5 in the A register.

The A-instruction is used for three different purposes. First, it provides the only way to enter a constant into the computer under program control. Second, it sets the stage for a subsequent C-instruction designed to manipulate a certain data memory location, by first setting A to the address of that location. Third, it sets the stage for a subsequent C-instruction that involves a jump, by first loading the address of the jump destination to the A register.

The C-Instruction

The C-instruction is the programming workhorse of the Hack platform -- the instruction that gets almost everything done. The instruction code is a specification that answers three questions: (a) what to compute? (b) Where to store the computed value? And (c) what to do next? Along with the A-instruction, these specifications determine all the possible operations of the computer.

Figure: C-Instruction syntax.

The MSB is the C-instruction code, which is 1. The next two bits are not used. The remaining bits form three fields that correspond to the three parts of the instruction's symbolic representation. Taken together, the semantics of the symbolic instruction dest=comp;jump is as follow. The comp field instructs the CPU what to compute. The dest field instructs where to store the computed value. The jump field specifies a jump condition. Either the dest field or the jump field or both may be empty. If the dest field is empty then the "=" sign may be omitted. If the jump field is empty then the ";" symbol may be omitted. We now turn to describe the format and semantics of each of the three fields.

The computation specification: The Hack ALU is designed to compute a fixed set of functions on the D, A, and M registers (where M=Memory[A]). The computed function is specified by the abit and the six c-bits comprising the instruction's comp field. This 7-bit pattern can potentially code 128 different functions, of which only the 28 listed in Table 5 are documented in the language specification.

	a=0						
mnemonic	c1	c2	c3	c4	c5	c6	
0	1	0	1	0	1	0	
1	1	1	1	1	1	1	
-1	1	1	1	0	1	0	
D	0	0	1	1	0	0	
A	1	1	0	0	0	0	M
!D	0	0	1	1	0	1	
!A	1	1	0	0	0	1	!M
-D	0	0	1	1	1	1	
-A	1	1	0	0	1	1	-M
D+1	0	1	1	1	1	1	
A+1	1	1	0	1	1	1	M+1
D-1	0	0	1	1	1	0	
A-1	1	1	0	0	1	0	M-1
D+A	0	0	0	0	1	0	D+M
D-A	0	1	0	0	1	1	D-M
A-D	0	0	0	1	1	1	M-D
D&A	0	0	0	0	0	0	D&M
D|A	0	1	0	1	0	1	D|M
	c1	c2	c3	c4	c5	c6	mnemonic
	a=1						

TABLE: The "compute" specification of the C-instruction. D and A are names of registers. M refers to the memory location addressed by A, i.e. to Memory[A]. The symbols "+" and "-" denote 16-bit 2's complement addition and subtraction, while "!", "|", and "&" denote the 16-bit bit-wise Boolean operators Not, Or, And, respectively.

Recall that the format of the C-instruction is "111a cccc ccdd djjj". Suppose we want to compute D-1, i.e. "the current value of the D register minus 1". According to Table 5, this can be done by issuing the instruction "1110 0011 10xx xxxx" (we use "x" to label bits that are irrelevant to the given example). To compute the value of D|M, we issue the instruction "1111 0101 01xx xxxx". To compute the constant -1, we issue the instruction "1110 1110 10xx xxxx", and so on.

The destination specification: The value computed by the comp part of the C-instruction can be simultaneously stored in several destinations, as specified by the instruction's dest part. The first and second d-bits code whether to store the computed value in the A register and in the D register, respectively. The third d-bit codes whether to store the computed value in M (i.e. in Memory[A]). One, more than one, or none of these bits may be asserted.

Table: The "destination" specification of the C-instruction.

d1	d2	d3	mnemonic	destination (where to store the computed value)
0	0	0	null	The value is not stored anywhere
0	0	1	M	Memory[A] (memory register addressed by A)
0	1	0	D	D register
0	1	1	MD	Memory[A] and D register
1	0	0	A	A register
1	0	1	AM	A register and Memory[A]
1	1	0	AD	A register and D register
1	1	1	AMD	A register, Memory[A], and D register

Recall that the format of the C-instruction is "111a cccc ccdd djjj". Suppose we want the computer to increment the value of Memory by 1, and also store the result in the D register. According to tables 5 and 6, this can be accomplished by the instructions:

```
0000 0000 0000 0111 // @7

1111 1101 1101 1xxx // DM=M+1 (x=irrelevant bits)
```

The A-instruction causes the computer to select the memory register whose address is 7 (the so called "M register"). The subsequent C-instruction computes the value of M+1 and stores the result in both D and M. The role of the 3 LSB bits of the second instruction is explained next.

The jump specification: The jump field of the C-instruction tells the computer what to do next. There are two possibilities: the computer should either fetch or execute the next instruction in the program, which is the default, or it should fetch and execute an instruction located elsewhere in the program. In the latter case, we assume that the A register has been previously set to the address to which we want to jump.

The jump itself is performed conditionally according to the value computed in the "comp" part of this instruction. The first j-bit specifies whether to jump in case this value is negative, the second j-bit in case the value is zero, and the third j-bit in case it is positive. This gives 8 possible jump conditions.

TABLE: The "jump" specification of the C-instruction. Out refers to the value computed by the instruction's comp part, and jump implies "continue execution with the instruction addressed by the A register".

j1 (out < 0)	j2 (out = 0)	j3 (out > 0)	Mnemonic	Effect
0	0	0	null	no jump
0	0	1	JGT	if $out > 0$ jump
0	1	0	JEQ	if $out = 0$ jump
0	1	1	JGE	if $out \geq 0$ jump
1	0	0	JLT	if $out < 0$ jump
1	0	1	JNE	if $out \neq 0$ jump
1	1	0	JLE	if $out \leq 0$ jump
1	1	1	JMP	jump

The following example illustrates the jump commands in action:

```
Logic                        Implementation

if Memory[3]=5 then          @3
    goto 100                 D=M      // D=Memory[3]
else goto 200                @5

                             D=D-A    // D=D-5
                             @100

                             D;JEQ    // if D=0 goto 100
                             @200

                             0;JMP    // goto 200
```

The last instruction ("0;JMP") effects an unconditional jump. Since the C-instruction syntax requires that we always effect some computation, we instruct the ALU to compute 0 (an arbitrary choice), which is ignored.

Conflicting uses of the A register: As was just illustrated, the programmer can use the A register in order to select either a data memory location for a subsequent C-instruction involving M, or an instruction memory location for a subsequent C-instruction involving a jump. Thus, in order to prevent conflicting use of the A register, we require that in well written programs, a C-instruction that may cause a jump (i.e. with some non-zero j bits) should not contain a reference to M.

Symbols

Assembly commands can refer to memory locations (addresses) using either constants or symbols. Symbols are introduced into assembly programs in three ways:

- Predefined symbols: A special subset of RAM (data memory) addresses can be referred to by any assembly program using pre-defined symbols, as follows.

    ◦ Virtual registers: the symbols R0 to R15 are pre-defined to refer to RAM addresses 0 to 15, respectively. This syntactic convention is designed to simplify assembly programming.

- ○ VM pointers: the symbols SP, LCL, ARG, THIS, and THAT are pre-defined to refer to RAM addresses 0 to 4, respectively. Note that each of these memory locations has two labels, e.g. address 2 can be referred to using either R2 or ARG. This syntactic convention will come to play in the implementation of the virtual machine, discussed in Chapters 7 and 8.

- ○ I/O Pointers: the symbols SCREEN and KBD are pre-defined to refer to RAM addresses 16384 (0x4000) and 24576 (0x6000), respectively, which are the base addresses of the screen and keyboard memory maps. The use of these I/O devices is explained below.

- Label symbols: These user-defined symbols, which serve to label destinations of goto commands, are declared by the pseudo command "(Xxx)". This directive defines the symbol Xxx to refer to the instruction memory location holding the next command in the program. A label can be defined only once and can be used anywhere in the assembly program, even before the line in which it is defined.

- Variable symbols: Any user-defined symbol Xxx appearing in an assembly program that is not predefined and is not defined elsewhere using the "(Xxx)" command is treated as a variable, and is mapped by the assembler to an available RAM location. Variables are mapped, as they are first encountered, to consecutive memory locations starting at RAM address 16 (0x0010).

Input / Output Handling the Hack platform can be connected to two peripheral devices: a screen and a keyboard. Both devices interact with the computer platform through memory maps. This means that drawing pixels on the screen is achieved by writing binary values into a memory segment associated with the screen. Likewise, "listening" to the keyboard is done by reading a memory location associated with the keyboard. The physical I/O devices and their memory maps are synchronized via continuous refresh loops.

Screen: The Hack computer can be connected to a black-and-white screen organized as 256 rows of 512 pixels per row. The screen's contents are represented by an 8K memory map that starts at RAM address 16384 (0x4000). Each row in the physical screen, starting at the screen's top left corner, is represented in the RAM by 32 consecutive 16-bit words. Thus the pixel at row r from the top and column c from the left is mapped on the c%16 bit (counting from LSB to MSB) of the word located at RAM[16384+r*32+c/16]. To write or read a pixel of the physical screen, one reads or writes the corresponding bit in the RAM-resident memory map (1=black, 0=white). Example:

```
// Draw a single black dot at the top left corner of the screen:

@SCREEN // Set the A register to point to the memory word that is mapped

  // to the 16 left-most pixels of the top row of the screen

M=1 // Blacken the left-most pixel
```

Keyboard: The Hack computer interfaces with the physical keyboard via a single-word memory map located in RAM address 24576 (0x6000). Whenever a key is pressed on the physical keyboard, its 16-bit ASCII code appears in RAM[24576]. When no key is pressed, the code 0 appears in this location. In addition to the usual ASCII codes, the Hack keyboard recognizes the following keys:

Table: Special keyboard codes in the Hack language.

Key pressed	Code	Key pressed	Code
new line	128	end	135
backspace	129	page up	136
left arrow	130	page down	137
right arrow	131	insert	138
up Arrow	132	delete	139
down arrow	133	esc	140
home	134	f1-f12	141-152

Syntax Conventions and Files Format

Binary code files: A binary code file is composed of text lines. Each line is a sequence of 16 "0" and "1" ASCII characters, coding a single machine language instruction. Taken together, all the lines in the file represent a machine language program. The contract is such that when a machine language program is loaded into the computer's instruction memory, the binary code represented by the file's n-th line is stored in address n of the instruction memory (the count of both program lines and memory addresses starts at 0).

By convention, machine language programs are stored in text files with a "hack" extension, e.g. Prog.hack.

Assembly language files: By convention, assembly language programs are stored in text files with an "asm" extension, e.g. Prog.asm. An assembly language file is composed of text lines, each representing either an instruction or a symbol declaration:

- Instruction: an A-instruction or a C-instruction.

- (Symbol): This pseudo-command causes the assembler to assign the label Symbol to the memory location into which the next command in the program will be stored. It is called "pseudo-command" since it generates no machine code.

Constants and symbols in assembly programs: Constants must be non-negative and are always written in decimal notation. A user-defined symbol can be any sequence of letters, digits, underscore ("_"), dot ("."), dollar sign ("$"), and colon (":") that does not begin with a digit.

Comments in assembly programs: text beginning with two slashes ("//") and ending at the end of the line is considered a comment and is ignored.

White space in assembly programs: space characters are ignored. Empty lines are ignored.

Case conventions: All the assembly mnemonics must be written in upper-case. The rest (userdefined labels and variable names) is case sensitive. The convention is to use upper-case for labels and lower-case for variable names.

Assembly Languages

Assembly Language is a low-level programming language. It helps in understanding the programming language to machine code. In computer, there is assembler that helps in converting the assembly code into machine code executable. Assembly language is designed to understand the instruction and provide to machine language for further processing. It mainly depends on the architecture of the system whether it is the operating system or computer architecture.

Assembly Language mainly consists of mnemonic processor instructions or data, and other statements or instructions. It is produced with the help of compiling the high-level language source code like C, C++. Assembly Language helps in fine-tuning the program.

Why is Assembly Language Useful?

Assembly language helps programmers to write the human-readable code that is almost similar to machine language. Machine language is difficult to understand and read as it is just a series of numbers. Assembly language helps in providing full control of what tasks a computer is performing.

Example: Find the below steps to print "Hello world" in Windows:

- Open the notepad.

- Write below code.

```
global _main
extern _printf
section.text
_main:
push message
call _printf
add  esp, 4
ret
message:
db 'Hello, World!', 10, 0
```

- Save the file with any name example XYZ.asm, the extension should be ".asm".

- The above file needs to compile with the help of assembler that is NASM (Netwide Assembler).

- Run the command nasm –f win32 XYZ.asm.

- After this, Nasm creates one object file that contains machine code but not the executable code that is XYZ.obj.

- To create the executable file for windows Minimal GNU is used that provides the GCC compiler.

- Run the command gcc –o XYZ.exe XYZ.obj.

- Execute the executable file now "XYZ".

- It will show the output as "Hello, world".

Why you should Learn Assembly Language?

The learning of assembly language is still important for programmers. It helps in taking complete control over the system and its resources. By learning assembly language, the programmer is able to write the code to access registers and able to retrieve the memory address of pointers and values. It mainly helps in speed optimization that increases efficiency and performance.

Assembly language learning helps in understanding the processor and memory functions. If the programmer is writing any program that needs to be a compiler that means the programmer should have a complete understanding of the processor. Assembly language helps in understanding the work of processor and memory. It is cryptic and symbolic language.

Assembly Language helps in contacting the hardware directly. This language is mainly based on computer architecture and it recognizes the certain type of processor and its different for different CPUs. Assembly language refers as transparent compared to other high-level languages. It has a small number of operations but it is helpful in understanding the algorithms and other flow of controls. It makes the code less complex and easy debugging as well.

Features

The features of the assembly language are mentioned below:

- It can use mnemonic than numeric operation code and it also provides the information of any error in the code.

- This language helps in specifying the symbolic operand that means it does not need to specify the machine address of that operand. It can be represented in the form of a symbol.

- The data can be declared by using decimal notation.

Assemblers

The assemblers are used to translate the assembly language into machine language. There are two types of assembler are:

- Single-pass assembler: A single assembler pass is referred as the complete scan of source program input to assembler or equivalent representation and translation by the statement on the basis of statement called as single pass assembler or one pass translation. It isolates the label, mnemonics and operand field of the system. It validates the code instructions by looking it up in mnemonic code table. It enters the symbol found in the label field and the address of the text available machine word into the symbol table. This pass is fast and effected, and no need to construct the intermediate code.

- Multi-pass assembler: In this, an assembler goes through assembly language several times and generates the object code. In this last pass is called a synthesis pass and this assembler requires any form of an intermediate code to generate each pass every time. It is comparatively slower than single pass assembler but there can be some actions that can be performed more than once means duplicated.

Advantages

- It allows complex jobs to run in a simpler way.
- It is memory efficient, as it requires less memory.
- It is faster in speed, as its execution time is less.
- It is mainly hardware oriented.
- It requires less instruction to get the result.
- It is used for critical jobs.
- It is not required to keep track of memory locations.
- It is a low-level embedded system.

Disadvantages

- It takes a lot of time and effort to write the code for the same.
- It is very complex and difficult to understand.
- The syntax is difficult to remember.
- It has a lack of portability of program between different computer architectures.
- It needs more size or memory of the computer to run the long programs written in Assembly Language.

High-level Languages

High level language is the next development in the evolution of computer languages. Examples of some high-level languages are given below:

- PROLOG (for "PROgramming LOGic").
- FORTRAN (for 'FORrmula TRANslation').
- LISP (for "LISt Processing").
- Pascal (named after the French scientist Blaise Pascal).

High-level languages are like English-like language, with less word also known as keywords and fewer ambiguities. Each high level language will have its own syntax and keywords. The meaning of the word syntax is grammar.

The Disadvantages of High-level Languages

- A high level language program can't get executed directly. It requires some translator to get it translated to machine language. There are two types of translators for high level language programs. They are interpreter and compiler. In case of interpreter, prior execution, each and every line will get translated and then executed. In case of compiler, the whole program will get translated as a whole and will create an executable file. And after that, as when required, the executable code will get executed. These translator programs, specially compilers, are huge one and so are quite expensive.

- The machine language code generated by the compiler might not be as compact as written straightaway in low-level language. Thus a program written in high-level language usually takes longer time to execute.

The Advantages of High-level Languages

- High-level language programs are easy to get developed. While coding if we do some errors then we can easily locate those errors and if we miss then during compilation those errors would get detected by the compiler. And the programmer will initiate respective corrections to do needful accordingly.

- By a glance through the program it is easy to visualize the function of the program.

- The programmer may not remain aware about the architecture of the hardware. So people with our hardware knowledge can also do high level language programming.

- The same high level language program works on any other computer, provided the respective compiler is available for the target new architecture. So high-level languages are portable.

- Productivity against high level language programming is enormously increased.

To conclude, high-level languages are almost always used nowadays except where very high-speed execution is required.

Example: As an example, let us consider the following program code written in high-level language C.

```
#include <stdio.h>

int main() {

 int a,b,c;

 printf("\n\n\t\t Welcome to the world of programming...");
```

```
printf("\n\n\t\t Please enter the first number...");

scanf("%d",&a);

printf("\n\n\t\t Please enter the second number...");

scanf("%d",&b);

c = a+b;

printf("\n\n\t\t So the sum of %d and %d is %d...",a,b,c);

printf("\n\n\t\t End of the program...");

}
```

Scripting Languages

A scripting language is a programming language that is interpreted, meaning it is translated into machine code when the code is run, rather than beforehand. Scripting languages are often used for short scripts over full computer programs. JavaScript, Python, and Ruby are all examples of scripting languages.

You may be surprised to learn that more than 700 programming languages have been invented throughout the history of computers. That's not nearly as many as the 6,900 human languages we have, but learning any new language is no small feat.

Scripting language (also known as scripting, or script) is plainly defined as a series of commands that are able to be executed without the need for compiling. While all scripting languages are programming languages, not all programming languages are scripting languages. PHP, Perl, and Python are common examples of scripting languages.

Scripting languages use a program known as an interpreter to translate commands and are directly interpreted from source code, not requiring a compilation step. Other programming languages, on the other hand, may require a compiler to translate commands into machine code before it can execute those commands.

Although it is important to know the difference between interpreted vs compiled programming languages, advanced hardware, and coding practices are beginning to make the distinction somewhat obsolete.

Interpreted vs Compiled Programming Languages

An interpreted programming language is a language designed to execute source code directly and without the need to compile a program into machine-language instructions. An interpreter will execute the program by translating statements into a series of one or more subroutines before finally translating them into another language, such as machine code.

In compiled programming languages, a compiler program translates code written in a high level programming language into a lower-level language in order for the program to execute. C or Java programs must usually be compiled first in order to run. Two well-known compilers are Eclipse for Java and gcc for C and C++.

Figure: Interpreted or compiled?

The easiest way to understand how a compiler functions is to think about various operating systems. For instance, Windows programs are compiled to run on Windows platforms and thus are not compatible with Mac.

Server-Side Scripting vs Client-Side Scripting

Figure: Whose side are you on?

There are two types of scripting languages: server side and client side. The only significant difference between the two is that the former requires a server for its processing.

Server-side scripting languages run on a web server. When a client sends a request, the server responds by sending content via HTTP. In contrast, client-side scripting languages run on the client end—on their web browser.

The benefit of client-side scripts is that they can reduce demand on the server, allowing web pages to load faster. Whereas, one significant benefit of server-side scripts is they are not viewable by the public like client-side scripts are.

When trying to decide which way to go on a project, keep in mind that client-side scripting is more focused on user interface and functionality. Conversely, server-side scripting focuses on faster processing, access to data, and resolving errors.

Examples of Server-Side Scripting Languages

The following are examples of server-side scripting languages.

Language	Comments
PHP	The most popular server-side language used on the web.
ASP.NET	Web-application framework developed by Microsoft.
Node.js	Can run on a multitude of platforms, including Windows, Linux, Unix, Mac, etc.
Java	Used in everything from your car stereo's Bluetooth to NASA applications.
Ruby	Dynamic. Focuses heavily on simplicity.
Perl	A bit of a mashup between C, shell script, AWK, and sed.
Python	Great for beginners to learn. Uses shorter code.

Examples of Client-Side Scripting Languages

The following are examples of client-side scripting languages.

Language	Comments
HTML	The foundation of web development.
CSS	Improves appearance and graphics on pages in your web browser.
JavaScript	Though typically client-side, can occasionally be used on server-side as well.

Applications of Scripting Languages

Figure: What are scripting languages used for?

Scripting languages are used in many areas, both on and off the web. In addition to server-side and client-side applications, scripting languages can be used in system administration. Examples of scripts used in system admin are Shell, Perl, and Python.

Scripting languages are also used in lots of games and multimedia. For example, Minecraft mods use Java to allow users to create their own worlds and items in the game. Additionally, Second Life, Trainz, and Wesnoth all allow users to create extensions on the games. Similar to the extensions used in games, extensions in other programs, such as Google's Chrome browser extensions, are all run using scripting languages.

Pros and Cons of Scripting Languages

Pros

The pros far outweigh the cons.

There are many benefits to using scripting languages over other programming languages. First, they are open-source. This allows users from around the world to join in the improvement process. Other pros include:

- No requirement to compile, although occasionally it is necessary.

- Easy to transfer between operating systems.

- Scripting languages make web pages look awesome.

- Easier to learn and write.

- Scripts can be used as a prototype to programs, saving time on test projects.

Cons

There are not a whole lot of cons to using scripting languages. One con is the fact that some companies don't want scripts to be read by everyone, so they use server-side scripts to avoid releasing them to the public. Also, installing an interpreter program can be a hassle. Finally, sometimes scripts are slower than programs.

Domain-specific Languages

Domain-specific languages are adjusted to a particular domain and provide notations close to it. Based on the features of the problem domain they improve the communication between developers and domain experts.

One of the first detailed publications on domain-specific languages was published by Jon Bentley in 1986. He referred to them as little languages. DSLs as little languages are tightly bound to a specific domain and their expressive power significantly differs from that of General Purpose Languages (GPLs). However, DSLs can improve development time and program correctness.

There are various techniques introduced to manage the complexity of the application development process. One of these is the so-called Domain-Driven Design (DDD) – introduced by Eric Evans.

He points out the fact that it is very important for the project's success to have a common language used between domain experts and developers. Without such language multiple transitions will be necessary. The overall cost of all translations, plus the possibility of misunderstanding, will put the project at risk. Ubiquitous in the team's work, that language should be structured around the domain model. In DDD a ubiquitous language can be materialized as one or more DSLs. These languages are also part of the Software Factories , where the process of modeling and implementing software product families realized in such a way that a given system can be automatically generated from a specification written in a domain-specific language.

There are several approaches to exploiting domain-specific languages in development. A DSL program could be interpreted or compiled, or can be used as a model to drive the process of code generation of GPL program chunks or even entire tiers of the developed system.

A well-designed DSL should be based on the following three principles:

- A DSL provides a direct mapping to the artifacts of the problem domain.

- DSL must use the common vocabulary of the problem domain. The vocabulary becomes the catalyst for better communication between developers and business users (domain experts).

- The DSL must abstract the underlying implementation. The DSL cannot contain accidental complexities that deal with implementation details.

Pros and Cons

There are many discussions on the web about the advantages and disadvantages of DSL. In fact, the better their design is, the easier the process of writing programs becomes.

Pros

Domain-specific languages have different expressive power compared to the general purpose languages, but they can significantly shorten the time for the development of an application, they can improve the correctness of the developed application, and the communication between the domain expert and the programmer. DSL can be used as mechanism to protect software systems as intellectual property and be a very powerful tool for creating a self-documented code. With DSL multiple programming paradigms can be combined and syntactic noise can be rapidly lowered.

Cons

Regardless of the lower final cost of the overall development a higher starting price of the application development is often pointed out as a disadvantage. Developing application that involves building appropriate DSL is a hard process that requires programmers to be language experts as well. In such cases the creation of DSL requires complete knowledge domain constraints. Debugging and unit testing is hard to perform when DSL is used in implementation. DSLs can lead to language cacophony. Proper selection of DSLs and adequate usage is crucial.

Taxonomy

The availability of language tools aka language workbench is important for the creation and future use of DSL. When can a language be qualified as domain-specific? A common indicator of a DSL is that it is not Turing-complete. These languages can be categorized as external or internal.

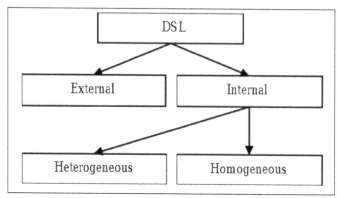

Figure: Taxonomy of DSL.

An external DSL is a language that is different from the main language (usually GPL). Common examples are languages like SQL, CSS and HTML. Most of them are bound to a particular technology or infrastructure. Often such DSLs are interpreted or translated through code generation tools into GPL code. Ever since XML gained popularity, many external DSLs have been modelled upon it. Some XML based languages were actually equipped with nice graphical outlook. The advantages of external DSLs include: loose specification and minimal or no following of common standards. In such a way developers can express the domain artifacts in compact and useful form. The quality of such a language strongly depends on the ability of the developer to write a high quality code generator or interpreter. External DSLs are not symbolically integrated with the main language and thus things such as refactoring are hard (or even impossible) to be automatically implemented. On the other hand, internal DSL is embedded into the main language and thus it is completely symbolically integrated in it. Internal DSLs are a particular way of using GPL. Internal DSLs provide domain friendly syntactic sugar to the existing API, using underlying programming language constructs. In fact there are two approaches for implementing internal DSLs – heterogeneous and homogeneous. Under the heterogeneous approach, the host language and the embedded language are not processed by the same compiler/interpreter. Two different compilers/interpreters are needed – hence the term heterogeneous. In the case of homogeneous implementation, the host compiler/interpreter is reused or extended so that the host and embedded language are processed by the same compiler/interpreter.

Some general purpose languages are well suited to be extended with internal DSLs. There is an ongoing discussion in the software developers' community on how the quality of internal DSL depends on the features of the host GPL. Martin Fowler and Eric Evans refer to internal DSL as a fluent interface. This term emphasizes the fact that an internal DSL is really just a particular kind of Application programming interface (API), but API designed in such a way that its vocabulary is suitable for sentence-like constructions, rather than sequence of method calls, and the constructions make sense even in a standalone context. Because internal DSLs comply the host language syntax they are not quite readable to non-developers as some of the external DSLs. The grammar of the host language imposes restrictions on the expressive possibilities of the internal DSLs.

Depending on the host language there are different approaches and efforts which need to be developed in order to extend the language with internal DSLs. Some of the host languages are already dynamic unlike others where it could be a challenge to achieve this flexibility. The approaches for DSL development could see them as interpreted, compiled, preprocessed, embedded or hybrid, or in the form of fluent interface. In their daily programming tasks software developers often need to choose between command-query API and fluent interface. How should they make a decision whether to build the API as a fluent interface or transform the well-known API into internal DSL? These questions are sometimes answered by developers in their daily tasks by way of creating different helper classes. Developers "carry" these helpers from project to project and they represent their vision how to improve the commonly used API. Sometimes these helper classes are written spontaneously and sometimes deliberately and carefully. In fact depending on the developers' experience, they can turn into proper DSL implementation that will remain stable throughout all similar projects or will be abandoned and completely overwritten in the next project.

Modeling with DSL

External DSLs are not Computer Aided Software Engineering (CASE) tools. After the rise of CASE during the 90s of the last century, CASE dramatically failed.

CASE tools failed for a number of reasons, but underlying it all was the fact that they couldn't come up with a coherent programming environment that would allow people to build general enterprise applications more effectively than the alternatives.

After the CASE another continuously evolving approach emerged. The Model Driven Architecture (MDA) was announced in 2001 by Object Management Group (OMG) as a tangible implementation of Model Driven Design based on Unified Modeling Language (UML) which was adopted by OMG in 1997.

In fact DSL appears to be a counterpart to MDA (and UML) approach. Domain-specific languages allow software engineers to focus on design decisions directly related to the particular domain (problem). DSL programs can be viewed as models and processed by model-driven (metadata-driven) code generators.

Models and Model Transformations

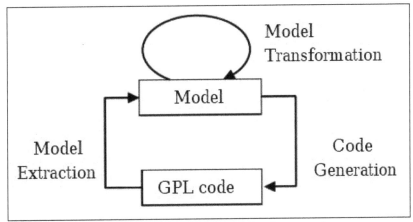

Figure: Model transformation and code generation.

Three major transformations can be identified, namely: model transformation, model extraction and code generation. Most of the present integrated development environments (IDE) can perform model extraction, for example the generation of class diagrams. Object-relational mapping (ORM) diagram generation from database schema is an example of model transformation. Transformation of ORM diagram to GPL code is an example for code generation.

Model-Driven Code Generation

Domain-Specific Model (DSM) driven development and transformation from DSM to code require careful design so that they can become really usable. Sometimes partitioning models (partial models) are proposed as improvement to maintainability and understanding. This also adds benefits to model management in multi-user environments. As an effective way to manage the complexity of software development, the modeling provides:

- Better understanding of software systems, and a way to create and communicate software designs before committing additional resources.

- An effective way of traceability through software development process.

- Ability to visualize entire systems and manage complexity.

- Preliminary software correctness through model verification.

- Better cost and time estimation.

Where can code generation techniques be applied effectively? People would argue that code generation should be used as much as possible, but experience shows that there will be a negative effect resulting from covering the whole application. This will dramatically complicate the DSLs used. Complex DSLs are hard to manage, especially when there are requirements changes.

Handling Changes and DSL Evolution

Requirements management is a very important part of project development as the change in requirements adds to the complexity of the project development. This is also true when DSL is utilized in the development process. The process of development should be adaptable to:

- Functional changes - such as the inclusion of new functionalities or change the existing ones.

- Non-functional changes: e.g. to change the security, reliability, usability and system performance.

- Changes in the platform - move to new hardware or OS platform.

Regardless of the applied methodology requirements are often not fully provided and programmers identify new requirements or requirements changes in the process of development of software product.

Some DSL are created from scratch just for developing a certain system. On the other hand technology related DSLs remain stable over time and undergo a long process of improvement and standardization. A well-designed DSL should not be affected by requirements changes, but the underlying code generation process and the resulting GPL code usually are. The language developer gains his knowledge for the domain during code writing and this affects the language itself.

Table: Influence of requirements changes.

	Model/DSL	Code Generator
Functional changes	●	○
Non-functional changes		●
Platform changes		●
● – high influence ○ – low influence		

Functional changes mostly affect the written model and if there are no DSL constructs, this can influence the language improvements. The evolution of language will cause changes in the code generator as well. On the other hand non-functional changes affect non-functional aspects weaved in the application. The weaving process is handled by the code generator. Moving a developed product to a different target platform should not affect functionality, business logic or appearance. Platform changes involve non-functional changes, for example different OS introduce different security issues whereas changing hardware can introduce performance issues. In addition, platform changes may advance in switching to different underlying GPL.

Whether you use DSL in single large project for a long time or in many projects for a short time, it will evolve along with the understanding of the problem domain, and it is crucially important for a strategy to be developed on how the domain-specific language should be maintained to mitigate the threat of abandonment at a later stage. The threat level may vary depending on the type of the language (internal or external), target of the language (architecture, technology, or problem domain), as well as the expected features of the language (such as backward compatibility, automatic migration to the new language version of all old programs/models), etc.

Table: Influence of requirements changes.

DSL		Abandonment Risk
	External	◆
Type	Internal Homogeneous	●
	Internal Heterogeneous	■
Target	Architecture	●
	Technology	●

Requirements	Problem Domain	◆
	Backward Compatibility	■
	Automatic Migration	◆
◆ – high, ■ – average, ● – low		

Empirical data on DSLs usage in different software development projects and the cases when DSLs have been abandoned are summarized in Table. External DSL rely on a larger number of tools than internal one. The maintenance of the developed product deteriorates with maintenance of these tools, which is sometimes hard. Moving a project to a new team is often accompanied by misuse or misunderstanding of external tools (even those not connected with particular DSL). Fluent interface, on the other hand, is easy to maintain because the refactoring of the product code and the internal DSL is blended. Requirements, such as backward compatibility and/or adding new tools' functionality for automatic migration to the newer version of domain-specific language, also bring high risk. The highest risk resulting from the abandonment of DSLs, however, is misunderstanding in the problem domain.

Generations of Programming Languages

There are five generation of Programming languages. They are:

- First Generation Languages: These are low-level languages like machine language.

- Second Generation Languages: These are low-level assembly languages used in kernels and hardware drives.

- Third Generation Languages: These are high-level languages like C, C++, Java, Visual Basic and JavaScript.

- Fourth Generation Languages: These are languages that consist of statements that are similar to statements in the human language. These are used mainly in database programming and scripting. Example of these languages include Perl, Python, Ruby, SQL, MatLab(MatrixLaboratory).

- Fifth Generation Languages: These are the programming languages that have visual tools to develop a program. Examples of fifth generation language include Mercury, OPS5, and Prolog.

The first two generations are called low level languages. The next three generations are called high level languages.

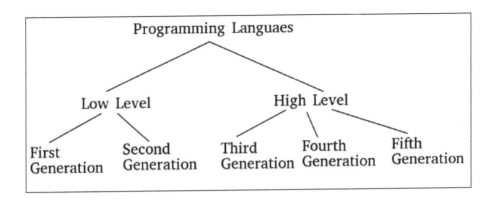

1st Generation

A first generation (programming) language (1GL) is a grouping of programming languages that are machine level languages used to program first-generation computers. The instructions were given through the front panel switches of these computers, directly to the CPU. There was originally no compiler or assembler to process the instructions in 1GL.

The instructions in 1GL are made of binary numbers, represented by 1s and 0s. This makes the language suitable for the understanding of the machine but very much more difficult to interpret and learn by the human programmer. Also known as a 1st generation language.

The main advantage of programming in 1GL is that the code can run very fast and very efficiently, precisely because the instructions are executed directly by the CPU. One the main disadvantages of programming in a low level language is that when an error occurs, the code is not as easy to fix.

The program is written as binary instructions, consisting of zeros and ones. This language is very much adapted to a specific computer and CPU, and code portability is therefore significantly reduced in comparison to higher level languages.

Modern day programmers still occasionally use machine level code, especially when programming lower level functions of the system, such as drivers, interfaces with firmware and hardware devices. Modern tools, such as native-code compilers are used to produce machine level from a higher-level language.

2nd Generation

A second generation programming language is also known as an assembly language. These archaic programming languages were popular during the late 1950s. A second-generation language uses alphabet letters, so programming is technically easier than just using complex series of zeros and ones. Second-generation languages offer various assembly mnemonics, which makes it easier for programmers to remember the codes. They are generally not used today by the public, but some third-generation language programs are still used.

The term generation summarizes major evolutionary advances in programming languages. First-generation languages were basic data instructions for processors to execute. Second-generation languages use an assembler to convert language statements into machine language. Third-generation languages use high-level language statements that are converted by a compiler into specific programming language statements. A third-generation language, such as C and Java, require a considerable amount of programming skills and knowledge.

Fourth-generation languages closely resemble human grammar and language. These languages are often used for accessing databases. Fifth-generation languages use a graphical interface to create language statements that are compiled with a third- or fourth-generation language compiler. Some of the biggest computer businesses, such as IBM and Microsoft, make fifth-generation visual programming solutions for creating new apps. Programming with a visual interface allows users to easily understand and complete object-oriented programming tasks.

Second-Generation Programming Languages Characteristics

Second-generation structures are based on first-generation structures, but the data structures use simple generalizations, such as dynamic arrays and different lower bounds. Like first-generation, they are still linear and closely based on machine-addressing modes. Second-generation languages usually have strong built-in types, hierarchical name structures and better control of name spaces, which allows for efficient dynamic memory allocation. This is because hierarchical structuring increases control flow, which eliminates the need for confusing networks.

These control structures offer recursive procedures, parameter-passing modes and syntactic structures. Second-generation languages use word policies that establish keyword-in-context rules. During their peak of popularity, many second-generation programmers took advantage of the unlimited generalization functionality, which produced both desirable results and undesirable consequences. These languages are specific to a particular type of processor family and processor environment. They are occasionally used in kernels and device drivers to produce processing intensive games and graphics.

3rd Generation

The period of third generation was from 1965-1971. The computers of third generation used Integrated Circuits (ICs) in place of transistors. A single IC has many transistors, resistors, and capacitors along with the associated circuitry.

The IC was invented by Jack Kilby. This development made computers smaller in size, reliable, and efficient. In this generation remote processing, time-sharing, multiprogramming operating system was used. High-level languages (FORTRAN-II TO IV, COBOL, PASCAL PL/1, BASIC, ALGOL-68 etc.) were used during this generation.

The main features of third generation are:

- IC used.

- More reliable in comparison to previous two generations.

- Smaller size.

- Generated less heat.

- Faster.

- Lesser maintenance.

- Costly.

- AC required.

- Consumed lesser electricity.

- Supported high-level language.

Some computers of this generation were:

- IBM-360 series.

- Honeywell-6000 series.

- PDP (Personal Data Processor).

- IBM-370/168.

- TDC-316.

4th Generation

A fourth generation (programming) language (4GL) is a grouping of programming languages that attempt to get closer than 3GLs to human language, form of thinking and conceptualization.

4GLs are designed to reduce the overall time, effort and cost of software development. The main domains and families of 4GLs are: database queries, report generators, data manipulation, analysis and reporting, screen painters and generators, GUI creators, mathematical optimization, web developmentand general purpose languages. Also known as a 4th generation language, a domain specific language, or a high productivity language.

4GLs are more programmer-friendly and enhance programming efficiency with usage of English-like words and phrases, and when appropriate, the use of icons, graphical interfaces and symbolical representations. The key to the realization of efficiency with 4GLs lies in an appropriate match between the tool and the application domain. Additionally, 4GLs have widened the population of professionals able to engage in software development.

Many 4GLs are associated with databases and data processing, allowing the efficient development of business-oriented systems with languages that closely match the way domain experts formulate business rules and processing sequences. Many of such data-oriented 4GLs are based on the Structured Query Language (SQL), invented by IBM and subsequently adopted by ANSI and ISO as the standard language for managing structured data.

Most 4GLs contain the ability to add 3GL-level code to introduce specific system logic into the 4GL program. The most ambitious 4GLs, also denoted as Fourth Generation Environments, attempt to produce entire systems from a design made in CASE tools and the additional specification of data structures, screens, reports and some specific logic.

5th Generation

A fifth generation (programming) language (5GL) is a grouping of programming languages build on the premise that a problem can be solved, and an application built to solve it, by providing constraints to the program (constraint-based programming), rather than specifying algorithmically how the problem is to be solved (imperative programming).

In essence, the programming language is used to denote the properties, or logic, of a solution, rather than how it is reached. Most constraint-based and logic programming languages are 5GLs. A common misconception about 5GLs pertains to the practice of some 4GL vendors to denote their products as 5GLs, when in essence the products are evolved and enhanced 4GL tools. Also known as a 5th generation language.

The leap beyond 4GLs is sought by taking a different approach to the computational challenge of solving problems. When the programmer dictates how the solution should look, by specifying conditions and constraints in a logical manner, the computer is then free to search for a suitable solution. Most of the applicable problems solved by this approach can currently be found in the domain of artificial intelligence.

Considerable research has been invested in the 1980s and 1990s, into the development of 5GLs. As larger programs were built, it became apparent that the approach of finding an algorithm given a problem description, logical instructions and a set of constraint is a very hard problem in itself. During the 1990s, the wave of hype that preceded the popularization of 5GLs and predictions that they will replace most other programming languages, gave way to a more sober realization.

PROLOG (acronym for PROgramming LOGic) is an example of a Logical Programming Language. It uses a form of mathematical logic (predicate calculus) to solve queries on a programmer-given database of facts and rules.

References

- What-is-assembly-language: educba.com, Retrieved 15, February 2020

- High-level-language-program: tutorialspoint.com, Retrieved 08, May 2020

- What-is-a-scripting-language: careerkarma.com, Retrieved 17, August 2020

- Domain_Specific_Languages_in_Practice-275725872: researchgate.net, Retrieved 11, January 2020

- Generation-programming-languages: geeksforgeeks.org, Retrieved 03, March 2020

- First-generation-programming-language-24304: techopedia.com, Retrieved 09, June 2020

3

Important Concepts in Programming Languages

All programming languages have particular aspects without which they would be rendered inoperative. Syntax, which refers to the set of rules determining correct statements or expressions, data type, structured programming, programming style, and control flow are certain aspects of programming languages are covered in this chapter.

Syntax

```python
def add5(x):
    return x+5

def dotwrite(ast):
    nodename = getNodename()
    label=symbol.sym_name.get(int(ast[0]),ast[0])
    print ' %s [label="%s' % (nodename, label),
    if isinstance(ast[1], str):
        if ast[1].strip():
            print '= %s"];' % ast[1]
        else:
            print '"]'
    else:
        print '"];'
        children = []
        for n, child in enumerate(ast[1:]):
            children.append(dotwrite(child))
        print ' %s -> {' % nodename,
        for name in children:
            print '%s' % name,
```

Syntax highlighting and indent style are often used to aid programmers in recognizing elements of source code. Color coded highlighting is used in this piece of code written in Python.

In computer science, the syntax of a computer language is the set of rules that defines the combinations of symbols that are considered to be a correctly structured document or fragment in that language. This applies both to programming languages, where the document represents source code, and markup languages, where the document represents data. The syntax of a language defines its surface form. Text-based computer languages are based on sequences of characters, while visual programming languages are based on the spatial layout and connections between symbols (which may be textual or graphical). Documents that are syntactically invalid are said to have a syntax error.

Syntax – the form – is contrasted with semantics – the meaning. In processing computer languages, semantic processing generally comes after syntactic processing, but in some cases semantic processing is necessary for complete syntactic analysis, and these are done together or concurrently. In a compiler, the syntactic analysis comprises the frontend, while semantic analysis comprises the backend (and middle end, if this phase is distinguished).

Levels of Syntax

Computer language syntax is generally distinguished into three levels:

- Words – the lexical level, determining how characters form tokens.

- Phrases – the grammar level, narrowly speaking, determining how tokens form phrases.

- Context – determining what objects or variables names refer to, if types are valid, etc.

Distinguishing in this way yields modularity, allowing each level to be described and processed separately, and often independently. First a lexer turns the linear sequence of characters into a linear sequence of tokens; this is known as "lexical analysis" or "lexing". Second the parser turns the linear sequence of tokens into a hierarchical syntax tree; this is known as "parsing" narrowly speaking. Thirdly the contextual analysis resolves names and checks types. This modularity is sometimes possible, but in many real-world languages an earlier step depends on a later step – for example, the lexer hack in C is because tokenization depends on context. Even in these cases, syntactical analysis is often seen as approximating this ideal model.

The parsing stage itself can be divided into two parts: the parse tree or "concrete syntax tree" which is determined by the grammar, but is generally far too detailed for practical use, and the abstract syntax tree (AST), which simplifies this into a usable form. The AST and contextual analysis steps can be considered a form of semantic analysis, as they are adding meaning and interpretation to the syntax, or alternatively as informal, manual implementations of syntactical rules that would be difficult or awkward to describe or implement formally.

The levels generally correspond to levels in the Chomsky hierarchy. Words are in a regular language, specified in the lexical grammar, which is a Type-3 grammar, generally given as regular expressions. Phrases are in a context-free language (CFL), generally a deterministic context-free language (DCFL), specified in a phrase structure grammar, which is a Type-2 grammar, generally given as production rules in Backus–Naur form (BNF). Phrase grammars are often specified in much more constrained grammars than full context-free grammars, in order to make them easier to parse; while the LR parser can parse any DCFL in linear time, the simple LALR parser and even simpler LL parser are more efficient, but can only parse grammars whose production rules are constrained. Contextual structure can in principle be described by a context-sensitive grammar, and automatically analyzed by means such as attribute grammars, though in general this step is done manually, via name resolution rules and type checking, and implemented via a symbol table which stores names and types for each scope.

Tools have been written that automatically generate a lexer from a lexical specification written in regular expressions and a parser from the phrase grammar written in BNF: this allows one to use declarative programming, rather than need to have procedural or functional programming. A notable example is the lex-yacc pair. These automatically produce a *concrete* syntax tree; the parser writer must then manually write code describing how this is converted to an *abstract* syntax tree. Contextual analysis is also generally implemented manually. Despite the existence of these automatic tools, parsing is often implemented manually, for various reasons – perhaps the phrase structure is not context-free, or an alternative implementation improves performance or error-reporting, or allows the grammar to be changed more easily. Parsers are often written in functional languages, such as Haskell, in scripting languages, such as Python or Perl, or in C or C++.

Examples of Errors

As an example, (add 1 1) is a syntactically valid Lisp program (assuming the 'add' function exists, else name resolution fails), adding 1 and 1. However, the following are invalid:

```
(_ 1 1)      lexical error: '_' is not valid

(add 1 1     parsing error: missing closing ')'
```

Note that the lexer is unable to identify the first error – all it knows is that, after producing the token LEFT_PAREN, '(' the remainder of the program is invalid, since no word rule begins with '_'. The second error is detected at the parsing stage: The parser has identified the "list" production rule due to the '(' token (as the only match), and thus can give an error message; in general it may be ambiguous.

Type errors and undeclared variable errors are sometimes considered to be syntax errors when they are detected at compile-time (which is usually the case when compiling strongly-typed languages), though it is common to classify these kinds of error as semantic errors instead.

As an example, the Python code,

```
'a' + 1
```

contains a type error because it adds a string literal to an integer literal. Type errors of this kind can be detected at compile-time: They can be detected during parsing (phrase analysis) if the compiler uses separate rules that allow "integerLiteral + integerLiteral" but not "stringLiteral + integerLiteral", though it is more likely that the compiler will use a parsing rule that allows all expressions of the form "LiteralOrIdentifier + LiteralOrIdentifier" and then the error will be detected during contextual analysis (when type checking occurs). In some cases this validation is not done by the compiler, and these errors are only detected at runtime.

In a dynamically typed language, where type can only be determined at runtime, many type errors can only be detected at runtime. For example, the Python code,

```
a + b
```

is syntactically valid at the phrase level, but the correctness of the types of a and b can only be determined at runtime, as variables do not have types in Python, only values do. Whereas there is disagreement about whether a type error detected by the compiler should be called a syntax error (rather than a static semantic error), type errors which can only be detected at program execution time are always regarded as semantic rather than syntax errors.

Syntax Definition

The syntax of textual programming languages is usually defined using a combination of regular expressions (for lexical structure) and Backus–Naur form (for grammatical structure) to inductively specify syntactic categories (nonterminals) and *terminal* symbols. Syntactic categories are defined by rules called *productions*, which specify the values that belong to a particular syntactic category. Terminal symbols are the concrete characters or strings of characters (for example keywords such as *define, if, let,* or *void*) from which syntactically valid programs are constructed.

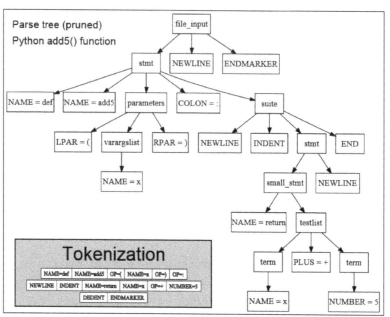

Parse tree of Python code with inset tokenization.

A language can have different equivalent grammars, such as equivalent regular expressions (at the lexical levels), or different phrase rules which generate the same language. Using a broader category of grammars, such as LR grammars, can allow shorter or simpler grammars compared with more restricted categories, such as LL grammar, which may require longer grammars with more rules. Different but equivalent phrase grammars yield different parse trees, though the underlying language (set of valid documents) is the same.

Example: Lisp

Below is a simple grammar, defined using the notation of regular expressions and Extended Backus–Naur form. It describes the syntax of Lisp, which defines productions for the syntactic categories *expression*, *atom*, *number*, *symbol*, and *list*:

```
expression = atom   | list

atom       = number | symbol

number     = [+-]?['0'-'9']+

symbol     = ['A'-'Z''a'-'z'].*

list       = '(', expression*, ')'
```

This grammar specifies the following:

- An *expression* is either an *atom* or a *list*.

- An *atom* is either a *number* or a *symbol*.

- A *number* is an unbroken sequence of one or more decimal digits, optionally preceded by a plus or minus sign.

- A *symbol* is a letter followed by zero or more of any characters (excluding whitespace).

- A *list* is a matched pair of parentheses, with zero or more *expressions* inside it.

Here the decimal digits, upper- and lower-case characters, and parentheses are terminal symbols.

The following are examples of well-formed token sequences in this grammar: '12345', '()', '(a b c232 (1))'.

Complex Grammars

The grammar needed to specify a programming language can be classified by its position in the Chomsky hierarchy. The phrase grammar of most programming languages can be specified using a Type-2 grammar, i.e., they are context-free grammars, though the overall syntax is context-sensitive (due to variable declarations and nested scopes), hence Type-1. However, there are exceptions, and for some languages the phrase grammar is Type-0 (Turing-complete).

In some languages like Perl and Lisp the specification (or implementation) of the language allows constructs that execute during the parsing phase. Furthermore, these languages have constructs that allow the programmer to alter the behavior of the parser. This combination effectively blurs the distinction between parsing and execution, and makes syntax analysis an undecidable problem in these languages, meaning that the parsing phase may not finish. For example, in Perl it is possible to execute code during parsing using a BEGIN statement, and Perl function prototypes may alter the syntactic interpretation, and possibly even the syntactic validity of the remaining code. Colloquially this is referred to as "only Perl can parse Perl" (because code must be executed during parsing, and can modify the grammar), or more strongly "even Perl cannot parse Perl" (because it is undecidable). Similarly, Lisp macros introduced by the defmacro syntax also execute during parsing, meaning that a Lisp compiler must have an entire Lisp run-time system present. In contrast C macros are merely string replacements, and do not require code execution.

Syntax Versus Semantics

The syntax of a language describes the form of a valid program, but does not provide any information about the meaning of the program or the results of executing that program. The meaning given to a combination of symbols is handled by semantics (either formal or hard-coded in a reference implementation). Not all syntactically correct programs are semantically correct. Many syntactically correct programs are nonetheless ill-formed, per the language's rules; and may (depending on the language specification and the soundness of the implementation) result in an error on translation or execution. In some cases, such programs may exhibit undefined behavior. Even when a program is well-defined within a language, it may still have a meaning that is not intended by the person who wrote it.

Using natural language as an example, it may not be possible to assign a meaning to a grammatically correct sentence or the sentence may be false:

- "Colorless green ideas sleep furiously." is grammatically well formed but has no generally accepted meaning.

- "John is a married bachelor." is grammatically well formed but expresses a meaning that cannot be true.

The following C language fragment is syntactically correct, but performs an operation that is not semantically defined (because p is a null pointer, the operations p->real and p->im have no meaning):

```
complex *p = NULL;

complex abs_p = sqrt (p->real * p->real + p->im * p->im);
```

As a simpler example,

```
int x;

printf("%d", x);
```

is syntactically valid, but not semantically defined, as it uses an uninitialized variable. Even though compilers for some programming languages (e.g., Java and C#) would detect uninitialized variable errors of this kind, they should be regarded as semantic errors rather than syntax errors.

Data Type

In computer science and computer programming, a data type or simply type is a classification of data which tells the compiler or interpreter how the programmer intends to use the data. Most programming languages support various types of data, for example: real, integer or Boolean. A Data type provides a set of values from which an expression (i.e. variable, function ...) may take its values. The type defines the operations that can be done on the data, the meaning of the data, and the way values of that type can be stored.

Overview

Data types are used within type systems, which offer various ways of defining, implementing and using them. Different type systems ensure varying degrees of type safety.

Almost all programming languages explicitly include the notion of data type, though different languages may use different terminology. Common data types include:

- Integers
- Booleans
- Characters
- Floating-point numbers
- Alphanumeric strings

For example, in the Java programming language, the "int" type represents the set of 32-bit integers ranging in value from -2,147,483,648 to 2,147,483,647, as well as the operations that can be performed on integers, such as addition, subtraction, and multiplication. Colors, on the other hand, are represented by three bytes denoting the amounts each of red, green, and blue, and one string representing that color's name; allowable operations include addition and subtraction, but not multiplication.

Most programming languages also allow the programmer to define additional data types, usually by combining multiple elements of other types and defining the valid operations of the new data type. For example, a programmer might create a new data type named "complex number" that would include real and imaginary parts. A data type also represents a constraint placed upon the interpretation of data in a type system, describing representation, interpretation and structure of values or objects stored in computer memory. The type system uses data type information to check correctness of computer programs that access or manipulate the data.

Most data types in statistics have comparable types in computer programming, and vice versa.

Definition of a "Type"

(Parnas, Shore & Weiss 1976) identified five definitions of a "type" that were used—sometimes implicitly—in the literature. Types including behavior align more closely with object-oriented models, whereas a structured programming model would tend to not include code, and are called plain old data structures.

The five types are:

Syntactic:

> A type is a purely syntactic label associated with a variable when it is declared. Such definitions of "type" do not give any semantic meaning to types.

Representation:

> A type is defined in terms of its composition of more primitive types—often machine types.

Representation and behaviour:

> A type is defined as its representation and a set of operators manipulating these representations.

Value space:

> A type is a set of possible values which a variable can possess. Such definitions make it possible to speak about (disjoint) unions or Cartesian products of types.

Value space and behaviour:

> A type is a set of values which a variable can possess and a set of functions that one can apply to these values.

The definition in terms of a representation was often done in imperative languages such as ALGOL and Pascal, while the definition in terms of a value space and behaviour was used in higher-level languages such as Simula and CLU.

Classes of Data Types

Machine Data Types

All data in computers based on digital electronics is represented as bits (alternatives 0 and 1) on the lowest level. The smallest addressable unit of data is usually a group of bits called a byte (usually an octet, which is 8 bits). The unit processed by machine code instructions is called a word (as of 2011, typically 32 or 64 bits). Most instructions interpret the word as a binary number, such that a 32-bit word can represent unsigned integer values from 0 to or signed integer values from 0 to $2^{32} - 1$. Because of two's complement, the machine language and machine doesn't need to distinguish between these unsigned and signed data types for the most part.

There is a specific set of arithmetic instructions that use a different interpretation of the bits in word as a floating-point number.

Machine data types need to be *exposed* or made available in systems or low-level programming languages, allowing fine-grained control over hardware. The C programming language, for instance, supplies integer types of various widths, such as short and long. If a corresponding native type does not exist on the target platform, the compiler will break them down into code using types that do exist. For instance, if a 32-bit integer is requested on a 16 bit platform, the compiler will tacitly treat it as an array of two 16 bit integers.

Several languages allow binary and hexadecimal literals, for convenient manipulation of machine data.

In higher level programming, machine data types are often hidden or *abstracted* as an implementation detail that would render code less portable if exposed. For instance, a generic numeric type might be supplied instead of integers of some specific bit-width.

Boolean Type

The Boolean type represents the values true and false. Although only two values are possible, they are rarely implemented as a single binary digit for efficiency reasons. Many programming languages do not have an explicit Boolean type, instead interpreting (for instance) 0 as false and other values as true. Boolean data simply refers to the logical structure of how the language is interpreted to the machine language. In this case a Boolean 0 refers to the logic False. True is always a non zero, especially a one which is known as Boolean 1.

Numeric Types

Such as:

- The integer data types, or "whole numbers". May be sub-typed according to their ability to contain negative values (e.g. unsigned in C and C++). May also have a small number of predefined subtypes (such as short and long in C/C++); or allow users to freely define sub-ranges such as 1..12 (e.g. Pascal/Ada).

- Floating point data types, usually represent values as high-precision fractional values (rational numbers, mathematically), but are sometimes misleadingly called reals (evocative of mathematical real numbers). They usually have predefined limits on both their maximum values and their precision. Output of these values are often represented in a decimal number format.

- Fixed point data types are convenient for representing monetary values. They are often implemented internally as integers, leading to predefined limits.

- Bignum or arbitrary precision numeric types lack predefined limits. They are not primitive types, and are used sparingly for efficiency reasons.

Composite Types

Composite types are derived from more than one primitive type. This can be done in a number of ways. The ways they are combined are called data structures. Composing a primitive type into a compound type generally results in a new type, e.g. *array-of-integer* is a different type to *integer*.

- An array stores a number of elements of the same type in a specific order. They are accessed randomly using an integer to specify which element is required (although the elements may be of almost any type). Arrays may be fixed-length or expandable.

  o A list is similar to an array, but its contents are strung together by a series of references to the next element.

- Record (also called tuple or struct) Records are among the simplest data structures. A record is a value that contains other values, typically in fixed number and sequence and typically indexed by names. The elements of records are usually called *fields* or *members*.

- Union. A union type definition will specify which of a number of permitted primitive types may be stored in its instances, e.g. "float or long integer". Contrast with a record, which could be defined to contain a float *and* an integer; whereas, in a union, there is only one type allowed at a time.

  o A tagged union (also called a variant, variant record, discriminated union, or disjoint union) contains an additional field indicating its current type, for enhanced type safety.

- A set is an abstract data structure that can store certain values, without any particular order, and no repeated values. Values themselves are not retrieved from sets, rather one tests a value for membership to obtain a boolean "in" or "not in".

- An object contains a number of data fields, like a record, and also a number of subroutines for accessing or modifying them, called methods.

Many others are possible, but they tend to be further variations and compounds of the above.

Enumerations

The enumerated type has distinct values, which can be compared and assigned, but which do not necessarily have any particular concrete representation in the computer's memory; compilers and interpreters can represent them arbitrarily. For example, the four suits in a deck of playing cards may be four enumerators named *CLUB*, *DIAMOND*, *HEART*, *SPADE*, belonging to an enumerated type named *suit*. If a variable *V* is declared having *suit* as its data type, one can assign any of those four values to it. Some implementations allow programmers to assign integer values to the enumeration values, or even treat them as type-equivalent to integers.

String and Text Types

Such as:

- Alphanumeric character. A letter of the alphabet, digit, blank space, punctuation mark, etc.

- Alphanumeric strings, a sequence of characters. They are typically used to represent words and text.

Character and string types can store sequences of characters from a character set such as ASCII. Since most character sets include the digits, it is possible to have a numeric string, such as "1234". However, many languages treat these as belonging to a different type to the numeric value 1234.

Character and string types can have different subtypes according to the required character "width". The original 7-bit wide ASCII was found to be limited, and superseded by 8 and 16-bit sets, which can encode a wide variety of non-Latin alphabets (Hebrew, Chinese) and other symbols. Strings may be either stretch-to-fit or of fixed size, even in the same programming language. They may also be subtyped by their maximum size.

Note: strings are not primitive in all languages, for instance C: they may be composed from arrays of characters.

Other Types

Types can be based on, or derived from, the basic types explained above. In some languages, such as C, functions have a type derived from the type of their return value.

Pointers and References

The main non-composite, derived type is the pointer, a data type whose value refers directly to (or "points to") another value stored elsewhere in the computer memory using its address. It is a primitive kind of reference. (In everyday terms, a page number in a book could be considered a piece of data that refers to another one). Pointers are often stored in a format similar to an integer; however, attempting to dereference or "look up" a pointer whose value was never a valid memory address would cause a program to crash. To ameliorate this potential problem, pointers are considered a separate type to the type of data they point to, even if the underlying representation is the same.

Function Types

Abstract Data Types

Any type that does not specify an implementation is an abstract data type. For instance, a stack (which is an abstract type) can be implemented as an array (a contiguous block of memory containing multiple values), or as a linked list (a set of non-contiguous memory blocks linked by pointers).

Abstract types can be handled by code that does not know or "care" what underlying types are contained in them. Programming that is agnostic about concrete data types is called generic programming. Arrays and records can also contain underlying types, but are considered concrete because they specify how their contents or elements are laid out in memory.

Examples include:

- A queue is a first-in first-out list. Variations are Deque and Priority queue.

- A set can store certain values, without any particular order, and with no repeated values.

- A stack is a last-in, first out data structure.

- A tree is a hierarchical structure.

- A graph.

- A hash, dictionary, map or associative array is a more flexible variation on a record, in which name-value pairs can be added and deleted freely.

- A smart pointer is the abstract counterpart to a pointer. Both are kinds of references.

Utility Types

For convenience, high-level languages may supply ready-made "real world" data types, for instance *times*, *dates* and *monetary values* and *memory*, even where the language allows them to be built from primitive types.

Type Systems

A type system associates types with each computed value. By examining the flow of these values, a type system attempts to prove that no *type errors* can occur. The type system in question determines what constitutes a type error, but a type system generally seeks to guarantee that operations expecting a certain kind of value are not used with values for which that operation does not make sense.

A compiler may use the static type of a value to optimize the storage it needs and the choice of algorithms for operations on the value. In many C compilers the float data type, for example, is represented in 32 bits, in accord with the IEEE specification for single-precision floating point numbers. They will thus use floating-point-specific microprocessor operations on those values (floating-point addition, multiplication, etc.).

The depth of type constraints and the manner of their evaluation affect the *typing* of the language. A programming language may further associate an operation with varying concrete algorithms on each type in the case of type polymorphism. Type theory is the study of type systems, although the concrete type systems of programming languages originate from practical issues of computer architecture, compiler implementation, and language design.

Type systems may be variously static or dynamic, strong or weak typing, and so forth.

Structured Programming

Structured programming is a programming paradigm aimed at improving the clarity, quality, and development time of a computer program by making extensive use of subroutines, block structures, for and while loops—in contrast to using simple tests and jumps such as the *go to* statement which could lead to "spaghetti code" causing difficulty to both follow and maintain.

It emerged in the late 1950s with the appearance of the ALGOL 58 and ALGOL 60 programming languages, with the latter including support for block structures. Contributing factors to its popularity and widespread acceptance, at first in academia and later among practitioners, include the discovery of what is now known as the structured program theorem in 1966, and the publication of the influential "Go To Statement Considered Harmful" open letter in 1968 by Dutch computer scientist Edsger W. Dijkstra, who coined the term "structured programming".

Structured programming is most frequently used with deviations that allow for clearer programs in some particular cases, such as when exception handling has to be performed.

Elements

Control Structures

Following the structured program theorem, all programs are seen as composed of control structures:

- "Sequence"; ordered statements or subroutines executed in sequence.

- "Selection"; one or a number of statements is executed depending on the state of the program. This is usually expressed with keywords such as if..then..else..endif.

- "Iteration"; a statement or block is executed until the program reaches a certain state, or operations have been applied to every element of a collection. This is usually expressed with keywords such as while, repeat, for or do..until. Often it is recommended that each loop should only have one entry point (and in the original structural programming, also only one exit point, and a few languages enforce this).

- "Recursion"; a statement is executed by repeatedly calling itself until termination conditions are met. While similar in practice to iterative loops, recursive loops may be more computationally efficient, and are implemented differently as a cascading stack.

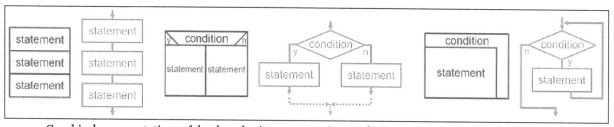

Graphical representations of the three basic patterns using NS diagrams (blue) and flow charts (green).

Subroutines

Subroutines; callable units such as procedures, functions, methods, or subprograms are used to allow a sequence to be referred to by a single statement.

Blocks

Blocks are used to enable groups of statements to be treated as if they were one statement. *Block-structured* languages have a syntax for enclosing structures in some formal way, such as an if-statement bracketed by if..fi as in ALGOL 68, or a code section bracketed by BEGIN..END, as in PL/I, whitespace indentation as in Python - or the curly braces {...} of C and many later languages.

Structured Programming Languages

It is possible to do structured programming in any programming language, though it is preferable to use something like a procedural programming language. Some of the languages initially used for structured programming include: ALGOL, Pascal, PL/I and Ada – but most new procedural programming languages since that time have included features to encourage structured programming, and sometimes deliberately left out features – notably GOTO – in an effort to make unstructured programming more difficult. *Structured programming* (sometimes known as modular programming) enforces a logical structure on the program being written to make it more efficient and easier to understand and modify.

History

Theoretical Foundation

The structured program theorem provides the theoretical basis of structured programming. It states that three ways of combining programs—sequencing, selection, and iteration—are sufficient to express any computable function. This observation did not originate with the structured programming movement; these structures are sufficient to describe the instruction cycle of a central processing unit, as well as the operation of a Turing machine. Therefore, a processor is always executing a "structured program" in this sense, even if the instructions it reads from memory are not part of a structured program. However, authors usually credit the result to a 1966 paper by Böhm and Jacopini, possibly because Dijkstra cited this paper himself. The structured program theorem does not address how to write and analyze a usefully structured program. These issues were addressed during the late 1960s and early 1970s, with major contributions by Dijkstra, Robert W. Floyd, Tony Hoare, Ole-Johan Dahl, and David Gries.

Debate

P. J. Plauger, an early adopter of structured programming, described his reaction to the structured program theorem:

> Us converts waved this interesting bit of news under the noses of the unreconstructed assembly-language programmers who kept trotting forth twisty bits of logic and saying, 'I

betcha can't structure this.' Neither the proof by Böhm and Jacopini nor our repeated successes at writing structured code brought them around one day sooner than they were ready to convince themselves.

Donald Knuth accepted the principle that programs must be written with provability in mind, but he disagreed (and still disagrees) with abolishing the GOTO statement. In his 1974 paper, "Structured Programming with Goto Statements", he gave examples where he believed that a direct jump leads to clearer and more efficient code without sacrificing provability. Knuth proposed a looser structural constraint: It should be possible to draw a program's flow chart with all forward branches on the left, all backward branches on the right, and no branches crossing each other. Many of those knowledgeable in compilers and graph theory have advocated allowing only reducible flow graphs.

Structured programming theorists gained a major ally in the 1970s after IBM researcher Harlan Mills applied his interpretation of structured programming theory to the development of an indexing system for the *New York Times* research file. The project was a great engineering success, and managers at other companies cited it in support of adopting structured programming, although Dijkstra criticized the ways that Mills's interpretation differed from the published work.

As late as 1987 it was still possible to raise the question of structured programming in a computer science journal. Frank Rubin did so in that year with an open letter titled ""GOTO considered harmful" considered harmful". Numerous objections followed, including a response from Dijkstra that sharply criticized both Rubin and the concessions other writers made when responding to him.

Outcome

By the end of the 20th century nearly all computer scientists were convinced that it is useful to learn and apply the concepts of structured programming. High-level programming languages that originally lacked programming structures, such as FORTRAN, COBOL, and BASIC, now have them.

Common Deviations

While goto has now largely been replaced by the structured constructs of selection (if/then/else) and repetition (while and for), few languages are purely structured. The most common deviation, found in many languages, is the use of a return statement for early exit from a subroutine. This results in multiple exit points, instead of the single exit point required by structured programming. There are other constructions to handle cases that are awkward in purely structured programming.

Early Exit

The most common deviation from structured programming is early exit from a function or loop. At the level of functions, this is a return statement. At the level of loops, this is a break statement (terminate the loop) or continue statement (terminate the current iteration, proceed with next iteration). In structured programming, these can be replicated by adding additional branches or tests, but for returns from nested code this can add significant complexity. C is an early and prominent example of these constructs. Some newer languages also have "labeled breaks", which allow breaking out of more than just the innermost loop. Exceptions also allow early exit, but have further consequences, and thus are treated below.

Multiple exits can arise for a variety of reasons, most often either that the subroutine has no more work to do (if returning a value, it has completed the calculation), or has encountered "exceptional" circumstances that prevent it from continuing, hence needing exception handling.

The most common problem in early exit is that cleanup or final statements are not executed – for example, allocated memory is not deallocated, or open files are not closed, causing memory leaks or resource leaks. These must be done at each return site, which is brittle and can easily result in bugs. For instance, in later development, a return statement could be overlooked by a developer, and an action which should be performed at the end of a subroutine (e.g., a trace statement) might not be performed in all cases. Languages without a return statement, such as standard Pascal don't have this problem.

Most modern languages provide language-level support to prevent such leaks. Most commonly this is done via unwind protection, which ensures that certain code is guaranteed to be run when execution exits a block; this is a structured alternative to having a cleanup block and a goto. This is most often known as try...finally, and considered a part of exception handling. Various techniques exist to encapsulate resource management. An alternative approach, found primarily in C++, is Resource Acquisition Is Initialization, which uses normal stack unwinding (variable deallocation) at function exit to call destructors on local variables to deallocate resources.

Kent Beck, Martin Fowler and co-authors have argued in their refactoring books that nested conditionals may be harder to understand than a certain type of flatter structure using multiple exits predicated by guard clauses. Their 2009 book flatly states that "one exit point is really not a useful rule. Clarity is the key principle: If the method is clearer with one exit point, use one exit point; otherwise don't". They offer a cookbook solution for transforming a function consisting only of nested conditionals into a sequence of guarded return (or throw) statements, followed by a single unguarded block, which is intended to contain the code for the common case, while the guarded statements are supposed to deal with the less common ones (or with errors). Herb Sutter and Andrei Alexandrescu also argue in their 2004 C++ tips book that the single-exit point is an obsolete requirement.

In his 2004 textbook, David Watt writes that "single-entry multi-exit control flows are often desirable". Using Tennent's framework notion of sequencer, Watt uniformly describes the control flow constructs found in contemporary programming languages and attempts to explain why certain types of sequencers are preferable to others in the context of multi-exit control flows. Watt writes that unrestricted gotos (jump sequencers) are bad because the destination of the jump is not self-explanatory to the reader of a program until the reader finds and examines the actual label or address that is the target of the jump. In contrast, Watt argues that the conceptual intent of a return sequencer is clear from its own context, without having to examine its destination. Watt writes that a class of sequencers known as *escape sequencers*, defined as a "sequencer that terminates execution of a textually enclosing command or procedure", encompasses both breaks from loops (including multi-level breaks) and return statements. Watt also notes that while jump sequencers (gotos) have been somewhat restricted in languages like C, where the target must be an inside the local block or an encompassing outer block, that restriction alone is not sufficient to make the intent of gotos in C self-describing and so they can still produce "spaghetti code". Watt also examines how exception sequencers differ from escape and jump sequencers.

In contrast to the above, Bertrand Meyer wrote in his 2009 textbook that instructions like break and continue "are just the old goto in sheep's clothing" and strongly advised against their use.

Exception Handling

Based on the coding error from the Ariane 501 disaster, software developer Jim Bonang argues that any exceptions thrown from a function violate the single-exit paradigm, and proposes that all inter-procedural exceptions should be forbidden. In C++ syntax, this is done by declaring all function signatures as throw() Bonang proposes that all single-exit conforming C++ should be written along the lines of:

```
bool myCheck1() throw()

{

  bool success = false;

  try {

    // do something that may throw exceptions

    if(myCheck2() == false) {

      throw SomeInternalException();

    }

    // other code similar to the above

    success = true;

  }

  catch(...) { // all exceptions caught and logged

  }

  return success;

}
```

Peter Ritchie also notes that, in principle, even a single throw right before the return in a function constitutes a violation of the single-exit principle, but argues that Dijkstra's rules were written in a time before exception handling became a paradigm in programming languages, so he proposes to allow any number of throw points in addition to a single return point. He notes that solutions which wrap exceptions for the sake of creating a single-exit have higher nesting depth and thus are more difficult to comprehend, and even accuses those who propose to apply such solutions to programming languages which support exceptions of engaging in cargo cult thinking.

David Watt also analyzes exception handling in the framework of sequencers. Watt notes that an abnormal situation (generally exemplified with arithmetic overflows or input/output failures like file not found) is a kind of error that "is detected in some low-level program unit, but [for which] a handler is more naturally located in a high-level program unit". For example, a program might contain several calls to read files, but the action to perform when a file is not found depends on the meaning (purpose) of the file in question to the program and thus a handling routine for this abnormal situation cannot be located in low-level system code. Watts further notes that introducing status flags testing in the caller, as single-exit structured programming or even (multi-exit) return sequencers would entail, results in a situation where "the application code tends to get cluttered by tests of status flags" and that "the programmer might forgetfully or lazily omit to test a status flag. In fact, abnormal situations represented by status flags are by default ignored!" He notes that in contrast to status flags testing, exceptions have the opposite default behavior, causing the program to terminate unless the programmer explicitly deals with the exception in some way, possibly by adding code to willfully ignore it. Based on these arguments, Watt concludes that jump sequencers or escape sequencers aren't as suitable as a dedicated exception sequencer with the semantics discussed above.

The textbook by Louden and Lambert emphasizes that exception handling differs from structured programming constructs like while loops because the transfer of control "is set up at a different point in the program than that where the actual transfer takes place. At the point where the transfer actually occurs, there may be no syntactic indication that control will in fact be transferred." Computer science professor Arvind Kumar Bansal also notes that in languages which implement exception handling, even control structures like for, which have the single-exit property in absence of exceptions, no longer have it in presence of exceptions, because an exception can prematurely cause an early exit in any part of the control structure; for instance if init() throws an exception in for (init(); check(); increm()), then the usual exit point after check() is not reached. Citing multiple prior studies by others (1999-2004) and their own results, Westley Weimer and George Necula wrote that a significant problem with exceptions is that they "create hidden control-flow paths that are difficult for programmers to reason about".

The necessity to limit code to single-exit points appears in some contemporary programming environments focused on parallel computing, such as OpenMP. The various parallel constructs from OpenMP, like parallel do, do not allow early exits from inside to the outside of the parallel construct; this restriction includes all manner of exits, from break to C++ exceptions, but all of these are permitted inside the parallel construct if the jump target is also inside it.

Multiple Entry

More rarely, subprograms allow multiple *entry*. This is most commonly only *re*-entry into a coroutine (or generator/semicoroutine), where a subprogram yields control (and possibly a value), but can then be resumed where it left off. There are a number of common uses of such programming, notably for streams (particularly input/output), state machines, and concurrency. From a code execution point of view, yielding from a coroutine is closer to structured programming than returning from a subroutine, as the subprogram has not actually terminated, and will continue when called again – it is not an early exit. However, coroutines mean that multiple subprograms have execution state – rather than a single call stack of subroutines – and thus introduce a different form of complexity.

It is very rare for subprograms to allow entry to an arbitrary position in the subprogram, as in this case the program state (such as variable values) is uninitialized or ambiguous, and this is very similar to a goto.

State Machines

Some programs, particularly parsers and communications protocols, have a number of states that follow each other in a way that is not easily reduced to the basic structures, and some programmers implement the state-changes with a jump to the new state. This type of state-switching is often used in the Linux kernel.

However, it is possible to structure these systems by making each state-change a separate subprogram and using a variable to indicate the active state. Alternatively, these can be implemented via coroutines, which dispense with the trampoline.

Programming Style

Programming style is a set of rules or guidelines used when writing the source code for a computer program. It is often claimed that following a particular programming style will help programmers to read and understand source code conforming to the style, and help to avoid introducing errors.

A classic work on the subject was *The Elements of Programming Style*, written in the 1970s, and illustrated with examples from the Fortran and PL/I languages prevalent at the time.

The programming style used in a particular program may be derived from the coding conventions of a company or other computing organization, as well as the preferences of the author of the code. Programming styles are often designed for a specific programming language (or language family): style considered good in C source code may not be appropriate for BASIC source code, and so on. However, some rules are commonly applied to many languages.

Elements of Good Style

Good style is a subjective matter, and is difficult to define. However, there are several elements common to a large number of programming styles. The issues usually considered as part of programming style include the layout of the source code, including indentation; the use of white space around operators and keywords; the capitalization or otherwise of keywords and variable names; the style and spelling of user-defined identifiers, such as function, procedure and variable names; and the use and style of comments.

Code Appearance

Programming styles commonly deal with the visual appearance of source code, with the goal of readability. Software has long been available that formats source code automatically, leaving coders to concentrate on naming, logic, and higher techniques. As a practical point, using a computer to format source code saves time, and it is possible to then enforce company-wide standards without debates.

Indentation

Indent styles assist in identifying control flow and blocks of code. In some programming languages indentation is used to delimit logical blocks of code; correct indentation in these cases is more than a matter of style. In other languages indentation and white space do not affect function, although logical and consistent indentation makes code more readable. Compare:

```
if (hours < 24 && minutes < 60 && seconds < 60) {

    return true;

} else {

    return false;

}
```

or

```
if (hours < 24 && minutes < 60 && seconds < 60)

{

    return true;

}

else

{

    return false;

}
```

with something like

```
if  ( hours    < 24

    && minutes < 60

    && seconds < 60

)

{return     true

;}          else

{return     false

;}
```

The first two examples are probably much easier to read because they are indented in an established way (a "hanging paragraph" style). This indentation style is especially useful when dealing with multiple nested constructs.

Note however that this example is the same as simply:

```
return hours < 24 && minutes < 60 && seconds < 60;
```

ModuLiq

The ModuLiq Zero Indent Style groups with carriage returns rather than indents. Compare all of the above to:

```
if (hours < 24 && minutes < 60 && seconds < 60)

return true;

else

return false;
```

Lua

Lua does not use the traditional curly braces or parenthesis. if/else statements only require the expression be followed by then, and closing the if/else statement with end.

```
if hours < 24 and minutes < 60 and seconds < 60 then

    return true

else

    return false

end
```

Indentation is optional. and,or,not are used in between true/false statements.

They are true/false statements, as

```
print(not true)
```

would mean false.

Python

Python uses indentation to indicate control structures, so *correct indentation* is required. By do-ing this, the need for bracketing with curly braces (i.e. { and }) is eliminated. On the other hand, copying and pasting Python code can lead to problems, because the indentation level of the pasted code may not be the same as the indentation level of the current line. Such reformatting can be tedious to do by hand, but some text editors and IDEs have features to do it automatically. There are also problems when Python code being rendered unusable when posted on a forum or web page that removes white space, though this problem can be avoided where it is possible to enclose code in white space-preserving tags such as "<pre> ... </pre>" (for HTML), "[code]" ... "[/code]" (for bbcode), etc.

```
if hours < 24 and minutes < 60 and seconds < 60:

    return True
```

```
else:

    return False
```

Notice that Python does not use curly braces, but a regular colon (e.g. else:).

Many Python programmers tend to follow a commonly agreed style guide known as PEP8. There are tools designed to automate PEP8 compliance.

Haskell

Haskell similarly has the off-side rule, i.e. it has a two dimension syntax where indentation is meaningful to define blocks. Although an alternate syntax uses curly braces and semicolons. Haskell is a declarative language, there are statements, but declarations within a Haskell script. Example:

```
let c_1 = 1

    c_2 = 2

in

    f x y = c_1 * x + c_2 * y
```

may be written in one line as:

```
let {c_1=1;c_2=2} in f x y = c_1 * x + c_2 * y
```

Haskell encourage the use of literate programming, where extended text explain the genesis of the code. In literate Haskell scripts (named with the lhs extension), everything is a comment except blocks marked as code. The program can be written in LATEX, in such case the code environment marks what is code. Also each active code paragraph can be marked by preceding and ending it with an empty line, and starting each line of code with a greater than sign and a space. Here an example using LATEX markup:

```
The function \verb+isValidDate+ test if date is valid

\begin{code}

isValidDate :: Date -> Bool

isValidDate date = hh>=0  && mm>=0 && ss>=0

                && hh<24 && mm<60 && ss<60

  where (hh,mm,ss) = fromDate date

\end{code}

observe that in this case the overloaded function is \verb+fromDate ::
Date -> (Int,Int,Int)+.
```

And an example using plain text:

```
The function isValidDate test if date is valid
```

```
> isValidDate :: Date -> Bool
> isValidDate date = hh>=0  && mm>=0 && ss>=0
>                      && hh<24 && mm<60 && ss<60
>  where (hh,mm,ss) = fromDate date
```

```
observe that in this case the overloaded function is fromDate :: Date ->
(Int,Int,Int).
```

Vertical Alignment

It is often helpful to align similar elements vertically, to make typo-generated bugs more obvious. Compare:

```
$search = array('a', 'b', 'c', 'd', 'e');
$replacement = array('foo', 'bar', 'baz', 'quux');
```

```
// Another example:
```

```
$value = 0;
$anothervalue = 1;
$yetanothervalue = 2;
with:
$search       = array('a',    'b',    'c',    'd',    'e');
$replacement = array('foo', 'bar', 'baz', 'quux');
```

```
// Another example:
$value           = 0;
$anothervalue    = 1;
$yetanothervalue = 2;
```

The latter example makes two things intuitively clear that were not clear in the former:

- The search and replace terms are related and match up: they are not discrete variables.

- There is one more search term than there are replacement terms. If this is a bug, it is now more likely to be spotted.

However, note that there are arguments *against* vertical alignment:

- Inter-line false dependencies; tabular formatting creates dependencies across lines. For example, if an identifier with a long name is added to a tabular layout, the column width may have to be increased to accommodate it. This forces a bigger change to the source code than necessary, and the essential change may be lost in the noise. This is detrimental to Revision control where inspecting differences between versions is essential.

- Brittleness; if a programmer does not neatly format the table when making a change, maybe legitimately with the previous point in mind, the result becomes a mess that deteriorates with further such changes. Simple refactoring operations, such as search-and-replace, may also break the formatting.

- Resistance to modification; tabular formatting requires more effort to maintain. This may put off a programmer from making a beneficial change, such as adding, correcting or improving the name of an identifier, because it will mess up the formatting.

- Reliance on mono-spaced font; tabular formatting assumes that the editor uses a fixed-width font. Many modern code editors support proportional fonts, and the programmer may prefer to use a proportional font for readability.

- Tool dependence; some of the effort of maintaining alignment can be alleviated by tools (e.g. a source code editor that supports elastic tabstops), although that creates a reliance on such tools.

For example, if a simple refactoring operation is performed on the code above, renaming variables "$replacement" to "$r" and "$anothervalue" to "$a", the resulting code will look like this:

```
$search      = array('a',    'b',    'c',    'd',    'e');

$r = array('foo', 'bar', 'baz', 'quux');

// Another example:

$value            = 0;

$a    = 1;

$yetanothervalue = 2;
```

The original sequential formatting will still look fine after such change:

```
$search = array('a', 'b', 'c', 'd', 'e');

$r = array('foo', 'bar', 'baz', 'quux');
```

```
// Another example:


$value = 0;

$a = 1;

$yetanothervalue = 2;
```

Spaces

In those situations where some white space is required, the grammars of most free-format languages are unconcerned with the amount that appears. Style related to white space is commonly used to enhance readability. There are currently no known hard facts (conclusions from studies) about which of the whitespace styles have the best readability.

For instance, compare the following syntactically equivalent examples of C code:

```
int i;

for(i=0;i<10;++i){

    printf("%d",i*i+i);

}
```

versus

```
int i;

for (i=0; i<10; ++i) {

    printf("%d", i*i+i);

}
```

versus

```
int i;

for (i = 0; i < 10; ++i) {

    printf("%d", i * i + i);

}
```

Tabs

The use of tabs to create white space presents particular issues when not enough care is taken because the location of the tabulation point can be different depending on the tools being used and even the preferences of the user.

As an example, one programmer prefers tab stops of four and has his toolset configured this way, and uses these to format his code.

```
int     ix;      // Index to scan array

long    sum;     // Accumulator for sum
```

Another programmer prefers tab stops of eight, and his toolset is configured this way. When he examines his code, he may well find it difficult to read.

```
int             ix;                     // Index to scan array

long    sum;     // Accumulator for sum
```

One widely used solution to this issue may involve forbidding the use of tabs for alignment or rules on how tab stops must be set. Note that tabs work fine provided they are used consistently, restricted to logical indentation, and not used for alignment:

```
class MyClass {
        int foobar(
                int qux, // first parameter
                int quux); // second parameter
        int foobar2(
                int qux, // first parameter
                int quux, // second parameter
                int quuux); // third parameter
};
```

Control Flow

In computer science, control flow (or flow of control) is the order in which individual statements, instructions or function calls of an imperative program are executed or evaluated. The emphasis on explicit control flow distinguishes an *imperative programming* language from a *declarative programming* language.

Within an imperative programming language, a *control flow statement* is a statement which execution results in a choice being made as to which of two or more paths to follow. For non-strict functional languages, functions and language constructs exist to achieve the same result, but they are usually not termed control flow statements.

A set of statements is in turn generally structured as a block, which in addition to grouping, also defines a lexical scope.

Interrupts and signals are low-level mechanisms that can alter the flow of control in a way similar to a subroutine, but usually occur as a response to some external stimulus or event (that can occur asynchronously), rather than execution of an *in-line* control flow statement.

At the level of machine language or assembly language, control flow instructions usually work by altering the program counter. For some central processing units (CPUs), the only control flow instructions available are conditional or unconditional branch instructions, also termed jumps.

Categories

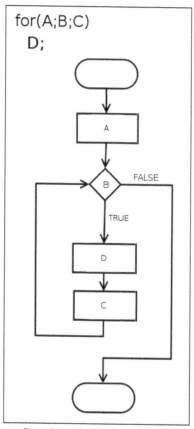

A flow chart showing control flow.

The kinds of control flow statements supported by different languages vary, but can be categorized by their effect:

- Continuation at a different statement (unconditional branch or jump).

- Executing a set of statements only if some condition is met (choice - i.e., conditional branch).

- Executing a set of statements zero or more times, until some condition is met (i.e., loop - the same as conditional branch).

- Executing a set of distant statements, after which the flow of control usually returns (subroutines, coroutines, and continuations).

- Stopping the program, preventing any further execution (unconditional halt).

Primitives

Labels

A label is an explicit name or number assigned to a fixed position within the source code, and which may be referenced by control flow statements appearing elsewhere in the source code. A label marks a position within source code, and has no other effect.

Line numbers are an alternative to a named label (and used in some languages such as Fortran and BASIC), that are whole numbers placed at the start of each line of text in the source code. Languages which use these often impose the constraint that the line numbers must increase in value in each following line, but may not require that they be consecutive. For example, in BASIC:

```
10 LET X = 3

20 PRINT X
```

In other languages such as C and Ada, a label is an identifier, usually appearing at the start of a line and immediately followed by a colon. For example, in C:

```
Success: printf("The operation was successful.\n");
```

The language ALGOL 60 allowed both whole numbers and identifiers as labels (both linked by colons to the following statement), but few if any other ALGOL variants allowed whole numbers.

Goto

The *goto* statement (a combination of the English words *go* and *to*, and pronounced accordingly) is the most basic form of unconditional transfer of control.

Although the keyword may either be in upper or lower case depending on the language, it is usually written as:

```
goto label
```

The effect of a goto statement is to cause the next statement to be executed to be the statement appearing at (or immediately after) the indicated label.

Goto statements have been considered harmful by many computer scientists, notably Dijkstra.

Subroutines

The terminology for subroutines varies; they may alternatively be known as routines, procedures, functions (especially if they return results) or methods (especially if they belong to classes or type classes).

In the 1950s, computer memories were very small by current standards so subroutines were used mainly to reduce program size. A piece of code was written once and then used many times from various other places in a program.

Today, subroutines are more often used to help make a program that is more structured, e.g., by isolating some algorithm or hiding some data access method. If many programmers are working on one program, subroutines are one kind of modularity that can help divide the work.

Sequence

In structured programming, the ordered sequencing of successive commands is considered one of the basic control structures, which is used as a building block for programs alongside iteration, recursion and choice.

Minimal Structured Control Flow

In May 1966, Böhm and Jacopini published an article in *Communications of the ACM* which showed that any program with gotos could be transformed into a goto-free form involving only choice (IF THEN ELSE) and loops (WHILE condition DO xxx), possibly with duplicated code and/ or the addition of Boolean variables (true/false flags). Later authors showed that choice can be replaced by loops (and yet more Boolean variables).

That such minimalism is possible does not mean that it is necessarily desirable; after all, computers theoretically need only one machine instruction (subtract one number from another and branch if the result is negative), but practical computers have dozens or even hundreds of machine instructions.

What Böhm and Jacopini's article showed was that all programs could be goto-free. Other research showed that control structures with one entry and one exit were much easier to understand than any other form, mainly because they could be used anywhere as a statement without disrupting the control flow. In other words, they were *composable*. (Later developments, such as non-strict programming languages – and more recently, composable software transactions – have continued this strategy, making components of programs even more freely composable.)

Some academics took a purist approach to the Böhm-Jacopini result and argued that even instructions like break and return from the middle of loops are bad practice as they are not needed in the Böhm-Jacopini proof, and thus they advocated that all loops should have a single exit point. This purist approach is embodied in the language Pascal (designed in 1968–1969), which up to the mid-1990s was the preferred tool for teaching introductory programming in academia. The direct application of the Böhm-Jacopini theorem may result in additional local variables being introduced in the structured chart, and may also result in some code duplication. The latter issue is called the loop and a half problem in this context. Pascal is affected by both of these problems and according to empirical studies cited by Eric S. Roberts, student programmers had difficulty formulating correct solutions in Pascal for several simple problems, including writing a function for searching an element in an array. A 1980 study by Henry Shapiro cited by Roberts found that using only the Pascal-provided control structures, the correct solution was given by only 20% of the subjects, while no subject wrote incorrect code for this problem if allowed to write a return from the middle of a loop.

Control Structures in Practice

Most programming languages with control structures have an initial keyword which indicates the type of control structure involved. Languages then divide as to whether or not control structures have a final keyword.

- No final keyword: ALGOL 60, C, C++, Haskell, Java, Pascal, Perl, PHP, PL/I, Python, PowerShell. Such languages need some way of grouping statements together:

  o   ALGOL 60 and Pascal: begin ... end

  o   C, C++, Java, Perl, PHP, and PowerShell: curly brackets { ... }

  o   PL/I: DO ... END

  o   Python: uses indent level

  o   Haskell: either indent level or curly brackets can be used, and they can be freely mixed

  o   Lua: uses do ... end

- Final keyword: Ada, ALGOL 68, Modula-2, Fortran 77, Mythryl, Visual Basic. The forms of the final keyword vary:

  o   Ada: final keyword is end + *space* + initial keyword e.g., if ... end if, loop ... end loop

  o   ALGOL 68, Mythryl: initial keyword spelled backwards e.g., if ... fi, case ... esac

  o   Fortran 77: final keyword is end + initial keyword e.g., IF ... ENDIF, DO ... ENDDO

  o   Modula-2: same final keyword END for everything

  o   Visual Basic: every control structure has its own keyword. If ... End If; For ... Next; Do ... Loop; While ... Wend

Choice

If-then-(Else) Statements

Conditional expressions and conditional constructs are features of a programming language which perform different computations or actions depending on whether a programmer-specified boolean *condition* evaluates to true or false.

- IF..GOTO. A form found in unstructured languages, mimicking a typical machine code instruction, would jump to (GOTO) a label or line number when the condition was met.

- IF..THEN..(ENDIF). Rather than being restricted to a jump, any simple statement, or nested block, could follow the THEN key keyword. This a structured form.

- IF..THEN..ELSE..(ENDIF). As above, but with a second action to be performed if the condition is false. This is one of the most common forms, with many variations. Some require a terminal ENDIF, others do not. C and related languages do not require a terminal keyword, or a 'then', but do require parentheses around the condition.

- Conditional statements can be and often are nested inside other conditional statements. Some languages allow ELSE and IF to be combined into ELSEIF, avoiding the need to have a series of ENDIF or other final statements at the end of a compound statement.

Less common variations include:

- Some languages, such as Fortran, have a *three-way* or *arithmetic if*, testing whether a numeric value is positive, negative or zero.

- Some languages have a functional form of an if statement, for instance Lisp's cond.

- Some languages have an operator form of an if statement, such as C's ternary operator.

- Perl supplements a C-style if with when and unless.

- Smalltalk uses ifTrue and ifFalse messages to implement conditionals, rather than any fundamental language construct.

Case and Switch Statements

Switch statements (or *case statements*, or *multiway branches*) compare a given value with specified constants and take action according to the first constant to match. There is usually a provision for a default action ("else", "otherwise") to be taken if no match succeeds. Switch statements can allow compiler optimizations, such as lookup tables. In dynamic languages, the cases may not be limited to constant expressions, and might extend to pattern matching, as in the shell script example on the right, where the *) implements the default case as a glob matching any string. Case logic can also be implemented in functional form, as in SQL's decode statement.

Pascal:	Ada:	C:	Shell script:	Lisp:
| ```
case someChar of

  'a': actionOnA;

  'x': actionOnX;

  'y','z':action-
OnYandZ;

  else actionOnNo-
Match;

end;
``` | ```
case someChar is

  when 'a' =>
actionOnA;

  when 'x' =>
actionOnX;

  when 'y' | 'z'
=>   actionOn-
YandZ;

  when others
=>  actionOnNoM-
atch;

end;
``` | ```
switch  (so-
meChar) {

  case 'a': ac-
tionOnA; break;

  case 'x': ac-
tionOnX; break;

  case 'y':

  case 'z': ac-
tionOnYandZ;
break;

  default: ac-
tionOnNoMatch;

}
``` | ```
case  $someChar
in

  a)    action-
OnA ;;

  x)    action-
OnX ;;

  [yz])  ac-
tionOnYandZ ;;

  *)    action-
OnNoMatch  ;;

esac
``` | ```
(case someChar

  ((#\a)    ac-
tionOnA)

  ((#\x)    ac-
tionOnX)

  ((#\y #\z) ac-
tionOnYandZ)

  (else    ac-
tionOnNoMatch))
``` |

Loops

A loop is a sequence of statements which is specified once but which may be carried out several times in succession. The code "inside" the loop (the *body* of the loop, shown as *xxx*) is obeyed a specified number of times, or once for each of a collection of items, or until some condition is met, or indefinitely.

In functional programming languages, such as Haskell and Scheme, loops can be expressed by
```

using recursion or fixed point iteration rather than explicit looping constructs. Tail recursion is a special case of recursion which can be easily transformed to iteration.

Count-controlled Loops

Most programming languages have constructions for repeating a loop a certain number of times. In most cases counting can go downwards instead of upwards and step sizes other than 1 can be used.

```
FOR I = 1 TO N           | for I := 1 to N do begin
                         |
     XXX                 |      XXX
                         |
NEXT I                   | end;

-----------------------------------------------------------

DO I = 1,N               | for ( I=1; I<=N; ++I ) {
                         |
     XXX                 |      XXX
                         |
END DO                   | }
```

In these examples, if N < 1 then the body of loop may execute once (with I having value 1) or not at all, depending on the programming language.

In many programming languages, only integers can be reliably used in a count-controlled loop. Floating-point numbers are represented imprecisely due to hardware constraints, so a loop such as,

```
for X := 0.1 step 0.1 to 1.0 do
```

might be repeated 9 or 10 times, depending on rounding errors and/or the hardware and/or the compiler version. Furthermore, if the increment of X occurs by repeated addition, accumulated rounding errors may mean that the value of X in each iteration can differ quite significantly from the expected sequence 0.1, 0.2, 0.3, ..., 1.0.

Condition-controlled Loops

Most programming languages have constructions for repeating a loop until some condition changes. Some variations test the condition at the start of the loop; others test it at the end. If the test is at the start, the body may be skipped completely; if it is at the end, the body is always executed at least once.

```
DO WHILE (test)          | repeat
                         |
     XXX                 |      XXX
                         |
LOOP                     | until test;

-------------------------------------------------

while (test) {           | do
```

```
        xxx                       |       xxx

    }                             | while (test);
```

A control break is a value change detection method used within ordinary loops to trigger process-ing for groups of values. Values are monitored within the loop and a change diverts program flow to the handling of the group event associated with them.

DO UNTIL (End-of-File)

  IF new-zipcode <> current-zipcode

    display_tally(current-zipcode, zipcount)

    current-zipcode = new-zipcode

    zipcount = 0

  ENDIF

  zipcount++

LOOP

Collection-controlled Loops

Several programming languages (e.g., Ada, D, C++11, Smalltalk, PHP, Perl, Object Pascal, Java, C#, MATLAB, Mythryl, Visual Basic, Ruby, Python, JavaScript, Fortran 95 and later) have special constructs which allow implicit looping through all elements of an array, or all members of a set or collection.

```
someCollection do: [:eachElement |xxx].

for Item in Collection do begin xxx end;

foreach (item; myCollection) { xxx }

foreach someArray { xxx }

foreach ($someArray as $k => $v) { xxx }

Collection<String> coll; for (String s : coll) {}

foreach (string s in myStringCollection) { xxx }

$someCollection | ForEach-Object { $_ }

forall ( index = first:last:step... )
```

Scala has for-expressions, which generalise collection-controlled loops, and also support other uses, such as asynchronous programming. Haskell has do-expressions and comprehensions, which together provide similar function to for-expressions in Scala.

General Iteration

General iteration constructs such as C's for statement and Common Lisp's do form can be used to express any of the above sorts of loops, and others, such as looping over some number of collections in parallel. Where a more specific looping construct can be used, it is usually preferred over the general iteration construct, since it often makes the purpose of the expression clearer.

Infinite Loops

Infinite loops are used to assure a program segment loops forever or until an exceptional condition arises, such as an error. For instance, an event-driven program (such as a server) should loop forever, handling events as they occur, only stopping when the process is terminated by an operator.

Infinite loops can be implemented using other control flow constructs. Most commonly, in unstructured programming this is jump back up (goto), while in structured programming this is an indefinite loop (while loop) set to never end, either by omitting the condition or explicitly setting it to true, as while (true) .... Some languages have special constructs for infinite loops, typically by omitting the condition from an indefinite loop. Examples include Ada (loop ... end loop), Fortran (DO ... END DO), Go (for { ... }), and Ruby (loop do ... end).

Often, an infinite loop is unintentionally created by a programming error in a condition-controlled loop, wherein the loop condition uses variables that never change within the loop.

Continuation with Next Iteration

Sometimes within the body of a loop there is a desire to skip the remainder of the loop body and continue with the next iteration of the loop. Some languages provide a statement such as continue (most languages), skip, or next (Perl and Ruby), which will do this. The effect is to prematurely terminate the innermost loop body and then resume as normal with the next iteration. If the iteration is the last one in the loop, the effect is to terminate the entire loop early.

Redo Current Iteration

Some languages, like Perl and Ruby, have a redo statement that restarts the current iteration from the start.

Restart Loop

Ruby has a retry statement that restarts the entire loop from the initial iteration.

Early Exit From Loops

When using a count-controlled loop to search through a table, it might be desirable to stop searching as soon as the required item is found. Some programming languages provide a statement such

as break (most languages), exit, or last (Perl), which effect is to terminate the current loop immediately, and transfer control to the statement immediately after that loop.

The following example is done in Ada which supports both *early exit from loops* and *loops with
test in the middle*. Both features are very similar and comparing both code snippets will show the
difference: *early exit* must be combined with an if statement while a *condition in the middle* is a
self-contained construct.

```ada
with Ada.Text IO;

with Ada.Integer Text IO;


procedure Print_Squares is

    X : Integer;
begin

    Read_Data : loop

        Ada.Integer Text IO.Get(X);

    exit Read_Data when X = 0;

        Ada.Text IO.Put (X * X);

        Ada.Text IO.New_Line;

    end loop Read_Data;

end Print_Squares;
```

Python supports conditional execution of code depending on whether a loop was exited early (with
a break statement) or not by using an else-clause with the loop. For example,

```python
for n in set_of_numbers:

    if isprime(n):

        print "Set contains a prime number"

        break

else:

    print "Set did not contain any prime numbers"
```

The else clause in the above example is linked to the for statement, and not the inner if statement.
Both Python's for and while loops support such an else clause, which is executed only if early exit
of the loop has not occurred.

Some languages support breaking out of nested loops; in theory circles, these are called multi-level breaks. One common use example is searching a multi-dimensional table. This can be done either via multilevel breaks (break out of N levels), as in bash and PHP, or via labeled breaks (break out and continue at given label), as in Java and Perl. Alternatives to multilevel breaks include single breaks, together with a state variable which is tested to break out another level; exceptions, which are caught at the level being broken out to; placing the nested loops in a function and using return to effect termination of the entire nested loop; or using a label and a goto statement. C does not include a multilevel break, and the usual alternative is to use a goto to implement a labeled break. Python does not have a multilevel break or continue – this was proposed in PEP 3136, and rejected on the basis that the added complexity was not worth the rare legitimate use.

The notion of multi-level breaks is of some interest in theoretical computer science, because it gives rise to what is today called the *Kosaraju hierarchy*. In 1973 S. Rao Kosaraju refined the structured program theorem by proving that it's possible to avoid adding additional variables in structured programming, as long as arbitrary-depth, multi-level breaks from loops are allowed. Furthermore, Kosaraju proved that a strict hierarchy of programs exists: for every integer n, there exists a program containing a multi-level break of depth n that cannot be rewritten as a program with multi-level breaks of depth less than n without introducing added variables.

One can also return out of a subroutine executing the looped statements, breaking out of both the nested loop and the subroutine. There are other proposed control structures for multiple breaks, but these are generally implemented as exceptions instead.

In his 2004 textbook, David Watt uses Tennent's notion of sequencer to explain the similarity between multi-level breaks and return statements. Watt notes that a class of sequencers known as *escape sequencers*, defined as "sequencer that terminates execution of a textually enclosing command or procedure", encompasses both breaks from loops (including multi-level breaks) and return statements. As commonly implemented, however, return sequencers may also carry a (return) value, whereas the break sequencer as implemented in contemporary languages usually cannot.

Loop Variants and Invariants

Loop variants and loop invariants are used to express correctness of loops.

In practical terms, a loop variant is an integer expression which has an initial non-negative value. The variant's value must decrease during each loop iteration but must never become negative during the correct execution of the loop. Loop variants are used to guarantee that loops will terminate.

A loop invariant is an assertion which must be true before the first loop iteration and remain true after each iteration. This implies that when a loop terminates correctly, both the exit condition and the loop invariant are satisfied. Loop invariants are used to monitor specific properties of a loop during successive iterations.

Some programming languages, such as Eiffel contain native support for loop variants and invariants. In other cases, support is an add-on, such as the Java Modeling Language's specification for loop statements in Java.

Loop Sublanguage

Some Lisp dialects provide an extensive sublanguage for describing Loops. An early example can be found in Conversional Lisp of Interlisp. Common Lisp provides a Loop macro which implements such a sublanguage.

Structured Non-local Control Flow

Many programming languages, especially those favoring more dynamic styles of programming, offer constructs for *non-local control flow*. These cause the flow of execution to jump out of a given context and resume at some predeclared point. *Conditions*, *exceptions* and *continuations* are three common sorts of non-local control constructs; more exotic ones also exist, such as generators, coroutines and the async keyword.

Conditions

PL/I has some 22 standard conditions (e.g., ZERODIVIDE SUBSCRIPTRANGE ENDFILE) which can be raised and which can be intercepted by: ON *condition* action; Programmers can also define and use their own named conditions.

Like the *unstructured if*, only one statement can be specified so in many cases a GOTO is needed to decide where flow of control should resume.

Unfortunately, some implementations had a substantial overhead in both space and time (especially SUBSCRIPTRANGE), so many programmers tried to avoid using conditions.

Common Syntax examples:

```
ON condition GOTO label
```

Exceptions

Modern languages have a specialized structured construct for exception handling which does not rely on the use of GOTO or (multi-level) breaks or returns. For example, in C++ one can write:

```
try {
    xxx1                               // Somewhere in here
    xxx2                               //    use: ``''throw'''' some-
Value;
    xxx3
} catch (someClass& someId) {         // catch value of someClass
    actionForSomeClass
} catch (someType& anotherId) {        // catch value of someType
    actionForSomeType
```

```
} catch (...) {                                      // catch anything not already
caught

    actionForAnythingElse

}
```

Any number and variety of catch clauses can be used above. If there is no catch matching a particular throw, control percolates back through subroutine calls and/or nested blocks until a matching catch is found or until the end of the main program is reached, at which point the program is forcibly stopped with a suitable error message.

Via C++'s influence, catch is the keyword reserved for declaring a pattern-matching exception handler in other languages popular today, like Java or C#. Some other languages like Ada use the keyword exception to introduce an exception handler and then may even employ a different keyword (when in Ada) for the pattern matching. A few languages like AppleScript incorporate placeholders in the exception handler syntax to automatically extract several pieces of information when the exception occurs. This approach is exemplified below by the on error construct from AppleScript:

```
try

    set myNumber to myNumber / 0

on error e  number n  from f  to t  partial result pr

    if ( e = "Can't divide by zero" ) then display dialog "You must not
do that"

end try
```

David Watt's 2004 textbook also analyzes exception handling in the framework of sequencers. Watt notes that an abnormal situation, generally exemplified with arithmetic overflows or input/output failures like file not found, is a kind of error that "is detected in some low-level program unit, but [for which] a handler is more naturally located in a high-level program unit". For example, a program might contain several calls to read files, but the action to perform when a file is not found depends on the meaning (purpose) of the file in question to the program and thus a handling routine for this abnormal situation cannot be located in low-level system code. Watts further notes that introducing status flags testing in the caller, as single-exit structured programming or even (multi-exit) return sequencers would entail, results in a situation where "the application code tends to get cluttered by tests of status flags" and that "the programmer might forgetfully or lazily omit to test a status flag. In fact, abnormal situations represented by status flags are by default ignored!" Watt notes that in contrast to status flags testing, exceptions have the opposite default behavior, causing the program to terminate unless the programmer explicitly deals with the exception in some way, possibly by adding explicit code to ignore it. Based on these arguments, Watt concludes that jump sequencers or escape sequencers aren't as suitable as a dedicated exception sequencer with the semantics discussed above.

In Object Pascal, D, Java, C#, and Python a finally clause can be added to the try construct. No matter how control leaves the try the code inside the finally clause is guaranteed to execute. This is useful when writing code that must relinquish an expensive resource (such as an opened file or a database connection) when finished processing:

```
FileStream stm = null;                              // C# example

try {

    stm = new FileStream ("logfile.txt", FileMode.Create);

    return ProcessStuff(stm);                       // may throw an exception

} finally {

    if (stm != null)

        stm.Close();

}
```

Since this pattern is fairly common, C# has a special syntax:

```
using (FileStream stm = new FileStream ("logfile.txt", FileMode.Create)) {

    return ProcessStuff(stm);                       // may throw an exception

}
```

Upon leaving the using-block, the compiler guarantees that the stm object is released, effectively binding the variable to the file stream while abstracting from the side effects of initializing and releasing the file. Python's with statement and Ruby's block argument to File.open are used to similar effect.

All the languages mentioned above define standard exceptions and the circumstances under which they are thrown. Users can throw exceptions of their own; in fact C++ allows users to throw and catch almost any type, including basic types like int, whereas other languages like Java aren't as permissive.

Continuations

Async

C# 5.0 introduced the async keyword for supporting asynchronous I/O in a "direct style".

Generators

Generators, also known as semicoroutines, allow control to be yielded to a consumer method temporarily, typically using a yield keyword. Like the async keyword, this supports programming in a "direct style".

Coroutines

Coroutines are functions that can yield control to each other - a form of co-operative multitasking without threads.

Coroutines can be implemented as a library if the programming language provides either continuations or generators - so the distinction between coroutines and generators in practice is a technical detail.

Non-local Control Flow Cross Reference

Proposed Control Structures

In a spoof Datamation article in 1973, R. Lawrence Clark suggested that the GOTO statement could be replaced by the COMEFROM statement, and provides some entertaining examples. COMEFROM was implemented in one esoteric programming language named INTERCAL.

Donald Knuth's 1974 article "Structured Programming with go to Statements", identifies two situations which were not covered by the control structures listed above, and gave examples of control structures which could handle these situations. Despite their utility, these constructs have not yet found their way into mainstream programming languages.

Loop with Test in the Middle

The following was proposed by Dahl in 1972:

```
loop                          loop

    xxx1                          read(char);

while test;                   while not atEndOfFile;

    xxx2                          write(char);

repeat;                       repeat;
```

If *xxx1* is omitted we get a loop with the test at the top. If xxx2 is omitted we get a loop with the test at the bottom. If while is omitted we get an infinite loop. Hence this single construction can replace several constructions in most programming languages. A possible variant is to allow more than one while test; within the loop, but the use of exitwhen appears to cover this case better.

Languages lacking this construct generally emulate it using an equivalent infinite-loop-with-break idiom:

```
while (true) {

    xxx1

    if (not test)

        break

    xxx2

}
```

In Ada, the above loop construct (loop-while-repeat) can be represented using a standard infinite loop (loop - end loop) that has an exit when clause in the middle.

```
with Ada.Text_IO;

with Ada.Integer_Text_IO;

procedure Print_Squares is

    X : Integer;

begin

    Read_Data : loop

        Ada.Integer_Text_IO.Get(X);

    exit Read_Data when X = 0;

        Ada.Text IO.Put (X * X);

        Ada.Text IO.New_Line;

    end loop Read_Data;

end Print_Squares;
```

Naming a loop (like *Read_Data* in this example) is optional but permits leaving the outer loop of several nested loops.

Multiple Early Exit/Exit from Nested Loops

This was proposed by Zahn in 1974. A modified version is presented here.

```
    exitwhen EventA or EventB or EventC;

        xxx

    exits

        EventA: actionA

        EventB: actionB

        EventC: actionC

    endexit;
```

exit when is used to specify the events which may occur within xxx, their occurrence is indicated by using the name of the event as a statement. When some event does occur, the relevant action is carried out, and then control passes just after endexit. This construction provides a very clear separation between determining that some situation applies, and the action to be taken for that situation.

exitwhen is conceptually similar to exception handling, and exceptions or similar constructs are used for this purpose in many languages.

The following simple example involves searching a two-dimensional table for a particular item.

```
exitwhen found or missing;

    for I := 1 to N do

        for J := 1 to M do

            if table[I,J] = target then found;

    missing;

exits

    found:   print ("item is in table");

    missing: print ("item is not in table");

endexit;
```

Security

One way to attack a piece of software is to redirect the flow of execution of a program. A variety of control-flow integrity techniques, including stack canaries, buffer overflow protection, shadow stacks, and vtable pointer verification, are used to defend against these attacks.

References

- Kenneth C. Louden; Kenneth A. Lambert (2011). Programming Languages: Principles and Practices (3 ed.). Cengage Learning. pp. 422–423. ISBN 1-111-52941-8

- Payer, Mathias; Kuznetsov, Volodymyr. "On differences between the CFI, CPS, and CPI properties". nebelwelt. net. Retrieved 2016-06-01

- Kozen, Dexter (2008). "The Böhm–Jacopini Theorem Is False, Propositionally". Lecture Notes in Computer Science: 177–192. doi:10.1007/978-3-540-70594-9_11

- David Anthony Watt; William Findlay (2004). Programming language design concepts. John Wiley & Sons. pp. 221–222. ISBN 978-0-470-85320-7

- "The Common Lisp Cookbook - Macros and Backquote". Cl-cookbook.sourceforge.net. 2007-01-16. Retrieved 2013-08-17

- David Anthony Watt; William Findlay (2004). Programming language design concepts. John Wiley & Sons. pp. 215–221. ISBN 978-0-470-85320-7

Types of Programming Paradigms

Programming paradigm refers to the style or way of programming. It is an approach to solving problems using the tools and techniques available to programming languages. Every programming language has its own unique paradigm. Object-oriented programming, aspect-oriented programming, automata-oriented programming, flow-based programming, non-structured programming, etc. are the types of programming paradigms which are examined closely in this chapter.

Programming Paradigm

Programming paradigms are a way to classify programming languages based on their features. Languages can be classified into multiple paradigms.

Some paradigms are concerned mainly with implications for the execution model of the language, such as allowing side effects, or whether the sequence of operations is defined by the execution model. Other paradigms are concerned mainly with the way that code is organized, such as grouping a code into units along with the state that is modified by the code. Yet others are concerned mainly with the style of syntax and grammar.

Common programming paradigms include:

- Imperative which allows side effects,

- Functional which disallows side effects,

- Declarative which does not state the order in which operations execute,

- Object-oriented which groups code together with the state the code modifies,

- Procedural which groups code into functions,

- Logic which has a particular style of execution model coupled to a particular style of syntax and grammar,

- Symbolic programming which has a particular style of syntax and grammar.

For example, languages that fall into the imperative paradigm have two main features: they state the order in which operations occur, with constructs that explicitly control that order, and they allow side effects, in which state can be modified at one point in time, within one unit of code, and then later read at a different point in time inside a different unit of code. The communication between the units of code is not explicit. Meanwhile, in object-oriented programming, code is organized into objects that contain state that is only modified by the code that is part of the object. Most object-oriented languages are also imperative languages. In contrast, languages that fit the declarative paradigm do not state the order in which to execute operations. Instead, they supply a number of operations that are available in the system, along with the conditions under which each is allowed to execute. The implementation of the language's execution model tracks which operations are free to execute and chooses the order on its own. More at Comparison of multi-paradigm programming languages.

Overview

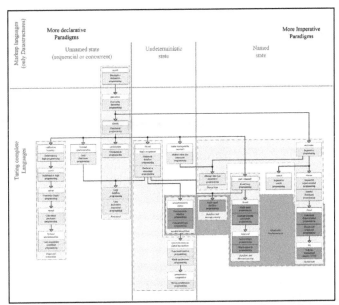

Overview of the various programming paradigms according to Peter Van Roy.

Just as software engineering (as a process) is defined by differing *methodologies*, so the programming languages (as models of computation) are defined by differing *paradigms*. Some languages are designed to support one paradigm (Smalltalk supports object-oriented programming, Haskell supports functional programming), while other programming languages support multiple paradigms (such as Object Pascal, C++, Java, C#, Scala, Visual Basic, Common Lisp, Scheme, Perl, PHP, Python, Ruby, Oz, and F#). For example, programs written in C++, Object Pascal or PHP can be purely procedural, purely object-oriented, or can contain elements of both or other paradigms. Software designers and programmers decide how to use those paradigm elements.

In object-oriented programming, programs are treated as a set of interacting objects. In functional programming, programs are treated as a sequence of stateless function evaluations. When programming computers or systems with many processors, in process-oriented programming, programs are treated as sets of concurrent processes acting on logically shared data structures.

Many programming paradigms are as well known for the techniques they *forbid* as for those they *enable*. For instance, pure functional programming disallows use of side-effects, while structured programming disallows use of the goto statement. Partly for this reason, new paradigms are often regarded as doctrinaire or overly rigid by those accustomed to earlier styles. Yet, avoiding certain techniques can make it easier to understand program behavior, and to prove theorems about program correctness.

Programming paradigms can also be compared with *programming models* which allow invoking an execution model by using only an API. Programming models can also be classified into paradigms, based on features of the execution model.

For parallel computing, using a programming model instead of a language is common. The reason is that details of the parallel hardware leak into the abstractions used to program the hardware. This causes the programmer to have to map patterns in the algorithm onto patterns in the execution model (which have been inserted due to leakage of hardware into the abstraction). As a consequence, no one parallel programming language maps well to all computation problems. It is thus more convenient to use a base sequential language and insert API calls to parallel execution models, via a programming model. Such parallel programming models can be classified according to abstractions that reflect the hardware, such as shared memory, distributed memory with message passing, notions of *place* visible in the code, and so forth. These can be considered flavors of programming paradigm that apply to only parallel languages and programming models.

History

Different approaches to programming have developed over time, being identified as such either at the time or retrospectively. An early approach consciously identified as such is structured programming, advocated since the mid 1960s. The concept of a "programming paradigm" as such dates at least to 1978, in the Turing Award lecture of Robert W. Floyd, entitled *The Paradigms of Programming*, which cites the notion of paradigm as used by Thomas Kuhn in his *The Structure of Scientific Revolutions* (1962).

Machine Code

The lowest-level programming paradigms are machine code, which directly represents the instructions (the contents of program memory) as a sequence of numbers, and assembly language where the machine instructions are represented by mnemonics and memory addresses can be given symbolic labels. These are sometimes called first- and second-generation languages.

In the 1960s, assembly languages were developed to support library COPY and quite sophisticated conditional macro generation and preprocessing abilities, CALL to (subroutines), external variables and common sections (globals), enabling significant code re-use and isolation from hardware specifics via use of logical operators such as READ/WRITE/GET/PUT. Assembly was, and still is, used for time critical systems and often in embedded systems as it gives the most direct control of what the machine does.

Procedural Languages

The next advance was the development of procedural languages. These third-generation languages (the first described as high-level languages) use vocabulary related to the problem being solved. For example,

- COmmon Business Oriented Language (COBOL) – uses terms like file, move and copy.

- FORmula TRANslation (FORTRAN) – using mathematical language terminology, it was developed mainly for scientific and engineering problems.

- ALGOrithmic Language (ALGOL) – focused on being an appropriate language to define algorithms, while using mathematical language terminology and targeting scientific and engineering problems just like FORTRAN.

- Programming Language One (PL/I) – a hybrid commercial-scientific general purpose language supporting pointers.

- Beginners All purpose Symbolic Instruction Code (BASIC) – it was developed to enable more people to write programs.

- C – a general-purpose programming language, initially developed by Dennis Ritchie between 1969 and 1973 at AT&T Bell Labs.

All these languages follow the procedural paradigm. That is, they describe, step by step, exactly the procedure that should, according to the particular programmer at least, be followed to solve a specific problem. The efficacy and efficiency of any such solution are both therefore entirely subjective and highly dependent on that programmer's experience, inventiveness, and ability.

Following the widespread use of procedural languages, object-oriented programming (OOP) languages were created, such as Simula, Smalltalk, C++, C#, Eiffel, PHP, and Java. In these languages, data and methods to manipulate it are kept as one unit called an object. The only way that another object or user can access the data is via the object's *methods*. Thus, the inner workings of an object may be changed without affecting any code that uses the object. There is still some controversy raised by Alexander Stepanov, Richard Stallman and other programmers, concerning the efficacy of the OOP paradigm versus the procedural paradigm. The need for every object to have associative methods leads some skeptics to associate OOP with software bloat; an attempt to resolve this dilemma came through polymorphism.

Because object-oriented programming is considered a paradigm, not a language, it is possible to create even an object-oriented assembler language. High Level Assembly (HLA) is an example of this that fully supports advanced data types and object-oriented assembly language programming – despite its early origins. Thus, differing programming paradigms can be seen rather like *motivational memes* of their advocates, rather than necessarily representing progress from one level to the next. Precise comparisons of the efficacy of competing paradigms are frequently made more difficult because of new and differing terminology applied to similar entities and processes together with numerous implementation distinctions across languages.

Further Paradigms

Literate programming, as a form of imperative programming, structures programs as a human-centered web, as in a hypertext essay: documentation is integral to the program, and the program is structured following the logic of prose exposition, rather than compiler convenience.

Independent of the imperative branch, declarative programming paradigms were developed. In these languages, the computer is told what the problem is, not how to solve the problem – the program is structured as a set of properties to find in the expected result, not as a procedure to follow. Given a database or a set of rules, the computer tries to find a solution matching all the desired properties. An archetype of a declarative language is the fourth generation language SQL, and the family of functional languages and logic programming.

Functional programming is a subset of declarative programming. Programs written using this paradigm use functions, blocks of code intended to behave like mathematical functions. Functional languages discourage changes in the value of variables through assignment, making a great deal of use of recursion instead.

The logic programming paradigm views computation as automated reasoning over a body of knowledge. Facts about the problem domain are expressed as logic formulae, and programs are executed by applying inference rules over them until an answer to the problem is found, or the set of formulae is proved inconsistent.

Symbolic programming is a paradigm that describes programs able to manipulate formulas and program components as data. Programs can thus effectively modify themselves, and appear to "learn", making them suited for applications such as artificial intelligence, expert systems, natural language processing and computer games. Languages that support this paradigm include Lisp and Prolog.

Multi-paradigm

A *multi-paradigm programming language* is a programming language that supports more than one programming paradigm. The design goal of such languages is to allow programmers to use the most suitable programming style and associated language constructs for a given job, considering that no single paradigm solves all problems in the easiest or most efficient way.

One example is C#, which includes imperative and object-oriented paradigms, together with a certain level of support for functional programming with features like delegates (allowing functions to be treated as first-order objects), type inference, anonymous functions and Language Integrated Query. Other examples are F#, Python and Scala, which provide similar functionality to C# but also include full support for functional programming (including currying, pattern matching, algebraic data types, lazy evaluation, tail recursion, immutability, etc.). Perhaps the most extreme example is Oz, which has subsets that adhere to logic (Oz descends from logic programming), functional, object-oriented, dataflow concurrent, and other paradigms. Oz was designed over a ten-year period to combine in a harmonious way concepts that are traditionally associated with different programming paradigms. Lisp, while often taught as a functional language, is known for its malleability and thus its ability to engulf many paradigms.

Object-oriented Programming

Object-oriented programming (OOP) is a programming paradigm based on the concept of "objects", which may contain data, in the form of fields, often known as *attributes;* and code, in the form of procedures, often known as *methods*. A feature of objects is that an object's procedures can access and often modify the data fields of the object with which they are associated (objects have a notion of "this" or "self"). In OOP, computer programs are designed by making them out of objects that interact with one another. There is significant diversity of OOP languages, but the most popular ones are class-based, meaning that objects are instances of classes, which typically also determine their type.

Many of the most widely used programming languages (such as C++, Delphi, Java, Python etc.) are multi-paradigm programming languages that support object-oriented programming to a greater or lesser degree, typically in combination with imperative, procedural programming. Significant object-oriented languages include Java, C++, C#, Python, PHP, Ruby, Perl, Object Pascal, Objective-C, Dart, Swift, Scala, Common Lisp, and Smalltalk.

Features

Object-oriented Programming uses objects, but not all of the associated techniques and structures are supported directly in languages that claim to support OOP. The features listed below are, however, common among languages considered strongly class- and object-oriented (or multi-paradigm with OOP support), with notable exceptions mentioned.

Shared with Non-OOP Predecessor Languages

Object-oriented programming languages typically share low-level features with high-level procedural programming languages (which were invented first). The fundamental tools that can be used to construct a program include:

- Variables that can store information formatted in a small number of built-in data types like integers and alphanumeric characters. This may include data structures like strings, lists, and hash tables that are either built-in or result from combining variables using memory pointers.

- Procedures – also known as functions, methods, routines, or subroutines – that take input, generate output, and manipulate data. Modern languages include structured programming constructs like loops and conditionals.

Modular programming support provides the ability to group procedures into files and modules for organizational purposes. Modules are namespaced so code in one module will not be accidentally confused with the same procedure or variable name in another file or module.

Objects and Classes

Languages that support object-oriented programming typically use inheritance for code reuse and extensibility in the form of either classes or prototypes. Those that use classes support two main concepts:

- Classes – the definitions for the data format and available procedures for a given type or class of object; may also contain data and procedures (known as class methods) themselves, i.e. classes contains the data members and member functions.

- Objects – instances of classes.

Objects sometimes correspond to things found in the real world. For example, a graphics program may have objects such as "circle", "square", "menu". An online shopping system might have objects such as "shopping cart", "customer", and "product". Sometimes objects represent more abstract entities, like an object that represents an open file, or an object that provides the service of translating measurements from U.S. customary to metric.

Each object is said to be an instance of a particular class (for example, an object with its name field set to "Mary" might be an instance of class Employee). Procedures in object-oriented programming are known as methods; variables are also known as fields, members, attributes, or properties. This leads to the following terms:

- Class variables – belong to the *class as a whole*; there is only one copy of each one.

- Instance variables or attributes – data that belongs to individual *objects*; every object has its own copy of each one.

- Member variables – refers to both the class and instance variables that are defined by a particular class.

- Class methods – belong to the *class as a whole* and have access only to class variables and inputs from the procedure call.

- Instance methods – belong to *individual objects*, and have access to instance variables for the specific object they are called on, inputs, and class variables.

Objects are accessed somewhat like variables with complex internal structure, and in many languages are effectively pointers, serving as actual references to a single instance of said object in memory within a heap or stack. They provide a layer of abstraction which can be used to separate internal from external code. External code can use an object by calling a specific instance method with a certain set of input parameters, read an instance variable, or write to an instance variable. Objects are created by calling a special type of method in the class known as a constructor. A program may create many instances of the same class as it runs, which operate independently. This is an easy way for the same procedures to be used on different sets of data.

Object-oriented programming that uses classes is sometimes called class-based programming, while prototype-based programming does not typically use classes. As a result, a significantly different yet analogous terminology is used to define the concepts of *object* and *instance*.

In some languages classes and objects can be composed using other concepts like traits and mixins.

Dynamic Dispatch/message Passing

It is the responsibility of the object, not any external code, to select the procedural code to execute in response to a method call, typically by looking up the method at run time in a table associated with the object. This feature is known as dynamic dispatch, and distinguishes an object from an abstract data type (or module), which has a fixed (static) implementation of the operations for all instances. If there are multiple methods that might be run for a given name, it is known as multiple dispatch.

A method call is also known as *message passing*. It is conceptualized as a message (the name of the method and its input parameters) being passed to the object for dispatch.

Encapsulation

Encapsulation is an Object Oriented Programming concept that binds together the data and functions that manipulate the data, and that keeps both safe from outside interference and misuse. Data encapsulation led to the important OOP concept of data hiding.

If a class does not allow calling code to access internal object data and permits access through methods only, this is a strong form of abstraction or information hiding known as encapsulation. Some languages (Java, for example) let classes enforce access restrictions explicitly, for example denoting internal data with the private keyword and designating methods intended for use by code outside the class with the public keyword. Methods may also be designed public, private, or intermediate levels such as protected (which allows access from the same class and its subclasses, but not objects of a different class). In other languages (like Python) this is enforced only by convention (for example, private methods may have names that start with an underscore). Encapsulation prevents external code from being concerned with the internal workings of an object. This facilitates code refactoring, for example allowing the author of the class to change how objects of that class represent their data internally without changing any external code (as long as "public" method calls work the same way). It also encourages programmers to put all the code that is concerned with a certain set of data in the same class, which organizes it for easy comprehension by other programmers. Encapsulation is a technique that encourages decoupling.

Composition, Inheritance and Delegation

Objects can contain other objects in their instance variables; this is known as object composition. For example, an object in the Employee class might contain (point to) an object in the Address class, in addition to its own instance variables like "first_name" and "position". Object composition is used to represent "has-a" relationships: every employee has an address, so every Employee object has a place to store an Address object.

Languages that support classes almost always support inheritance. This allows classes to be arranged in a hierarchy that represents "is-a-type-of" relationships. For example, class Employee might inherit from class Person. All the data and methods available to the parent class also appear in the child class with the same names. For example, class Person might define variables "first_name" and "last_name" with method "make_full_name()". These will also be available in class Employee, which might add the variables "position" and "salary". This technique allows easy re-use of the same procedures and data definitions, in addition to potentially mirroring real-world relationships in an intuitive way. Rather than utilizing database tables and programming subroutines, the developer utilizes objects the user may be more familiar with: objects from their application domain.

Subclasses can override the methods defined by superclasses. Multiple inheritance is allowed in some languages, though this can make resolving overrides complicated. Some languages have special support for mixins, though in any language with multiple inheritance, a mixin is simply a class that does not represent an is-a-type-of relationship. Mixins are typically used to add the same methods to multiple classes. For example, class UnicodeConversionMixin might provide a method unicode_to_ascii() when included in class FileReader and class WebPageScraper, which don't share a common parent.

Abstract classes cannot be instantiated into objects; they exist only for the purpose of inheritance into other "concrete" classes which can be instantiated. In Java, the final keyword can be used to prevent a class from being subclassed.

The doctrine of composition over inheritance advocates implementing has-a relationships using composition instead of inheritance. For example, instead of inheriting from class Person, class Employee could give each Employee object an internal Person object, which it then has the opportunity to hide from external code even if class Person has many public attributes or methods. Some languages, like Go do not support inheritance at all.

The "open/closed principle" advocates that classes and functions "should be open for extension, but closed for modification".

Delegation is another language feature that can be used as an alternative to inheritance.

Polymorphism

Subtyping, a form of polymorphism, is when calling code can be agnostic as to whether an object belongs to a parent class or one of its descendants. For example, a function might call "make_full_name()" on an object, which will work whether the object is of class Person or class Employee. This is another type of abstraction which simplifies code external to the class hierarchy and enables strong separation of concerns.

Open Recursion

In languages that support open recursion, object methods can call other methods on the same object (including themselves), typically using a special variable or keyword called this or self. This variable is *late-bound*; it allows a method defined in one class to invoke another method that is defined later, in some subclass thereof.

History

Terminology invoking "objects" and "oriented" in the modern sense of object-oriented programming made its first appearance at MIT in the late 1950s and early 1960s. In the environment of the artificial intelligence group, as early as 1960, "object" could refer to identified items (LISP atoms) with properties (attributes); Alan Kay was later to cite a detailed understanding of LISP internals as a strong influence on his thinking in 1966. Another early MIT example was Sketchpad created by Ivan Sutherland in 1960–61; in the glossary of the 1963 technical report based on his dissertation about Sketchpad, Sutherland defined notions of "object" and "instance" (with the class concept covered by "master" or "definition"), albeit specialized to graphical interaction. Also, an MIT ALGOL version, AED-0, established a direct link between data structures ("plexes", in that dialect) and procedures, prefiguring what were later termed "messages", "methods", and "member functions".

The formal programming concept of objects was introduced in the mid-1960s with Simula 67, a major revision of Simula I, a programming language designed for discrete event simulation, created by Ole-Johan Dahl and Kristen Nygaard of the Norwegian Computing Center in Oslo.

Simula 67 was influenced by SIMSCRIPT and C.A.R. "Tony" Hoare's proposed "record classes". Simula introduced the notion of classes and instances or objects (as well as subclasses, virtual procedures, coroutines, and discrete event simulation) as part of an explicit programming paradigm. The language also used automatic garbage collection that had been invented earlier for the functional programming language Lisp. Simula was used for physical modeling, such as models to study and improve the movement of ships and their content through cargo ports. The ideas of Simula 67 influenced many later languages, including Smalltalk, derivatives of LISP (CLOS), Object Pascal, and C++.

The Smalltalk language, which was developed at Xerox PARC (by Alan Kay and others) in the 1970s, introduced the term *object-oriented programming* to represent the pervasive use of objects and messages as the basis for computation. Smalltalk creators were influenced by the ideas introduced in Simula 67, but Smalltalk was designed to be a fully dynamic system in which classes could be created and modified dynamically rather than statically as in Simula 67. Smalltalk and with it OOP were introduced to a wider audience by the August 1981 issue of *Byte Magazine*.

In the 1970s, Kay's Smalltalk work had influenced the Lisp community to incorporate object-based techniques that were introduced to developers via the Lisp machine. Experimentation with various extensions to Lisp (such as LOOPS and Flavors introducing multiple inheritance and mixins) eventually led to the Common Lisp Object System, which integrates functional programming and object-oriented programming and allows extension via a Meta-object protocol. In the 1980s, there were a few attempts to design processor architectures that included hardware support for objects in memory but these were not successful. Examples include the Intel iAPX 432 and the Linn Smart Rekursiv.

In 1985, Bertrand Meyer produced the first design of the Eiffel language. Focused on software quality, Eiffel is among the purely object-oriented languages, but differs in the sense that the language itself is not only a programming language, but a notation supporting the entire software lifecycle. Meyer described the Eiffel software development method, based on a small number of key ideas from software engineering and computer science, in Object-Oriented Software Construction. Essential to the quality focus of Eiffel is Meyer's reliability mechanism, Design by Contract, which is an integral part of both the method and language.

Object-oriented programming developed as the dominant programming methodology in the early and mid 1990s when programming languages supporting the techniques became widely available. These included Visual FoxPro 3.0, C++, and Delphi. Its dominance was further enhanced by the rising popularity of graphical user interfaces, which rely heavily upon object-oriented programming techniques. An example of a closely related dynamic GUI library and OOP language can be found in the Cocoa frameworks on Mac OS X, written in Objective-C, an object-oriented, dynamic messaging extension to C based on Smalltalk. OOP toolkits also enhanced the popularity of event-driven programming (although this concept is not limited to OOP).

At ETH Zürich, Niklaus Wirth and his colleagues had also been investigating such topics as data abstraction and modular programming (although this had been in common use in the 1960s or earlier). Modula-2 (1978) included both, and their succeeding design, Oberon, included a distinctive approach to object orientation, classes, and such.

Object-oriented features have been added to many previously existing languages, including Ada, BASIC, Fortran, Pascal, and COBOL. Adding these features to languages that were not initially designed for them often led to problems with compatibility and maintainability of code.

More recently, a number of languages have emerged that are primarily object-oriented, but that are also compatible with procedural methodology. Two such languages are Python and Ruby.

Probably the most commercially important recent object-oriented languages are Java, developed by Sun Microsystems, as well as C# and Visual Basic.NET (VB.NET), both designed for Microsoft's .NET platform. Each of these two frameworks shows, in its own way, the benefit of using OOP by creating an abstraction from implementation. VB.NET and C# support cross-language inheritance, allowing classes defined in one language to subclass classes defined in the other language.

Oop Languages

Simula (1967) is generally accepted as being the first language with the primary features of an object-oriented language. It was created for making simulation programs, in which what came to be called objects were the most important information representation. Smalltalk (1972 to 1980) is another early example, and the one with which much of the theory of OOP was developed. Concerning the degree of object orientation, the following distinctions can be made:

- Languages called "pure" OO languages, because everything in them is treated consistently as an object, from primitives such as characters and punctuation, all the way up to whole classes, prototypes, blocks, modules, etc. They were designed specifically to facilitate, even enforce, OO methods. Examples: Python, Ruby, Scala, Smalltalk, Eiffel, Emerald, JADE, Self.

- Languages designed mainly for OO programming, but with some procedural elements. Examples: Java, C++, C#, Delphi/Object Pascal, VB.NET.

- Languages that are historically procedural languages, but have been extended with some OO features. Examples: PHP, Perl, Visual Basic (derived from BASIC), MATLAB, COBOL 2002, Fortran 2003, ABAP, Ada 95, Pascal.

- Languages with most of the features of objects (classes, methods, inheritance), but in a distinctly original form. Examples: Oberon (Oberon-1 or Oberon-2).

- Languages with abstract data type support which may be used to resemble OO programming, but without all features of object-orientation. This includes object-*based* and prototype-based languages. Examples: JavaScript, Lua, Modula-2, CLU.

- Chameleon languages that support multiple paradigms, including OO. Tcl stands out among these for TclOO, a hybrid object system that supports both prototype-based programming and class-based OO.

OOP in Dynamic Languages

In recent years, object-oriented programming has become especially popular in dynamic programming languages. Python, PowerShell, Ruby and Groovy are dynamic languages built on OOP principles, while Perl and PHP have been adding object-oriented features since Perl 5 and PHP 4, and ColdFusion since version 6.

The Document Object Model of HTML, XHTML, and XML documents on the Internet has bindings to the popular JavaScript/ECMAScript language. JavaScript is perhaps the best known prototype-based programming language, which employs cloning from prototypes rather than inheriting from a class (contrast to class-based programming). Another scripting language that takes this approach is Lua.

OOP in a Network Protocol

The messages that flow between computers to request services in a client-server environment can be designed as the linearizations of objects defined by class objects known to both the client and the server. For example, a simple linearized object would consist of a length field, a code point identifying the class, and a data value. A more complex example would be a command consisting of the length and code point of the command and values consisting of linearized objects representing the command's parameters. Each such command must be directed by the server to an object whose class (or superclass) recognizes the command and is able to provide the requested service. Clients and servers are best modeled as complex object-oriented structures. Distributed Data Management Architecture (DDM) took this approach and used class objects to define objects at four levels of a formal hierarchy:

- Fields defining the data values that form messages, such as their length, codepoint and data values.

- Objects and collections of objects similar to what would be found in a Smalltalk program for messages and parameters.

- Managers similar to AS/400 objects, such as a directory to files and files consisting of metadata and records. Managers conceptually provide memory and processing resources for their contained objects.

- A client or server consisting of all the managers necessary to implement a full processing environment, supporting such aspects as directory services, security and concurrency control.

The initial version of DDM defined distributed file services. It was later extended to be the foundation of Distributed Relational Database Architecture (DRDA).

Design Patterns

Challenges of object-oriented design are addressed by several methodologies. Most common is known as the design patterns codified by Gamma *et al.*. More broadly, the term "design patterns" can be used to refer to any general, repeatable solution to a commonly occurring problem in software design. Some of these commonly occurring problems have implications and solutions particular to object-oriented development.

Inheritance and Behavioral Subtyping

It is intuitive to assume that inheritance creates a semantic "is a" relationship, and thus to infer that objects instantiated from subclasses can always be *safely* used instead of those instantiated from the superclass. This intuition is unfortunately false in most OOP languages, in particular in all those that allow mutable objects. Subtype polymorphism as enforced by the type checker in OOP languages (with mutable objects) cannot guarantee behavioral subtyping in any context. Behavioral subtyping is undecidable in general, so it cannot be implemented by a program (compiler). Class or object hierarchies must be carefully designed, considering possible incorrect uses that cannot be detected syntactically. This issue is known as the Liskov substitution principle.

Gang of Four Design Patterns

Design Patterns: Elements of Reusable Object-Oriented Software is an influential book published in 1995 by Erich Gamma, Richard Helm, Ralph Johnson, and John Vlissides, often referred to humorously as the "Gang of Four". Along with exploring the capabilities and pitfalls of object-oriented programming, it describes 23 common programming problems and patterns for solving them. As of April 2007, the book was in its 36th printing.

The book describes the following patterns:

- *Creational patterns* (5): Factory method pattern, Abstract factory pattern, Singleton pattern, Builder pattern, Prototype pattern.

- *Structural patterns* (7): Adapter pattern, Bridge pattern, Composite pattern, Decorator pattern, Facade pattern, Flyweight pattern, Proxy pattern.

- *Behavioral patterns* (11): Chain-of-responsibility pattern, Command pattern, Interpreter pattern, Iterator pattern, Mediator pattern, Memento pattern, Observer pattern, State pattern, Strategy pattern, Template method pattern, Visitor pattern.

Object-orientation and Databases

Both object-oriented programming and relational database management systems (RDBMSs) are extremely common in software today. Since relational databases don't store objects directly (though some RDBMSs have object-oriented features to approximate this), there is a general need to bridge the two worlds. The problem of bridging object-oriented programming accesses and data patterns with relational databases is known as object-relational impedance mismatch. There are a number of approaches to cope with this problem, but no general solution without downsides. One of the most common approaches is object-relational mapping, as found in IDE languages such as Visual FoxPro and libraries such as Java Data Objects and Ruby on Rails' ActiveRecord.

There are also object databases that can be used to replace RDBMSs, but these have not been as technically and commercially successful as RDBMSs.

Real-world Modeling and Relationships

OOP can be used to associate real-world objects and processes with digital counterparts. However, not everyone agrees that OOP facilitates direct real-world mapping or that real-world mapping is even a worthy goal; Bertrand Meyer argues in *Object-Oriented Software Construction* that a program is not a model of the world but a model of some part of the world; "Reality is a cousin twice removed". At the same time, some principal limitations of OOP have been noted. For example, the circle-ellipse problem is difficult to handle using OOP's concept of inheritance.

However, Niklaus Wirth (who popularized the adage now known as Wirth's law: "Software is getting slower more rapidly than hardware becomes faster") said of OOP in his paper, "Good Ideas through the Looking Glass", "This paradigm closely reflects the structure of systems 'in the real world', and it is therefore well suited to model complex systems with complex behaviours" (contrast KISS principle).

Steve Yegge and others noted that natural languages lack the OOP approach of strictly prioritizing *things* (objects/nouns) before *actions* (methods/verbs). This problem may cause OOP to suffer more convoluted solutions than procedural programming.

OOP and Control Flow

OOP was developed to increase the reusability and maintainability of source code. Transparent representation of the control flow had no priority and was meant to be handled by a compiler. With the increasing relevance of parallel hardware and multithreaded coding, developing transparent control flow becomes more important, something hard to achieve with OOP.

Responsibility- vs. Data-driven Design

Responsibility-driven design defines classes in terms of a contract, that is, a class should be defined around a responsibility and the information that it shares. This is contrasted by Wirfs-Brock and Wilkerson with data-driven design, where classes are defined around the data-structures that must be held. The authors hold that responsibility-driven design is preferable.

SOLID and GRASP Guidelines

SOLID is a mnemonic invented by Michael Feathers that stands for and advocates five programming practices:

- Single responsibility principle.

- Open/closed principle.

- Liskov substitution principle.

- Interface segregation principle.

- Dependency inversion principle.

GRASP (General Responsibility Assignment Software Patterns) is another set of guidelines advocated by Craig Larman.

Criticism

The OOP paradigm has been criticised for a number of reasons, including not meeting its stated goals of reusability and modularity, and for overemphasizing one aspect of software design and modeling (data/objects) at the expense of other important aspects (computation/algorithms).

Luca Cardelli has claimed that OOP code is "intrinsically less efficient" than procedural code, that OOP can take longer to compile, and that OOP languages have "extremely poor modularity properties with respect to class extension and modification", and tend to be extremely complex. The latter point is reiterated by Joe Armstrong, the principal inventor of Erlang, who is quoted as saying:

The problem with object-oriented languages is they've got all this implicit environment that they carry around with them. You wanted a banana but what you got was a gorilla holding the banana and the entire jungle.

A study by Potok et al. has shown no significant difference in productivity between OOP and procedural approaches.

Christopher J. Date stated that critical comparison of OOP to other technologies, relational in particular, is difficult because of lack of an agreed-upon and rigorous definition of OOP; however, Date and Darwen have proposed a theoretical foundation on OOP that uses OOP as a kind of customizable type system to support RDBMS.

In an article Lawrence Krubner claimed that compared to other languages (LISP dialects, functional languages, etc.) OOP languages have no unique strengths, and inflict a heavy burden of unneeded complexity.

Alexander Stepanov compares object orientation unfavourably to generic programming:

I find OOP technically unsound. It attempts to decompose the world in terms of interfaces that vary on a single type. To deal with the real problems you need multisorted algebras — families of interfaces that span multiple types. I find OOP philosophically unsound. It claims that everything is an object. Even if it is true it is not very interesting — saying that everything is an object is saying nothing at all.

Paul Graham has suggested that OOP's popularity within large companies is due to "large (and frequently changing) groups of mediocre programmers". According to Graham, the discipline imposed by OOP prevents any one programmer from "doing too much damage".

Steve Yegge noted that, as opposed to functional programming:

Object Oriented Programming puts the Nouns first and foremost. Why would you go to such lengths to put one part of speech on a pedestal? Why should one kind of concept take precedence over another? It's not as if OOP has suddenly made verbs less important in the way we actually think. It's a strangely skewed perspective.

Rich Hickey, creator of Clojure, described object systems as overly simplistic models of the real world. He emphasized the inability of OOP to model time properly, which is getting increasingly problematic as software systems become more concurrent.

Eric S. Raymond, a Unix programmer and open-source software advocate, has been critical of claims that present object-oriented programming as the "One True Solution", and has written that object-oriented programming languages tend to encourage thickly layered programs that destroy transparency. Raymond compares this unfavourably to the approach taken with Unix and the C programming language.

Rob Pike, a programmer involved in the creation of UTF-8 and Go, has called object-oriented programming "the Roman numerals of computing" and has said that OOP languages frequently shift the focus from data structures and algorithms to types. Furthermore, he cites an instance of a Java professor whose "idiomatic" solution to a problem was to create six new classes, rather than to simply use a lookup table.

Formal Semantics

Objects are the run-time entities in an object-oriented system. They may represent a person, a place, a bank account, a table of data, or any item that the program has to handle.

There have been several attempts at formalizing the concepts used in object-oriented programming. The following concepts and constructs have been used as interpretations of OOP concepts:

- Co algebraic data types.

- Abstract data types (which have existential types) allow the definition of modules but these do not support dynamic dispatch.

- Recursive types.

- Encapsulated state.

- Inheritance.

- Records are basis for understanding objects if function literals can be stored in fields (like in functional programming languages), but the actual calculi need be considerably more complex to incorporate essential features of OOP. Several extensions of System $F_{<:}$ that deal with mutable objects have been studied; these allow both subtype polymorphism and parametric polymorphism (generics).

Attempts to find a consensus definition or theory behind objects have not proven very successful (however, Abadi & Cardelli, *A Theory of Objects* for formal definitions of many OOP concepts and constructs), and often diverge widely. For example, some definitions focus on mental activities, and some on program structuring. One of the simpler definitions is that OOP is the act of using "map" data structures or arrays that can contain functions and pointers to other maps, all with some syntactic and scoping sugar on top. Inheritance can be performed by cloning the maps (sometimes called "prototyping").

Aspect-oriented Programming

In computing, aspect-oriented programming (AOP) is a programming paradigm that aims to increase modularity by allowing the separation of cross-cutting concerns. It does so by adding additional behavior to existing code (an advice) *without* modifying the code itself, instead separately specifying which code is modified via a "pointcut" specification, such as "log all function calls when the function's name begins with 'set'". This allows behaviors that are not central to the business logic (such as logging) to be added to a program without cluttering the code core to the functionality. AOP forms a basis for aspect-oriented software development.

AOP includes programming methods and tools that support the modularization of concerns at the level of the source code, while "aspect-oriented software development" refers to a whole engineering discipline.

Aspect-oriented programming entails breaking down program logic into distinct parts (so-called *concerns*, cohesive areas of functionality). Nearly all programming paradigms support some level of grouping and encapsulation of concerns into separate, independent entities by providing abstractions (e.g., functions, procedures, modules, classes, methods) that can be used for implementing, abstracting and composing these concerns. Some concerns "cut across" multiple abstractions in a program, and defy these forms of implementation. These concerns are called *cross-cutting concerns* or horizontal concerns.

Logging exemplifies a crosscutting concern because a logging strategy necessarily affects every logged part of the system. Logging thereby *crosscuts* all logged classes and methods.

All AOP implementations have some crosscutting expressions that encapsulate each concern in one place. The difference between implementations lies in the power, safety, and usability of the constructs provided. For example, interceptors that specify the methods to intercept express a limited form of crosscutting, without much support for type-safety or debugging. AspectJ has a number of such expressions and encapsulates them in a special class, an aspect. For example, an aspect can alter the behavior of the base code (the non-aspect part of a program) by applying advice (additional behavior) at various join points (points in a program) specified in a quantification or query called a pointcut (that detects whether a given join point matches). An aspect can also make binary-compatible structural changes to other classes, like adding members or parents.

History

AOP has several direct antecedents A1 and A2: reflection and metaobject protocols, subject-oriented programming, Composition Filters and Adaptive Programming.

Gregor Kiczales and colleagues at Xerox PARC developed the explicit concept of AOP, and followed this with the AspectJ AOP extension to Java. IBM's research team pursued a tool approach over a language design approach and in 2001 proposed Hyper/J and the Concern Manipulation Environment, which have not seen wide usage. The examples use AspectJ as it is the most widely known AOP language.

The Microsoft Transaction Server is considered to be the first major application of AOP followed by Enterprise JavaBeans.

Motivation and Basic Concepts

Typically, an aspect is *scattered* or *tangled* as code, making it harder to understand and maintain. It is scattered by virtue of the function (such as logging) being spread over a number of unrelated functions that might use *its* function, possibly in entirely unrelated systems, different source languages, etc. That means to change logging can require modifying all affected modules. Aspects become tangled not only with the mainline function of the systems in which they are expressed but also with each other. That means changing one concern entails understanding all the tangled concerns or having some means by which the effect of changes can be inferred.

For example, consider a banking application with a conceptually very simple method for transferring an amount from one account to another:

```
void transfer(Account fromAcc, Account toAcc, int amount) throws Exception {

    if (fromAcc.getBalance() < amount)

        throw new InsufficientFundsException();
```

```
    fromAcc.withdraw(amount);

    toAcc.deposit(amount);

}
```

However, this transfer method overlooks certain considerations that a deployed application would require: it lacks security checks to verify that the current user has the authorization to perform this operation; a database transaction should encapsulate the operation in order to prevent accidental data loss; for diagnostics, the operation should be logged to the system log, etc.

A version with all those new concerns, for the sake of example, could look somewhat like this:

void transfer(Account fromAcc, Account toAcc, int amount, User user,

```
    Logger logger, Database database) throws Exception {

  logger.info("Transferring money...");

  if (!isUserAuthorised(user, fromAcc)) {

    logger.info("User has no permission.");

    throw new UnauthorisedUserException();

  }

  if (fromAcc.getBalance() < amount) {

    logger.info("Insufficient funds.");

    throw new InsufficientFundsException();

  }

  fromAcc.withdraw(amount);

  toAcc.deposit(amount);

  database.commitChanges();  // Atomic operation.


  logger.info("Transaction successful.");

}
```

In this example other interests have become *tangled* with the basic functionality (sometimes called the *business logic concern*). Transactions, security, and logging all exemplify *cross-cutting concerns*.

Now consider what happens if we suddenly need to change (for example) the security considerations for the application. In the program's current version, security-related operations appear *scattered* across numerous methods, and such a change would require a major effort.

AOP attempts to solve this problem by allowing the programmer to express cross-cutting concerns in stand-alone modules called *aspects*. Aspects can contain *advice* (code joined to specified points in the program) and *inter-type declarations* (structural members added to other classes). For example, a security module can include advice that performs a security check before accessing a bank account. The pointcut defines the times (join points) when one can access a bank account, and the code in the advice body defines how the security check is implemented. That way, both the check and the places can be maintained in one place. Further, a good pointcut can anticipate later program changes, so if another developer creates a new method to access the bank account, the advice will apply to the new method when it executes.

So for the above example implementing logging in an aspect:

```
aspect Logger {

  void Bank.transfer(Account fromAcc, Account toAcc, int amount, User
user, Logger logger)  {

    logger.info("Transferring money...");

  }


  void Bank.getMoneyBack(User user, int transactionId, Logger logger)  {

    logger.info("User requested money back.");

  }

  // Other crosscutting code.

}
```

One can think of AOP as a debugging tool or as a user-level tool. Advice should be reserved for the cases where you cannot get the function changed (user level) or do not want to change the function in production code (debugging).

Join Point Models

The advice-related component of an aspect-oriented language defines a join point model (JPM). A JPM defines three things:

- When the advice can run. These are called *join points* because they are points in a running program where additional behavior can be usefully joined. A join point needs to be addressable and understandable by an ordinary programmer to be useful. It should also be stable across inconsequential program changes in order for an aspect to be stable across such changes. Many AOP implementations support method executions and field references as join points.

- A way to specify (or *quantify*) join points, called *pointcuts*. Pointcuts determine whether a given join point matches. Most useful pointcut languages use a syntax like the base language (for example, AspectJ uses Java signatures) and allow reuse through naming and combination.

- A means of specifying code to run at a join point. AspectJ calls this *advice*, and can run it before, after, and around join points. Some implementations also support things like defining a method in an aspect on another class.

Join-point models can be compared based on the join points exposed, how join points are specified, the operations permitted at the join points, and the structural enhancements that can be expressed.

AspectJ's Join-point Model

- The join points in AspectJ include method or constructor call or execution, the initialization of a class or object, field read and write access, exception handlers, etc. They do not include loops, super calls, throws clauses, multiple statements, etc.

- Pointcuts are specified by combinations of *primitive pointcut designators* (PCDs).

   "Kinded" PCDs match a particular kind of join point (e.g., method execution) and tend to take as input a Java-like signature. One such pointcut looks like this:

```
execution(* set*(*))
```

   This pointcut matches a method-execution join point, if the method name starts with "set" and there is exactly one argument of any type.

"Dynamic" PCDs check runtime types and bind variables. For example,

```
this(Point)
```

   This pointcut matches when the currently executing object is an instance of class Point. Note that the unqualified name of a class can be used via Java's normal type lookup.

"Scope" PCDs limit the lexical scope of the join point. For example:

```
within(com.company.*)
```

   This pointcut matches any join point in any type in the com.company package. The * is one form of the wildcards that can be used to match many things with one signature.

Pointcuts can be composed and named for reuse. For example:

```
pointcut set()  :  execution(* set*(*) ) && this(Point) && within(com.
company.*);
```

   This pointcut matches a method-execution join point, if the method name starts with "set" and this is an instance of type Point in the com.company package. It can be referred to using the name "set()".

- Advice specifies to run at (before, after, or around) a join point (specified with a pointcut) certain code (specified like code in a method). The AOP runtime invokes Advice automatically when the pointcut matches the join point. For example:

```
after() : set() {

  Display.update();

}
```

This effectively specifies: "if the *set()* pointcut matches the join point, run the code Display. update() after the join point completes."

Other Potential Join Point Models

There are other kinds of JPMs. All advice languages can be defined in terms of their JPM. For example, a hypothetical aspect language for UML may have the following JPM:

- Join points are all model elements.

- Pointcuts are some boolean expression combining the model elements.

- The means of affect at these points are a visualization of all the matched join points.

Inter-type Declarations

Inter-type declarations provide a way to express crosscutting concerns affecting the structure of modules. Also known as *open classes* and *extension methods*, this enables programmers to declare in one place members or parents of another class, typically in order to combine all the code related to a concern in one aspect. For example, if a programmer implemented the crosscutting display-update concern using visitors instead, an inter-type declaration using the visitor pattern might look like this in AspectJ:

```
aspect DisplayUpdate {

  void Point.acceptVisitor(Visitor v) {

    v.visit(this);

  }

  // other crosscutting code...

}
```

This code snippet adds the acceptVisitor method to the Point class.

It is a requirement that any structural additions be compatible with the original class, so that clients of the existing class continue to operate, unless the AOP implementation can expect to control all clients at all times.

Implementation

AOP programs can affect other programs in two different ways, depending on the underlying languages and environments:

1. a combined program is produced, valid in the original language and indistinguishable from an ordinary program to the ultimate interpreter.

2. the ultimate interpreter or environment is updated to understand and implement AOP features.

The difficulty of changing environments means most implementations produce compatible combination programs through a process known as *weaving* - a special case of program transformation. An aspect weaver reads the aspect-oriented code and generates appropriate object-oriented code with the aspects integrated. The same AOP language can be implemented through a variety of weaving methods, so the semantics of a language should never be understood in terms of the weaving implementation. Only the speed of an implementation and its ease of deployment are affected by which method of combination is used.

Systems can implement source-level weaving using preprocessors (as C++ was implemented originally in CFront) that require access to program source files. However, Java's well-defined binary form enables bytecode weavers to work with any Java program in .class-file form. Bytecode weavers can be deployed during the build process or, if the weave model is per-class, during class loading. AspectJ started with source-level weaving in 2001, delivered a per-class bytecode weaver in 2002, and offered advanced load-time support after the integration of AspectWerkz in 2005.

Any solution that combines programs at runtime has to provide views that segregate them properly to maintain the programmer's segregated model. Java's bytecode support for multiple source files enables any debugger to step through a properly woven .class file in a source editor. However, some third-party decompilers cannot process woven code because they expect code produced by Javac rather than all supported bytecode forms.

Deploy-time weaving offers another approach. This basically implies post-processing, but rather than patching the generated code, this weaving approach *subclasses* existing classes so that the modifications are introduced by method-overriding. The existing classes remain untouched, even at runtime, and all existing tools (debuggers, profilers, etc.) can be used during development. A similar approach has already proven itself in the implementation of many Java EE application servers, such as IBM's WebSphere.

Terminology

Standard terminology used in Aspect-oriented programming may include.

Cross-cutting concerns:

> Even though most classes in an OO model will perform a single, specific function, they often share common, secondary requirements with other classes. For example, we may want to add logging to classes within the data-access layer and also to classes in the UI layer whenever a thread enters or exits a method. Further concerns can be related to security such as access control or information flow control. Even though each class has a very

different primary functionality, the code needed to perform the secondary functionality is often identical.

Advice:

This is the additional code that you want to apply to your existing model. In our example, this is the logging code that we want to apply whenever the thread enters or exits a method.

Pointcut:

This is the term given to the point of execution in the application at which cross-cutting concern needs to be applied. In our example, a pointcut is reached when the thread enters a method, and another pointcut is reached when the thread exits the method.

Aspect:

The combination of the pointcut and the advice is termed an aspect. In the example above, we add a logging aspect to our application by defining a pointcut and giving the correct advice.

Comparison to Other Programming Paradigms

Aspects emerged from object-oriented programming and computational reflection. AOP languages have functionality similar to, but more restricted than metaobject protocols. Aspects relate closely to programming concepts like subjects, mixins, and delegation. Other ways to use aspect-oriented programming paradigms include Composition Filters and the hyperslices approach. Since at least the 1970s, developers have been using forms of interception and dispatch-patching that resemble some of the implementation methods for AOP, but these never had the semantics that the cross-cutting specifications provide written in one place.

Designers have considered alternative ways to achieve separation of code, such as C#'s partial types, but such approaches lack a quantification mechanism that allows reaching several join points of the code with one declarative statement.

Though it may seem unrelated, in testing, the use of mocks or stubs requires the use of AOP techniques, like around advice, and so forth. Here the collaborating objects are for the purpose of the test, a cross cutting concern. Thus the various Mock Object frameworks provide these features. For example, a process invokes a service to get a balance amount. In the test of the process, where the amount comes from is unimportant, only that the process uses the balance according to the requirements.

Adoption Issues

Programmers need to be able to read code and understand what is happening in order to prevent errors. Even with proper education, understanding crosscutting concerns can be difficult without proper support for visualizing both static structure and the dynamic flow of a program. Beginning in 2002, AspectJ began to provide IDE plug-ins to support the visualizing of crosscutting concerns. Those features, as well as aspect code assist and refactoring are now common.

Given the power of AOP, if a programmer makes a logical mistake in expressing crosscutting, it can lead to widespread program failure. Conversely, another programmer may change the join points in a program – e.g., by renaming or moving methods – in ways that the aspect writer did not anticipate, with unforeseen consequences. One advantage of modularizing crosscutting concerns is enabling one programmer to affect the entire system easily; as a result, such problems present as a conflict over responsibility between two or more developers for a given failure. However, the solution for these problems can be much easier in the presence of AOP, since only the aspect needs to be changed, whereas the corresponding problems without AOP can be much more spread out.

Criticism

The most basic criticism of the effect of AOP is that control flow is obscured, and is not only worse than the much-maligned GOTO, but is in fact closely analogous to the joke COME FROM statement. The *obliviousness of application*, which is fundamental to many definitions of AOP (the code in question has no indication that an advice will be applied, which is specified instead in the pointcut), means that the advice is not visible, in contrast to an explicit method call. For example, compare the COME FROM program:

```
 5 input x

10 print 'result is :'

15 print x


20 come from 10

25     x = x * x

30 return
```

with an AOP fragment with analogous semantics:

```
main() {

    input x

    print(result(x))

}

input result(int x) { return x }

around(int x): call(result(int)) && args(x) {

    int temp = proceed(x)

//    return temp * temp

}
```

Indeed, the pointcut may depend on runtime condition and thus not be statically deterministic. This can be mitigated but not solved by static analysis and IDE support showing which advices *potentially* match.

General criticisms are that AOP purports to improve "both modularity and the structure of code", but some counter that it instead undermines these goals and impedes "independent development and understandability of programs". Specifically, quantification by pointcuts breaks modularity: "one must, in general, have whole-program knowledge to reason about the dynamic execution of an aspect-oriented program." Further, while its goals (modularizing cross-cutting concerns) are well-understood, its actual definition is unclear and not clearly distinguished from other well-established techniques. Cross-cutting concerns potentially cross-cut each other, requiring some resolution mechanism, such as ordering. Indeed, aspects can apply to themselves, leading to problems such as the liar paradox.

Technical criticisms include that the quantification of pointcuts (defining where advices are executed) is "extremely sensitive to changes in the program", which is known as the *fragile pointcut problem*. The problems with pointcuts are deemed intractable: if one replaces the quantification of pointcuts with explicit annotations, one obtains attribute-oriented programming instead, which is simply an explicit subroutine call and suffers the identical problem of scattering that AOP was designed to solve.

Implementations

The following programming languages have implemented AOP, within the language, or as an external library:

- .NET Framework languages (C# / VB.NET):

    ○ PostSharp is a commercial AOP implementation with a free but limited edition.

    ○ Unity, It provides an API to facilitate proven practices in core areas of programming including data access, security, logging, exception handling and others.

- ActionScript

- Ada

- AutoHotkey

- C / C++

- COBOL

- The Cocoa Objective-C frameworks

- ColdFusion

- Common Lisp

- Delphi

- Delphi Prism

- e (IEEE 1647)

- Emacs Lisp

- Groovy

- Haskell

- Java:

  o AspectJ

- JavaScript

- Logtalk

- Lua

- make

- Matlab

- ML

- Perl

- PHP

- Prolog

- Python

- Racket

- Ruby

- Squeak Smalltalk

- UML 2.0

- XML

Automata-based Programming

Automata-based programming is a programming paradigm in which the program or part of it is thought of as a model of a finite state machine (FSM) or any other (often more complicated) formal automaton. Sometimes a potentially infinite set of possible states is introduced, and such a set can have a complicated structure, not just an enumeration.

FSM-based programming is generally the same, but, formally speaking, doesn't cover all possible variants, as FSM stands for finite state machine, and automata-based programming doesn't necessarily employ FSMs in the strict sense.

The following properties are key indicators for automata-based programming:

1. The time period of the program's execution is clearly separated down to the *steps of the automaton*. Each of the *steps* is effectively an execution of a code section (same for all the steps), which has a single entry point. Such a section can be a function or other routine, or just a cycle body. The step section might be divided down to subsections to be executed depending on different states, although this is not necessary.

2. Any communication between the steps is only possible via the explicitly noted set of variables named *the state*. Between any two steps, the program (or its part created using the automata-based technique) can not have implicit components of its state, such as local (stack) variables' values, return addresses, the current instruction pointer, etc. That is, the state of the whole program, taken at any two moments of entering the step of the automaton, can only differ in the values of the variables being considered as the state of the automaton.

The whole execution of the automata-based code is a (possibly explicit) cycle of the automaton's steps.

Another reason for using the notion of automata-based programming is that the programmer's style of thinking about the program in this technique is very similar to the style of thinking used to solve mathematical tasks using Turing machines, Markov algorithms, etc.

Example

Consider a program in C that reads a text from *standard input stream*, line by line, and prints the first word of each line. It is clear we need first to read and skip the leading spaces, if any, then read characters of the first word and print them until the word ends, and then read and skip all the remaining characters until the end-of-line character is encountered. Upon reaching the end of line character (regardless of the stage), we restart the algorithm from the beginning, and upon encountering the *end of file* condition (regardless of the stage), we terminate the program.

Traditional (Imperative) Program in C

The program which solves the example task in traditional (imperative) style can look something like this:

```
#include <stdio.h>

#include <ctype.h>

int main(void)

{

    int c;

    do {

        do {
```

```c
        c = getchar();
    } while(c == ' ');
    while(c != EOF && !isspace(c) && c != '\n') {
        putchar(c);
        c = getchar();
    }
    putchar('\n');
    while(c != EOF && c != '\n')
        c = getchar();
} while(c != EOF);
return 0;
}
```

Automata-based Style Program

The same task can be solved by thinking in terms of finite state machines. Note that line parsing has three stages: skipping the leading spaces, printing the word and skipping the trailing characters. Let's call them states before, inside and after. The program may now look like this:

```c
#include <stdio.h>
#include <ctype.h>
int main(void)
{
    enum states {
        before, inside, after
    } state;
    int c;
    state = before;
    while((c = getchar()) != EOF) {
        switch(state) {
            case before:
```

```
            if(c != ` `) {

                putchar(c);

                if(c != '\n')

                    state = inside;

            }

            break;

        case inside:

            if(!isspace(c))

                putchar(c);

            else {

                putchar('\n');

                if(c == '\n')

                    state = before;

                else

                    state = after;

            }

            break;

        case after:

            if(c == '\n')

                state = before;

        }

    }

    return 0;

}
```

Although the code now looks longer, it has at least one significant advantage: there's only one *reading* (that is, call to the getchar() function) instruction in the program. Besides that, there's only one loop instead of the four the previous versions had.

In this program, the body of the while loop is the automaton step, and the loop itself is the *cycle of the automaton's work*.

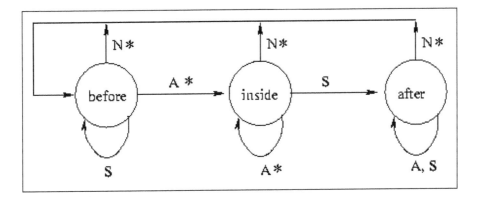

The program implements (models) the work of a *finite state machine* shown on the picture. The N denotes the end of line character, the S denotes spaces, and the **A** stands for all the other characters. The automaton follows exactly one *arrow* on each step depending on the current state and the encountered character. Some state switches are accompanied with printing the character; such arrows are marked with asterisks.

It is not absolutely necessary to divide the code down to separate handlers for each unique state. Furthermore, in some cases the very notion of the *state* can be composed of several variables' values, so that it could be impossible to handle each possible state explicitly. In the discussed program it is possible to reduce the code length by noticing that the actions taken in response to the end of line character are the same for all the possible states. The following program is equal to the previous one but is a bit shorter:

```c
#include <stdio.h>

#include <ctype.h>

int main(void)

{

    enum states {

        before, inside, after

    } state;

    int c;

    state = before;

    while((c = getchar()) != EOF) {

        if(c == '\n') {

            putchar('\n');

            state = before;

        } else
```

```
        switch(state) {
            case before:
                if(c != ' ') {
                    putchar(c);
                    state = inside;
                }
                break;
            case inside:
                if(c == ' ') {
                    state = after;
                } else {
                    putchar(c);
                }
                break;
            case after:
                break;
        }
    }
    if(state != before)
        putchar('\n');
    return 0;
}
```

A Separate Function for the Automation Step

The most important property of the previous program is that the automaton step code section is clearly localized. With a separate function for it, we can better demonstrate this property:

```
#include <stdio.h>

enum states { before, inside, after };

void step(enum states *state, int c)
```

```
{
    if(c == '\n') {
        putchar('\n');
        *state = before;
    } else
    switch(*state) {
        case before:
            if(c != ' ') {
                putchar(c);
                *state = inside;
            }
            break;
        case inside:
            if(c == ' ') {
                *state = after;
            } else {
                putchar(c);
            }
            break;
        case after:
            break;
    }
}
int main(void)
{
    int c;
    enum states state = before;
    while((c = getchar()) != EOF) {
```

```
        step(&state, c);

    }

    if(state != before)

        putchar('\n');

    return 0;

}
```

This example clearly demonstrates the basic properties of automata-based code:

1. Time periods of automaton step executions may not overlap.

2. The only information passed from the previous step to the next is the explicitly specified *automaton state*.

Explicit State Transition Table

A finite automaton can be defined by an explicit state transition table. Generally speaking, an automata-based program code can naturally reflect this approach. In the program below there's an array named the_table, which defines the table. The rows of the table stand for three *states*, while columns reflect the input characters (first for spaces, second for the end of line character, and the last is for all the other characters).

For every possible combination, the table contains the new state number and the flag, which determines whether the automaton must print the symbol. In a real life task, this could be more complicated; e.g., the table could contain pointers to functions to be called on every possible combination of conditions.

```
#include <stdio.h>

enum states { before = 0, inside = 1, after = 2 };

struct branch {

    unsigned char new_state:2; //BIT [1:0]

    unsigned char should_putchar:1; //BIT

};

struct branch the_table = {

                    /* ' '             '\n'           others */

    /* before */ { {before,0}, {before,1}, {inside,1} },

    /* inside */ { {after, 1}, {before,1}, {inside,1} },

    /* after  */ { {after, 0}, {before,1}, {after, 0} }
```

```
};

void step(enum states *state, int c)

{

    int idx2 = (c == ` `) ? 0 : (c == `\n`) ? 1 : 2;

    struct branch *b = & the_table[*state][idx2];

    *state = (enum states)(b->new_state);

    if(b->should_putchar) putchar(c);

}
```

Automation and Automata

Automata-based programming indeed closely matches the programming needs found in the field of automation.

A production cycle is commonly modelled as:

- A sequence of stages stepping according to input data (from captors).

- A set of actions performed depending on the current stage.

Various dedicated programming languages allow expressing such a model in more or less sophisticated ways.

Example Program

The example presented above could be expressed according to this view like in the following program. Here pseudo-code uses such conventions:

- 'set' and 'reset' respectively activate & inactivate a logic variable (here a stage)

- ':' is assignment, '=' is equality test

```
SPC : ` `

EOL : `\n`

states : (before, inside, after, end, endplusnl)

setState(c) {

    if c=EOF then if inside or after then set endplusnl else set end

    if before and (c!=SPC and c!=EOL) then set inside

    if inside and (c=SPC or c=EOL) then set after

    if after and c=EOL then set before
```

```
}

doAction(c) {

    if inside then write(c)

    else if c=EOL or endplusnl then write(EOL)

}


cycle {

    set before

    loop {

        c : readCharacter

        setState(c)

        doAction(c)

    }

    until end or endplusnl

}
```

The separation of routines expressing cycle progression on one side, and actual action on the other (matching input & output) allows clearer and simpler code.

Automation & Events

In the field of automation, stepping from step to step depends on input data coming from the machine itself. This is represented in the program by reading characters from a text. In reality, those data inform about position, speed, temperature, etc. of critical elements of a machine.

Like in GUI programming, changes in the machine state can thus be considered as events causing the passage from a state to another, until the final one is reached. The combination of possible states can generate a wide variety of events, thus defining a more complex production cycle. As a consequence, cycles are usually far to be simple linear sequences. There are commonly parallel branches running together and alternatives selected according to different events, schematically represented below:

```
    s:stage     c:condition



    s1

    |
```

```
    |-c2

    |

    s2

    |

    ----------

    |           |

    |-c31       |-c32

    |           |

   s31          s32

    |           |

    |-c41       |-c42

    |           |

    ----------

    |

    s4
```

Using Object-oriented Capabilities

If the implementation language supports object-oriented programming, a simple refactoring is to encapsulate the automaton into an object, thus hiding its implementation details. For example, an object-oriented version in C++ of the same program is below. A more sophisticated refactoring could employ the State pattern.

```cpp
#include <stdio.h>

class StateMachine {
    enum states { before = 0, inside = 1, after = 2 } state;
    struct branch {
        unsigned char new_state:2;
        unsigned char should_putchar:1;
    };
    static struct branch the_table;
public:
    StateMachine() : state(before) {}
```

```cpp
    void FeedChar(int c) {

        int idx2 = (c == ' ') ? 0 : (c == '\n') ? 1 : 2;

        struct branch *b = & the_table[state][idx2];

        state = (enum states)(b->new_state);

        if(b->should_putchar) putchar(c);

    }
};

struct StateMachine::branch StateMachine::the_table = {

                    /* ' '              '\n'          others */

    /* before */ { {before,0}, {before,1}, {inside,1} },

    /* inside */ { {after, 0}, {before,1}, {inside,1} },

    /* after  */ { {after, 0}, {before,1}, {after, 0} }

};

int main(void)

{

    int c;

    StateMachine machine;

    while((c = getchar()) != EOF)

        machine.FeedChar(c);

    return 0;

}
```

Note: To minimize changes not directly related to the subject of the article, the input/output functions from the standard library of C are being used. Note the use of the ternary operator, which could also be implemented as if-else.

Applications

Automata-based programming is widely used in lexical and syntactic analyses.

Besides that, thinking in terms of automata (that is, breaking the execution process down to *automaton steps* and passing information from step to step through the explicit *state*) is necessary for event-driven programming as the only alternative to using parallel processes or threads.

The notions of states and state machines are often used in the field of formal specification. For instance, UML-based software architecture development uses state diagrams to specify the behaviour of the program. Also various communication protocols are often specified using the explicit notion of *state*.

Thinking in terms of automata (steps and states) can also be used to describe semantics of some programming languages. For example, the execution of a program written in the Refal language is described as a sequence of *steps* of a so-called abstract Refal machine; the state of the machine is a *view* (an arbitrary Refal expression without variables).

Continuations in the Scheme language require thinking in terms of steps and states, although Scheme itself is in no way automata-related (it is recursive). To make it possible the call/cc feature to work, implementation needs to be able to catch a whole state of the executing program, which is only possible when there's no implicit part in the state. Such a *caught state* is the very thing called *continuation*, and it can be considered as the *state* of a (relatively complicated) automaton. The step of the automaton is deducing the next continuation from the previous one, and the execution process is the cycle of such steps.

Alexander Ollongren in his book explains the so-called *Vienna method* of programming languages semantics description which is fully based on formal automata.

The STAT system is a good example of using the automata-based approach; this system, besides other features, includes an embedded language called *STATL* which is purely automata-oriented.

History

Automata-based techniques were used widely in the domains where there are algorithms based on automata theory, such as formal language analyses.

One of the early papers on this is by Johnson et al., 1968.

One of the earliest mentions of automata-based programming as a general technique is found in the paper by Peter Naur, 1963. The author calls the technique *Turing machine approach*, however no real Turing machine is given in the paper; instead, the technique based on states and steps is described.

Compared Against Imperative and Procedural Programming

The notion of state is not exclusive property of automata-based programming. Generally speaking, *state* (or program state) appears during execution of any computer program, as a combination of all information that can change during the execution. For instance, a *state* of.a traditional imperative program consists of:

1. Values of all variables and the information stored within dynamic memory.

2. Values stored in registers.

3. Stack contents (including local variables' values and return addresses).

4. Current value of the instruction pointer.

These can be divided to the explicit part (such as values stored in variables) and the implicit part (return addresses and the instruction pointer).

Having said this, an automata-based program can be considered as a special case of an imperative program, in which implicit part of the state is minimized. The state of the whole program taken at the two distinct moments of entering the *step* code section can differ in the automaton state only. This simplifies the analysis of the program.

Object-oriented Programming Relationship

In the theory of object-oriented programming an object is said to have an internal *state* and is capable of *receiving messages*, *responding* to them, *sending* messages to other objects and changing the internal state during message handling. In more practical terminology, *to call an object's method* is considered the same as *to send a message to the object*.

Thus, on the one hand, objects from object-oriented programming can be considered as automata (or models of automata) whose *state* is the combination of internal fields, and one or more methods are considered to be the *step*. Such methods must not call each other nor themselves, neither directly nor indirectly, otherwise the object can not be considered to be implemented in an automata-based manner.

On the other hand, it is obvious that *object* is good for implementing a model of an automaton. When the automata-based approach is used within an object-oriented language, an automaton model is usually implemented by a class, the *state* is represented with internal (private) fields of the class, and the *step* is implemented as a method; such a method is usually the only non-constant public method of the class (besides constructors and destructors). Other public methods could query the state but don't change it. All the secondary methods (such as particular state handlers) are usually hidden within the private part of the class.

Flow-based Programming

In computer programming, flow-based programming (FBP) is a programming paradigm that defines applications as networks of "black box" processes, which exchange data across predefined connections by message passing, where the connections are specified *externally* to the processes. These black box processes can be reconnected endlessly to form different applications without having to be changed internally. FBP is thus naturally component-oriented.

FBP is a particular form of dataflow programming based on bounded buffers, information packets with defined lifetimes, named ports, and separate definition of connections.

Introduction

Flow-based programming defines applications using the metaphor of a "data factory". It views an application not as a single, sequential process, which starts at a point in time, and then does one thing at a time until it is finished, but as a network of asynchronous processes communicating by means of streams of structured data chunks, called "information packets" (IPs). In this view, the focus is on the application data and the transformations applied to it to produce the desired outputs. The network is defined externally to the processes, as a list of connections which is interpreted by a piece of software, usually called the "scheduler".

The processes communicate by means of fixed-capacity connections. A connection is attached to a process by means of a port, which has a name agreed upon between the process code and the network definition. More than one process can execute the same piece of code. At any point in time, a given IP can only be "owned" by a single process, or be in transit between two processes. Ports may either be simple, or array-type, as used e.g. for the input port of the Collate component described below. It is the combination of ports with asynchronous processes that allows many long-running primitive functions of data processing, such as Sort, Merge, Summarize, etc., to be supported in the form of software black boxes.

Because FBP processes can continue executing as long they have data to work on and somewhere to put their output, FBP applications generally run in less elapsed time than conventional programs, and make optimal use of all the processors on a machine, with no special programming required to achieve this.

The network definition is usually diagrammatic, and is converted into a connection list in some lower-level language or notation. FBP is often a visual programming language at this level. More complex network definitions have a hierarchical structure, being built up from subnets with "sticky" connections. Many other flow based languages/runtimes are built around more traditional programming languages, the most notable example is RaftLib which uses C++ iostream-like operators to specify the flow graph.

FBP has much in common with the Linda language in that it is, in Gelernter and Carriero's terminology, a "coordination language": it is essentially language-independent. Indeed, given a scheduler written in a sufficiently low-level language, components written in different languages can be linked together in a single network. FBP thus lends itself to the concept of domain-specific languages or "mini-languages".

FBP exhibits "data coupling", on coupling as the loosest type of coupling between components. The concept of loose coupling is in turn related to that of service-oriented architectures, and FBP fits a number of the criteria for such an architecture, albeit at a more fine-grained level than most examples of this architecture.

FBP promotes high-level, functional style of specifications that simplify reasoning about system behavior. An example of this is the distributed data flow model for constructively specifying and analyzing the semantics of distributed multi-party protocols.

History

Flow-Based Programming was invented by J. Paul Morrison in the early 1970s, and initially implemented in software for a Canadian bank. FBP at its inception was strongly influenced by some IBM simulation languages of the period, in particular GPSS, but its roots go all the way back to Conway's seminal paper on what he called coroutines.

FBP has undergone a number of name changes over the years: the original implementation was called AMPS (Advanced Modular Processing System). One large application in Canada went live in 1975, and, as of 2013, has been in continuous production use, running daily, for almost 40 years. Because IBM considered the ideas behind FBP "too much like a law of nature" to be patentable they instead put the basic concepts of FBP into the public domain, by means of a Technical Disclosure Bulletin, "Data Responsive Modular, Interleaved Task Programming System", in 1971. An article describing its concepts and experience using it was published in 1978 in the IBM Research IBM Systems Journal under the name DSLM. A second implementation was done as a joint project of IBM Canada and IBM Japan, under the name "Data Flow Development Manager" (DFDM), and was briefly marketed in Japan in the late '80s under the name "Data Flow Programming Manager".

Generally the concepts were referred to within IBM as "Data Flow", but this term was felt to be too general, and eventually the name flow-based programming was adopted.

From the early '80s to 1993 J. Paul Morrison and IBM architect Wayne Stevens refined and promoted the concepts behind FBP. Stevens wrote several articles describing and supporting the FBP concept, and included material about it in several of his books. In 1994 Morrison published a book describing FBP, and providing empirical evidence that FBP led to reduced development times.

Concepts

The following diagram shows the major entities of an FBP diagram (apart from the Information Packets). Such a diagram can be converted directly into a list of connections, which can then be executed by an appropriate engine (software or hardware).

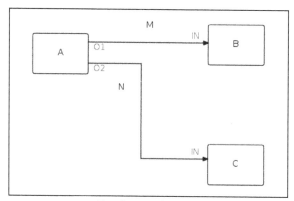

Simple FBP diagram.

A, B and C are processes executing code components. O1, O2, and the two INs are ports connecting the connections M and N to their respective processes. It is permitted for processes B and C to be executing the same code, so each process must have its own set of working storage, control blocks, etc. Whether or not they do share code, B and C are free to use the same port names, as port names only have meaning within the components referencing them (and at the network level, of course).

M and N are what are often referred to as "bounded buffers", and have a fixed capacity in terms of the number of IPs that they can hold at any point in time.

The concept of *ports* is what allows the same component to be used at more than one place in the network. In combination with a parametrization ability, called Initial Information Packets (IIPs), ports provide FBP with a component reuse ability, making FBP a component-based architecture. FBP thus exhibits what Raoul de Campo and Nate Edwards of IBM Research have termed configurable modularity.

Information Packets or IPs are allocated in what might be called "IP space" (just as Linda's tuples are allocated in "tuple space"), and have a well-defined lifetime until they are disposed of and their space is reclaimed - in FBP this must be an explicit action on the part of an owning process. IPs traveling across a given connection (actually it is their "handles" that travel) constitute a "stream", which is generated and consumed asynchronously - this concept thus has similarities to the lazy cons concept described in the 1976 article by Friedman and Wise.

IPs are usually structured chunks of data - some IPs, however, may not contain any real data, but are used simply as signals. An example of this is "bracket IPs", which can be used to group data IPs into sequential patterns within a stream, called "substreams". Substreams may in turn be nested. IPs may also be chained together to form "IP trees", which travel through the network as single objects.

The system of connections and processes described above can be "ramified" to any size. During the development of an application, monitoring processes may be added between pairs of processes, processes may be "exploded" to subnets, or simulations of processes may be replaced by the real process logic. FBP therefore lends itself to rapid prototyping.

This is really an assembly line image of data processing: the IPs travelling through a network of processes may be thought of as widgets travelling from station to station in an assembly line. "Machines" may easily be reconnected, taken off line for repair, replaced, and so on. Oddly enough, this image is very similar to that of unit record equipment that was used to process data before the days of computers, except that decks of cards had to be hand-carried from one machine to another.

Implementations of FBP may be non-preemptive or preemptive - the earlier implementations tended to be non-preemptive (mainframe and C language), whereas the latest Java implementation uses Java Thread class and is preemptive.

Examples

Telegram Problem

FBP components often form complementary pairs. This example uses two such pairs. The problem described seems very simple as described in words, but in fact is surprisingly difficult to accomplish using conventional procedural logic. The task, called the "Telegram Problem", originally described by Peter Naur, is to write a program which accepts lines of text and generates output lines containing as many words as possible, where the number of characters in each line does not exceed a certain length. The words may not be split and we assume no word is longer than the size of the output lines. This is analogous to the word-wrapping problem in text editors.

In conventional logic, the programmer rapidly discovers that neither the input nor the output structures can be used to drive the call hierarchy of control flow. In FBP, on the other hand, the problem description itself suggests a solution.

- "Words" are mentioned explicitly in the description of the problem, so it is reasonable for the designer to treat words as information packets (IPs).

- In FBP there is no single call hierarchy, so the programmer is not tempted to force a sub-pattern of the solution to be the top level.

Here is the most natural solution in FBP (there is no single "correct" solution in FBP, but this seems like a natural fit):

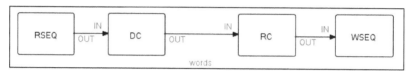

Peter Naur's "Telegram problem".

where DC and RC stand for "DeCompose" and "ReCompose", respectively.

As mentioned above, Initial Information Packets (IIPs) can be used to specify parametric information such as the desired output record length (required by the rightmost two components), or file names. IIPs are data chunks associated with a port in the network definition which become "normal" IPs when a "receive" is issued for the relevant port.

Batch Update

This type of program involves passing a file of "details" (changes, adds and deletes) against a "master file", and producing (at least) an updated master file, and one or more reports. Update programs are generally quite hard to code using synchronous, procedural code, as two (sometimes more) input streams have to be kept synchronized, even though there may be masters without corresponding details, or vice versa.

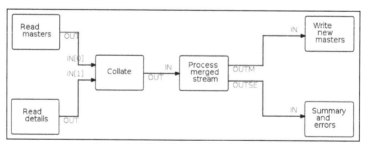

Canonical "batch update" structure.

In FBP, a reusable component (Collate), based on the unit record idea of a Collator, makes writing this type of application much easier as Collate merges the two streams and inserts bracket IPs to indicate grouping levels, significantly simplifying the downstream logic. Suppose that one stream ("masters" in this case) consists of IPs with key values of 1, 2 and 3, and the second stream IPs ("details") have key values of 11, 12, 21, 31, 32, 33 and 41, where the first digit corresponds to the master key values. Using bracket characters to represent "bracket" IPs, the collated output stream will be as follows:

```
( m1 d11 d12 )  ( m2 d21 )  ( m3 d31 d32 d33 )  (d41)
```

As there was no master with a value of 4, the last group consists of a single detail (plus brackets).

The structure of the above stream can be described succinctly using a BNF-like notation such as,

```
{ ( [m] d* ) }*
```

Collate is a reusable black box which only needs to know where the control fields are in its incoming IPs (even this is not strictly necessary as transformer processes can be inserted upstream to place the control fields in standard locations), and can in fact be generalized to any number of input streams, and any depth of bracket nesting. Collate uses an array-type port for input, allowing a variable number of input streams.

Multiplexing Processes

Flow-based programming supports process multiplexing in a very natural way. Since components are read-only, any number of instances of a given component ("processes") can run asynchronously with each other.

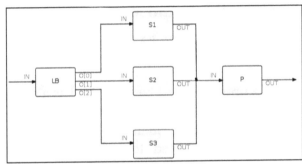

Example of multiplexing.

When computers usually had a single processor, this was useful when a lot of I/O was going on; now that machines usually have multiple processors, this is starting to become useful when processes are CPU-intensive as well. The diagram in this section shows a single "Load Balancer" process distributing data between 3 processes, labeled S1, S2 and S3, respectively, which are instances of a single component, which in turn feed into a single process on a "first-come, first served" basis.

Simple Interactive Network

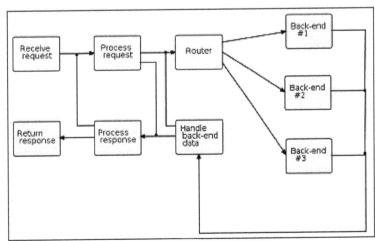

Schematic of general interactive application.

In this general schematic, requests (transactions) coming from users enter the diagram at the upper left, and responses are returned at the lower left. The "back ends" (on the right side) communicate with systems at other sites, e.g. using CORBA, MQSeries, etc. The cross-connections represent requests that do not need to go to the back ends, or requests that have to cycle through the network more than once before being returned to the user.

As different requests may use different back-ends, and may require differing amounts of time for the back-ends (if used) to process them, provision must be made to relate returned data to the appropriate requesting transactions, e.g. hash tables or caches.

The above diagram is schematic in the sense that the final application may contain many more processes: processes may be inserted between other processes to manage caches, display connection traffic, monitor throughput, etc. Also the blocks in the diagram may represent "subnets" - small networks with one or more open connections.

Comparison with Other Paradigms and Methodologies

Jackson Structured Programming (JSP) and Jackson System Development (JSD)

This methodology assumes that a program must be structured as a single procedural hierarchy of subroutines. Its starting point is to describe the application as a set of "main lines", based on the input and output data structures. One of these "main lines" is then chosen to drive the whole program, and the others are required to be "inverted" to turn them into subroutines (hence the name "Jackson inversion"). This sometimes results in what is called a "clash", requiring the program to be split into multiple programs or coroutines. When using FBP, this inversion process is not required, as every FBP component can be considered a separate "main line".

FBP and JSP share the concept of treating a program (or some components) as a parser of an input stream.

In Jackson's later work, Jackson System Development (JSD), the ideas were developed further.

In JSD the design is maintained as a network design until the final implementation stage. The model is then transformed into a set of sequential processes to the number of available processors. Jackson discusses the possibility of directly executing the network model that exists prior to this step, in section 1.3 of his book:

> The specification produced at the end of the System Timing step is, in principle, capable of direct execution. The necessary environment would contain a processor for each process, a device equivalent to an unbounded buffer for each data stream, and some input and output devices where the system is connected to the real world. *Such an environment could, of course, be provided by suitable software running on a sufficiently powerful machine. Sometimes, such direct execution of the specification will be possible, and may even be a reasonable choice.*

FBP was recognized by M A Jackson as an approach that follows his method of "Program decomposition into sequential processes communicating by a coroutine-like mechanism".

Applicative Programming

W.B. Ackerman defines an applicative language as one which does all of its processing by means of operators applied to values. The earliest known applicative language was LISP.

An FBP component can be regarded as a function transforming its input stream(s) into its output stream(s). These functions are then combined to make more complex transformations, as shown here:

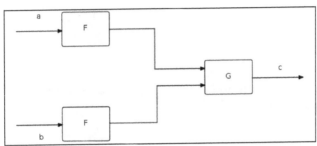

Two functions feeding one

If we label streams, as shown, with lower case letters, then the above diagram can be represented succinctly as follows:

```
c = G(F(a),F(b));
```

Just as in functional notation F can be used twice because it only works with values, and therefore has no side effects, in FBP two instances of a given component may be running concurrently with each other, and therefore FBP components must not have side-effects either. Functional notation could clearly be used to represent at least a part of an FBP network.

The question then arises whether FBP components can themselves be expressed using functional notation. W.H. Burge showed how stream expressions can be developed using a recursive, applicative style of programming, but this work was in terms of (streams of) atomic values. In FBP, it is necessary to be able to describe and process structured data chunks (FBP IPs).

Furthermore, most applicative systems assume that all the data is available in memory at the same time, whereas FBP applications need to be able to process long-running streams of data while still using finite resources. Friedman and Wise suggested a way to do this by adding the concept of "lazy cons" to Burge's work. This removed the requirement that both of the arguments of "cons" be available at the same instant of time. "Lazy cons" does not actually build a stream until both of its arguments are realized - before that it simply records a "promise" to do this. This allows a stream to be dynamically realized from the front, but with an unrealized back end. The end of the stream stays unrealized until the very end of the process, while the beginning is an ever-lengthening sequence of items.

Linda

Many of the concepts in FBP seem to have been discovered independently in different systems over the years. Linda, mentioned above, is one such. The difference between the two techniques is illustrated by the Linda "school of piranhas" load balancing technique - in FBP, this requires an extra "load balancer" component which routes requests to the component in a list which has the smallest number of IPs waiting to be processed. Clearly FBP and Linda are closely related, and one could easily be used to simulate the other.

Object-oriented Programming

An object in OOP can be described as a semi-autonomous unit comprising both information and behaviour. Objects communicate by means of "method calls", which are essentially subroutine calls, done indirectly via the class to which the receiving object belongs. The object's internal data can only be accessed by means of method calls, so this is a form of information hiding or "encapsulation". Encapsulation, however, predates OOP - David Parnas wrote one of the seminal articles on it in the early 70s - and is a basic concept in computing. Encapsulation is the very essence of an FBP component, which may be thought of as a black box, performing some conversion of its input data into its output data. In FBP, part of the specification of a component is the data formats and stream structures that it can accept, and those it will generate. This constitutes a form of design by contract. In addition, the data in an IP can only be accessed directly by the currently owning process. Encapsulation can also be implemented at the network level, by having outer processes protect inner ones.

A paper by C. Ellis and S. Gibbs distinguishes between active objects and passive objects. Passive objects comprise information and behaviour, as stated above, but they cannot determine the *timing* of this behaviour. Active objects on the other hand can do this. In their article Ellis and Gibbs state that active objects have much more potential for the development of maintainable systems than do passive objects. An FBP application can be viewed as a combination of these two types of object, where FBP processes would correspond to active objects, while IPs would correspond to passive objects.

Non-structured Programming

Non-structured programming is the historically earliest programming paradigm capable of creating Turing-complete algorithms. It is often contrasted with structured programming paradigms, including procedural, functional, and object-oriented programming.

Unstructured programming has been heavily criticized for producing hardly-readable ("spaghetti") code and is sometimes considered a bad approach for creating major projects, but has been praised for the freedom it offers to programmers and has been compared to how Mozart wrote music.

There are both high- and low-level programming languages that use non-structured programming. Some languages commonly cited as being non-structured include JOSS, FOCAL, TELCOMP, assembly languages, MS-DOS batch files, and early versions of BASIC, Fortran, COBOL, and MUMPS.

Features and Typical Concepts

Basic Concepts

A program in a non-structured language usually consists of sequentially ordered commands, or statements, usually one in each line. The lines are usually numbered or may have labels: this allows the flow of execution to jump to any line in the program.

Non-structured programming introduces basic control flow concepts such as loops, branches and jumps. Although there is no concept of procedures in the non-structured paradigm, subroutines are allowed. Unlike a procedure, a subroutine may have several entry and exit points, and a direct jump into or out of subroutine is (theoretically) allowed. This flexibility allows realization of coroutines.

There is no concept of locally scoped variables in non-structured programming (although for assembly programs, general purpose registers may serve the same purpose after saving on entry), but labels and variables can have a limited area of effect (for example, a group of lines). This means there is no (automatic) context refresh when calling a subroutine, so all variables might retain their values from the previous call. This makes general recursion difficult, but some cases of recursion—where no subroutine state values are needed after the recursive call—are possible if variables dedicated to the recursive subroutine are explicitly cleared (or re-initialized to their original value) on entry to the subroutine. The depth of nesting also may be limited to one or two levels.

Data Types

Non-structured languages allow only basic data types, such as numbers, strings and arrays (numbered sets of variables of the same type). The introduction of arrays into non-structured languages was a notable step forward, making stream data processing possible despite the lack of structured data types.

Event-driven Programming

In computer programming, event-driven programming is a programming paradigm in which the flow of the program is determined by events such as user actions (mouse clicks, key presses), sensor outputs, or messages from other programs/threads. Event-driven programming is the dominant paradigm used in graphical user interfaces and other applications (e.g. JavaScript web applications) that are centered on performing certain actions in response to user input. This is also true of programming for device drivers (e.g. P in USB device driver stacks).

In an event-driven application, there is generally a main loop that listens for events, and then triggers a callback function when one of those events is detected. In embedded systems the same may be achieved using hardware interrupts instead of a constantly running main loop. Event-driven programs can be written in any programming language, although the task is easier in languages that provide high-level abstractions, such as closures.

Event Handlers

A Trivial Event Handler

Because the code for checking for events and the main loop do not depend on the application, many programming frameworks take care of their implementation and expect the user to provide only the code for the event handlers. In this simple example there may be a call to an event handler called OnKeyEnter() that includes an argument with a string of characters, corresponding to what the user typed before hitting the ENTER key. To add two numbers, storage outside the event handler must be used. The implementation might look like below.

```
globally declare the counter K and the integer T.

OnKeyEnter(character C)

{

    convert C to a number N

    if K is zero store N in T and increment K

    otherwise add N to T, print the result and reset K to zero

}
```

While keeping track of history is straightforward in a batch program, it requires special attention and planning in an event-driven program.

Exception Handlers

In PL/1, even though a program itself may not be predominantly event-driven, certain abnormal events such as a hardware error, overflow or "program checks" may occur that possibly prevent further processing. Exception handlers may be provided by "ON statements" in (unseen) callers to provide housekeeping routines to clean up afterwards before termination.

Creating Event Handlers

The first step in developing an event-driven program is to write a series of subroutines, or methods, called event-handler routines. These routines handle the events to which the main program will respond. For example, a single left-button mouse-click on a command button in a GUI program may trigger a routine that will open another window, save data to a database or exit the application. Many modern-day programming environments provide the programmer with event templates, allowing the programmer to focus on writing the event code.

The second step is to bind event handlers to events so that the correct function is called when the event takes place. Graphical editors combine the first two steps: double-click on a button, and the editor creates an (empty) event handler associated with the user clicking the button and opens a text window so you can edit the event handler.

The third step in developing an event-driven program is to write the main loop. This is a function that checks for the occurrence of events, and then calls the matching event handler to process it. Most event-driven programming environments already provide this main loop, so it need not be specifically provided by the application programmer. RPG, an early programming language from IBM, whose 1960s design concept was similar to event-driven programming discussed above, provided a built-in main I/O loop (known as the "program cycle") where the calculations responded in accordance to 'indicators' (flags) that were set earlier in the cycle.

Common Uses

Most of existing GUI development tools and architectures rely on event-driven programming.

In addition, systems such as Node.js are also event-driven.

Criticism

The design of those programs which rely on event-action model has been criticised, and it has been suggested that event-action model leads programmers to create error prone, difficult to extend and excessively complex application code. Table-driven state machines have been advocated as a viable alternative. On the other hand, table-driven state machines themselves suffer from significant weaknesses including "state explosion" phenomenon.

Stackless Threading

An event-driven approach is used in hardware description languages. A thread context only needs a CPU stack while actively processing an event, once done the CPU can move on to process other event-driven threads, which allows an extremely large number of threads to be handled. This is essentially a finite-state machine approach.

Comparison of Multi-paradigm Programming Languages

Programming languages can be grouped by the number and types of paradigms supported.

Criticism

Some programming language researchers criticise the notion of paradigms as a classification of programming languages, e.g. Krishnamurthi. They argue that many programming languages cannot be strictly classified into one paradigm, but rather include features from several paradigms. This is clearly demonstrated in the table below (which is silent on the level of support of different 'paradigms').

Paradigm Summaries

A concise reference for the programming paradigms are listed.

- Concurrent programming – have language constructs for concurrency, these may involve multi-threading, support for distributed computing, message passing, shared resources (including shared memory), or futures.

  - Actor programming – concurrent computation with *actors* that make local decisions in response to the environment (capable of selfish or competitive behavior).

- Constraint programming – relations between variables are expressed as constraints (or constraint networks), directing allowable solutions (uses constraint satisfaction or simplex algorithm).

- Dataflow programming – forced recalculation of formulas when data values change (e.g. spreadsheets).

- Declarative programming – describes actions (e.g. HTML describes a page but not how to actually display it).

- Distributed programming – have support for multiple autonomous computers that communicate via computer networks.

- Functional programming – uses evaluation of mathematical functions and avoids state and mutable data.

- Generic programming – uses algorithms written in terms of to-be-specified-later types that are then instantiated as needed for specific types provided as parameters.

- Imperative programming – explicit statements that change a program state.

- Logic programming – uses explicit mathematical logic for programming.

- Metaprogramming – writing programs that write or manipulate other programs (or themselves) as their data, or that do part of the work at compile time that would otherwise be done at runtime.

  o Template metaprogramming – metaprogramming methods in which templates are used by a compiler to generate temporary source code, which is merged by the compiler with the rest of the source code and then compiled.

  o Reflective programming – metaprogramming methods in which a program modifies or extends itself.

- Object-oriented programming – uses data structures consisting of data fields and methods together with their interactions (objects) to design programs.

  o Class-based – object-oriented programming in which inheritance is achieved by defining classes of objects, versus the objects themselves.

  o Prototype-based – object-oriented programming that avoids classes and implements inheritance via cloning of instances.

- Pipeline programming – a simple syntax change to add syntax to nest function calls to language originally designed with none.

- Rule-based programming – a network of rules of thumb that comprise a knowledge base and can be used for expert systems and problem deduction & resolution.

- Visual programming – manipulating program elements graphically rather than by specifying them textually (e.g. Simulink); also termed *diagrammatic programming*.

References

- Michael A. Covington (2010-08-23). "CSCI/ARTI 4540/6540: First Lecture on Symbolic Programming and LISP" (PDF). University of Georgia. Retrieved 2013-11-20

- Ross, Doug. "The first software engineering language". LCS/AI Lab Timeline:. MIT Computer Science and Artificial Intelligence Laboratory. Retrieved 13 May 2010

- Dahl, Ole Johan (2004). "The Birth of Object Orientation: the Simula Languages" (PDF). doi:10.1007/978-3-540-39993-3_3. Retrieved 9 June 2016

- Nørmark, Kurt. Overview of the four main programming paradigms. Aalborg University, 9 May 2011. Retrieved 22 September 2012

- "Automata-based programming" (PDF). Scientific and Technical Journal of Information Technologies, Mechanics and Optics (53). 2008

- Vivek Gupta, Ethan Jackson, Shaz Qadeer and Sriram Rajamani. "P: Safe Asynchronous Event-Driven Programming". Retrieved 20 February 2017

- John C. Mitchell, Concepts in programming languages, Cambridge University Press, 2003, ISBN 0-521-78098-5, p.278.

- Gabe Stein (August 2013). "How an Arcane Coding Method From 1970s Banking Software Could Save the Sanity of Web Developers Everywhere". Retrieved 24 January 2016

- Peter Van Roy (2009-05-12). "Programming Paradigms for Dummies: What Every Programmer Should Know" (PDF). info.ucl.ac.be. Retrieved 2014-01-27

- Kindler, E.; Krivy, I. (2011). "Object-Oriented Simulation of systems with sophisticated control". International Journal of General Systems: 313–343

- Lewis, John; Loftus, William (2008). Java Software Solutions Foundations of Programming Design 6th ed. Pearson Education Inc. ISBN 0-321-53205-8. , section 1.6 "Object-Oriented Programming"

Widely Used Programming Languages

Certain programming languages are extensively used worldwide by programmers due to their accessibility, availability or ease-of-usage. This chapter sheds light on some prominent programming languages like C++, Java, Python and the C programming language for a thorough understanding of the subject matter.

C Programming Language

C is a general-purpose, high-level language that was originally developed by Dennis M. Ritchie to develop the UNIX operating system at Bell Labs. C was originally first implemented on the DEC PDP-11 computer in 1972.

In 1978, Brian Kernighan and Dennis Ritchie produced the first publicly available description of C, now known as the K&R standard.

The UNIX operating system, the C compiler, and essentially all UNIX application programs have been written in C. C has now become a widely used professional language for various reasons:

- Easy to learn.
- Structured language.
- It produces efficient programs.
- It can handle low-level activities.
- It can be compiled on a variety of computer platforms.

Facts About C

- C was invented to write an operating system called UNIX.
- C is a successor of B language which was introduced around the early 1970s.
- The language was formalized in 1988 by the American National Standard Institute (ANSI).
- The UNIX OS was totally written in C.
- Today C is the most widely used and popular System Programming Language.
- Most of the state-of-the-art software have been implemented using C.
- Today's most popular Linux OS and RDBMS MySQL have been written in C.

Reasons to use C

C was initially used for system development work, particularly the programs that make-up the operating system. C was adopted as a system development language because it produces code that runs nearly as fast as the code written in assembly language. Some examples of the use of C might be:

- Operating Systems
- Language Compilers
- Assemblers
- Text Editors
- Print Spoolers
- Network Drivers
- Modern Programs
- Databases
- Language Interpreters
- Utilities

C Programs

A C program can vary from 3 lines to millions of lines and it should be written into one or more text files with extension ".c"; for example, hello.c. You can use "vi", "vim" or any other text editor to write your C program into a file.

Local Environment Setup

If you want to set up your environment for C programming language, you need the following two software tools available on your computer, (a) Text Editor and (b) The C Compiler.

Text Editor

This will be used to type your program. Examples of a few editors include Windows Notepad, OS Edit command, Brief, Epsilon, EMACS, and vim or vi.

The name and version of text editors can vary on different operating systems. For example, Notepad will be used on Windows, and vim or vi can be used on Windows as well as on Linux or UNIX.

The files you create with your editor are called the source files and they contain the program source codes. The source files for C programs are typically named with the extension ".c".

Before starting your programming, make sure you have one text editor in place and you have enough experience to write a computer program, save it in a file, compile it and finally execute it.

The C Compiler

The source code written in source file is the human readable source for your program. It needs to be "compiled" into machine language so that your CPU can actually execute the program as per the instructions given.

The compiler compiles the source codes into final executable programs. The most frequently used and free available compiler is the GNU C/C++ compiler, otherwise you can have compilers either from HP or Solaris if you have the respective operating systems.

Installation on UNIX/Linux

If you are using Linux or UNIX, then check whether GCC is installed on your system by entering the following command from the command line:

```
$ gcc -v
```

If you have GNU compiler installed on your machine, then it should print a message as follows:

```
Using built-in specs.

Target: i386-redhat-linux

Configured with: ../configure --prefix=/usr .......

Thread model: posix

gcc version 4.1.2 20080704 (Red Hat 4.1.2-46)
```

If GCC is not installed, then you will have to install it yourself using the detailed instruction.

Installation on Mac OS

If you use Mac OS X, the easiest way to obtain GCC is to download the Xcode development environment from Apple's web site and follow the simple installation instructions. Once you have Xcode setup, you will be able to use GNU compiler for C/C++.

Installation on Windows

To install GCC on Windows, you need to install MinGW. To install MinGW, go to the MinGW homepage, www.mingw.org, and follow the link to the MinGW download page. Download the latest version of the MinGW installation program, which should be named MinGW-<version>.exe.

While installing Min GW, at a minimum, you must install gcc-core, gcc-g++, binutils, and the MinGW runtime, but you may wish to install more.

Add the bin subdirectory of your MinGW installation to your PATHenvironment variable, so that you can specify these tools on the command line by their simple names.

After the installation is complete, you will be able to run gcc, g++, ar, ranlib, dlltool, and several other GNU tools from the Windows command line.

Program Structure

Hello World Example

A C program basically consists of the following parts:

- Preprocessor Commands
- Functions
- Variables
- Statements & Expressions
- Comments

Let us look at a simple code that would print the words "Hello World":

```
#include <stdio.h>


int main() {

   /* my first program in C */

   printf("Hello, World! \n");


   return 0;

}
```

Let us take a look at the various parts of the above program:

- The first line of the program *#include <stdio.h>* is a preprocessor command, which tells a C compiler to include stdio.h file before going to actual compilation.
- The next line *int main()* is the main function where the program execution begins.
- The next line /*...*/ will be ignored by the compiler and it has been put to add additional comments in the program. So such lines are called comments in the program.
- The next line *printf(...)* is another function available in C which causes the message "Hello, World!" to be displayed on the screen.
- The next line return 0; terminates the main() function and returns the value 0.

Compile and Execute C Program

Let us see how to save the source code in a file, and how to compile and run it. Following are the simple steps:

- Open a text editor and add the above-mentioned code.

- Save the file as *hello.c.*

- Open a command prompt and go to the directory where you have saved the file.

- Type *gcc hello.c* and press enter to compile your code.

- If there are no errors in your code, the command prompt will take you to the next line and would generate *a.out* executable file.

- Now, type *a.out* to execute your program.

- You will see the output *"Hello World"* printed on the screen.

```
$ gcc hello.c

$ ./a.out

Hello, World!
```

Make sure the gcc compiler is in your path and that you are running it in the directory containing the source file hello.c.

Basic Syntax

Tokens in C

A C program consists of various tokens and a token is either a keyword, an identifier, a constant, a string literal, or a symbol. For example, the following C statement consists of five tokens:

```
printf("Hello, World! \n");
```

The individual tokens are:

```
printf

(

"Hello, World! \n"

)

;
```

Semicolons

In a C program, the semicolon is a statement terminator. That is, each individual statement must be ended with a semicolon. It indicates the end of one logical entity.

Given below are two different statements:

```
printf("Hello, World! \n");

return 0;
```

Comments

Comments are like helping text in your C program and they are ignored by the compiler. They start with /* and terminate with the characters */ as shown below:

```
/* my first program in C */
```

You cannot have comments within comments and they do not occur within a string or character literals.

Identifiers

A C identifier is a name used to identify a variable, function, or any other user-defined item. An identifier starts with a letter A to Z, a to z, or an underscore '_' followed by zero or more letters, underscores, and digits (0 to 9).

C does not allow punctuation characters such as @, $, and % within identifiers. C is a case-sensitive programming language. Thus, *Manpower* and *manpower* are two different identifiers in C. Here are some examples of acceptable identifiers:

```
mohd     zara   abc   move_name a_123

myname50  _temp  j   a23b9   retVal
```

Keywords

The following list shows the reserved words in C. These reserved words may not be used as constants or variables or any other identifier names.

auto	else	long	switch
break	enum	register	typedef
case	extern	return	union
char	float	short	unsigned
const	for	signed	void
continue	goto	sizeof	volatile
default	if	static	while
do	int	struct	_Packed
double			

Whitespace in C

A line containing only whitespace, possibly with a comment, is known as a blank line, and a C compiler totally ignores it.

Whitespace is the term used in C to describe blanks, tabs, newline characters and comments. Whitespace separates one part of a statement from another and enables the compiler to identify where one element in a statement, such as int, ends and the next element begins. Therefore, in the following statement –

```
int age;
```

there must be at least one whitespace character (usually a space) between int and age for the compiler to be able to distinguish them. On the other hand, in the following statement –

```
fruit = apples + oranges;   // get the total fruit
```

no whitespace characters are necessary between fruit and =, or between = and apples, although you are free to include some if you wish to increase readability.

Benefits of C Language

1. As a middle level language, C combines the features of both high level and low level languages. It can be used for low-level programming, such as scripting for drivers and kernels and it also supports functions of high level programming languages, such as scripting for software applications etc.

2. C is a structured programming language which allows a complex program to be broken into simpler programs called functions. It also allows free movement of data across these functions.

3. Various features of C including direct access to machine level hardware APIs, presence of C compilers, deterministic resource use and dynamic memory allocation make C language an optimum choice for scripting applications and drivers of embedded systems.

4. C language is case-sensitive which means lowercase and uppercase letters are treated differently.

5. C is highly portable and is used for scripting system applications which form a major part of Windows, UNIX and Linux operating system.

6. C is a general purpose programming language and can efficiently work on enterprise applications, games, graphics, and applications requiring calculations etc.

7. C language has a rich library which provides a number of built-in functions. It also offers dynamic memory allocation.

8. C implements algorithms and data structures swiftly, facilitating faster computations in programs. This has enabled the use of C in applications requiring higher degrees of calculations like MATLAB and Mathematica.

Disadvantages of C Language

1. C does not have concept of OOPs, that's why C++ is developed.

2. There is no runtime checking in C language.

3. There is no strict type checking. For example, we can pass an integer value.

4. for the floating data type.

5. C doesn't have the concept of namespace.

6. C doesn't have the concept of constructor or destructor.

C++ is an enhanced C language typically used for object oriented programming. It traces its origins back well over thirty years. Although it's far from the oldest computer language, it's one of the older ones that is in common usage today – so you might say it gets an A for its ability to adapt to changing technological times.

C++ was developed by Bjarne Stroustrup, who did the first development work as part of his PhD project. During the early years, he called the language "C with Classes". He had begun developing a new language because he felt that no existing language was ideal for large scale projects. Later, when he was working at AT&T Bell Labs, he again felt limited. He dusted off his "C with Classes" and added features of other languages. Simula had a strong influence; AlLGOL 68 played a role. Ultimately, a lot more than classes got added: virtual functions, templates, and operator overloading. *C++has influenced later languages like PHP, Java, and (not surprisingly) C# (C-Sharp).*

C++ has grown far beyond a one man operation. The name actually came from another developer, Rick Mascitti. It was partly a play on the name of the "++" operator and partly a reference to the enhancement.

The language was first standardized in 1998. Standards were again issued in 2003, 2007, and 2011. C++ is maintained by the ISO, a large standards committee. The current version is C++11. the biggest improvement is in abstraction mechanisms. Among the other goals of the most recent revision: to make C++ a better language for embedded systems and to better support novices.

Development has been guided by certain ideals. C++ strives to be portable; there is an attempt to avoid reliance on features that are platform-dependent.

Goals of the most recent revision include: to make C++ a better language for embedded systems and to better support novices. The standard, of course, isn't all there is; there are libraries that exist outside it.

Syntax and Structure of C++ Program

Here we will discuss one simple and basic C++ program to print "Hello this is C++" and its structure in parts with details and uses.

First C++ Program

```
#include <iostream.h>

using namespace std;

int main()

{

cout << "Hello this is C++";

}
```

Header files are included at the beginning just like in C program. Here iostream is a header file which provides us with input & output streams. Header files contained predeclared function libraries, which can be used by users for their ease.

Using namespace std, tells the compiler to use standard namespace. Namespace collects identifiers used for class, object and variables. NameSpace can be used by two ways in a program, either by the use of using statement at the beginning, like we did in above mentioned program or by using name of namespace as prefix before the identifier with scope resolution (::) operator.

Example: `std::cout << "A";`

main(), is the function which holds the executing part of program its return type is int.

cout <<, is used to print anything on screen, same as printf in C language. cin and cout are same as scanf and printf, only difference is that you do not need to mention format specifiers like, %d for int etc, in cout & cin.

Comments

For single line comments, use // before mentioning comment, like:

```
cout<<"single line";   // This is single line comment
```

For multiple line comment, enclose the comment between /* and */

```
/*this is

 a multiple line

 comment */
```

Using Classes

Classes name must start with capital letter, and they contain data variables and member functions.

```
class Abc

{

 int i;        //data variable

 void display()      //Member Function

  {

   cout<<"Inside Member Function";

  }

}; // Class ends here


int main()

{

 Abc obj; // Creatig Abc class's object

 obj.display(); //Calling member function using class object

}
```

This is how class is defined, its object is created and the member functions are used.

Variables can be declared anywhere in the entire program, but must be declared, before they are used. Hence, we don't need to declare variable at the start of the program.

Variables

Variable are used in C++, where we need storage for any value, which will change in program. Variable can be declared in multiple ways each with different memory requirements and functioning. Variable is the name of memory location allocated by the compiler depending upon the datatype of the variable.

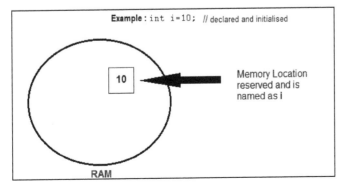

Basic Types of Variables

Each variable while declaration must be given a datatype, on which the memory assigned to the variable depends. Following are the basic types of variables,

`bool`	For variable to store boolean values(True or False)
`char`	For variables to store character types.
`int`	for variable with integral values
`float` and `double` are also types for variables with large and floating point values	

Declaration and Initialization

Variable must be declared before they are used. Usually it is preferred to declare them at the starting of the program, but in C++ they can be declared in the middle of program too, but must be done before using them.

Example:

```
int i;    // declared but not initialised

char c;

int i, j, k; // Multiple declaration
```

Initialization means assigning value to an already declared variable,

```
int i;   // declaration

i = 10; // initialization
```

Initialization and declaration can be done in one single step also,

```
int i=10;      //initialization and declaration in same step

int i=10, j=11;
```

If a variable is declared and not initialized by default it will hold a garbage value. Also, if a variable is once declared and if try to declare it again, we will get a compile time error.

```
int i,j;

i=10;

j=20;

int j=i+j;  //compile time error, cannot redeclare a variable in same scope
```

Scope of Variables

All the variables have their area of functioning, and out of that boundary they don't hold their value, this boundary is called scope of the variable. For most of the cases its between the curly braces,in which variable is declared that a variable exists, not outside it. We can broadly divide variables into two main types:

- Global Variables
- Local variables

Global Variables

Global variables are those, which ar once declared and can be used throughout the lifetime of the program by any class or any function. They must be declared outside the main() function. If only declared, they can be assigned different values at different time in program lifetime. But even if they are declared and initialized at the same time outside the main() function, then also they can be assigned any value at any point in the program.

Example: Only declared, not initialized

```
include <iostream>

using namespace std;

int x;          // Global variable declared

int main()

{

 x=10;             // Initialized once

 cout <<"first value of x = "<< x;

 x=20;           // Initialized again

 cout <<"Initialized again with value = "<< x;

}
```

Local Variables

Local variables are the variables which exist only between the curly braces, in which its declared. Outside that they are unavailable and leads to compile time error.

Example:

```
include <iostream>

using namespace std;

int main()

{

 int i=10;

 if(i<20)      // if condition scope starts
```

```
{
  int n=100;   // Local variable declared and initialized
}         // if condition scope ends
 cout << n;   // Compile time error, n not available here
}
```

Some Special Types of Variable

There are also some special keywords, to impart unique characteristics to the variables in the program.

1. Final - Once initialized, its value cant be changed.

2. Static - These variables holds their value between function calls.

Example :

```
#include <iostream.h>
using namespace std;
int main()
{
 final int i=10;
 static int y=20;
}
```

Operators in C++

Operators are special type of functions, that takes one or more arguments and produces a new value. For example : addition (+), substraction (-), multiplication (*) etc, are all operators. Operators are used to perform various operations on variables and constants.

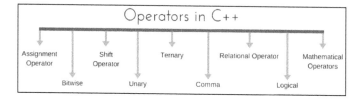

Types of Operators

1. Assignment Operator

2. Mathematical Operators

3. Relational Operators

4. Logical Operators

5. Bitwise Operators

6. Shift Operators

7. Unary Operators

8. Ternary Operator

9. Comma Operator

Assignment Operator (=)

Operates '=' is used for assignment, it takes the right-hand side (called rvalue) and copy it into the left-hand side (called lvalue). Assignment operator is the only operator which can be overloaded but cannot be inherited.

Mathematical Operators

There are operators used to perform basic mathematical operations. Addition (+), subtraction (-), diversion (/) multiplication (*) and modulus (%) are the basic mathematical operators. Modulus operator cannot be used with floating-point numbers.

C++ and C also use a shorthand notation to perform an operation and assignment at same type. *Example,*

```
int x=10;

x += 4 // will add 4 to 10, and hence assign 14 to X

x -= 5 // will subtract 5 from 10 and assign 5 to x
```

Relational Operators

These operators establish a relationship between operands. The relational operators are : less than (<) , grater thatn (>) , less than or equal to (<=), greater than equal to (>=), equivalent (==) and not equivalent (!=).

You must notice that assignment operator is (=) and there is a relational operator, for equivalent (==). These two are different from each other, the assignment operator assigns the value to any variable, whereas equivalent operator is used to compare values, like in if-else conditions, *Example:*

```
int x = 10; //assignment operator

x=5;      // again assignment operator

if(x == 5)  // here we have used equivalent relational operator, for com-
parison

{
```

```
cout <<"Successfully compared";

}
```

Logical Operators

The logical operators are AND (&&) and OR (||). They are used to combine two different expressions together.

If two statement are connected using AND operator, the validity of both statements will be considered, but if they are connected using OR operator, then either one of them must be valid. These operators are mostly used in loops (especially while loop) and in Decision making.

Bitwise Operators

There are used to change individual bits into a number. They work with only integral data types like char, int and long and not with floating point values.

* Bitwise AND operators &.

* Bitwise OR operator |.

* And bitwise XOR operator ^.

* And, bitwise NOT operator ~.

They can be used as shorthand notation too, & = , |= , ^= , ~= etc.

Shift Operators

Shift Operators are used to shift Bits of any variable. It is of three types,

1. Left Shift Operator <<.

2. Right Shift Operator >>.

3. Unsigned Right Shift Operator >>>.

Unary Operators

These are the operators which work on only one operand. There are many unary operators, but increment ++ and decrement -- operators are most used.

Other Unary Operators : address of &, dereference *, new and delete, bitwise not ~, logical not !, unary minus - and unary plus +.

Ternary Operator

The ternary if-else ? : is an operator which has three operands.

```
int a = 10;

a > 5 ? cout << "true" : cout << "false"
```

Comma Operator

This is used to separate variable names and to separate expressions. In case of expressions, the value of last expression is produced and used.

Example :

```
int a,b,c; // variables declaration using comma operator

a=b++, c++; // a = c++ will be done.
```

Size of Operator in C++

Size of is also an operator not a function, it is used to get information about the amount of memory allocated for data types & Objects. It can be used to get size of user defined data types too.

size of operator can be used with and without parentheses. If you apply it to a variable you can use it without parentheses.

```
cout << sizeOf(double);   //Will print size of double

int x = 2;

int i = sizeOf x;
```

Typedef Operator

Typedef is a keyword used in C language to assign alternative names to existing types. Its mostly used with user defined data types, when names of data types get slightly complicated. Following is the general syntax for using typedef,

```
typedef existing_name alias_name
```

Lets take an example and see how typedef actually works.

```
typedef unsigned long ulong;
```

The above statement define a term ulong for an unsigned long type. Now this ulong identifier can be used to define unsigned long type variables.

```
ulong i, j;
```

Typedef and Pointers

Typedef can be used to give an alias name to pointers also. Here we have a case in which use of typedef is beneficial during pointer declaration.

In Pointers * binds to the right and not the left.

```
int* x, y ;
```

By this declaration statement, we are actually declaring **x** as a pointer of type int, whereas **y** will be declared as a plain integer.

```
typedef int* IntPtr ;

IntPtr x, y, z;
```

But if we use typedef like in above example, we can declare any number of pointers in a single statement.

Real-world Applications of C++

Games

C++ overrides the complexities of 3D games, optimizes resource management and facilitates multiplayer with networking. The language is extremely fast, allows procedural programming for CPU intensive functions and provides greater control over hardware, because of which it has been widely used in development of gaming engines. For instance, the science fiction game Doom 3 is cited as an example of a game that used C++ well and the Unreal Engine, a suite of game development tools, is written in C++.

Graphic User Interface (GUI) Based Applications

Many highly used applications, such as Image Ready, Adobe Premier, Photoshop and Illustrator, are scripted in C++.

Web Browsers

With the introduction of specialized languages such as PHP and Java, the adoption of C++ is limited for scripting of websites and web applications. However, where speed and reliability are required, C++ is still preferred. For instance, a part of Google's back-end is coded in C++, and the rendering engine of a few open source projects, such as web browser Mozilla Firefox and email client Mozilla Thunderbird, are also scripted in the programming language.

Advance Computations and Graphics

C++ provides the means for building applications requiring real-time physical simulations, high-performance image processing, and mobile sensor applications. Maya 3D software, used for integrated 3D modeling, visual effects and animation, is coded in C++.

Database Software

C++ and C have been used for scripting MySQL, one of the most popular database management software. The software forms the backbone of a variety of database-based enterprises, such as Google, Wikipedia, Yahoo and YouTube etc.

Operating Systems

C++ forms an integral part of many of the prevalent operating systems including Apple's OS X and various versions of Microsoft Windows, and the erstwhile Symbian mobile OS.

Enterprise Software

C++ finds a purpose in banking and trading enterprise applications, such as those deployed by Bloomberg and Reuters. It is also used in development of advanced software, such as flight simulators and radar processing.

Medical and Engineering Applications

Many advanced medical equipments, such as MRI machines, use C++ language for scripting their software. It is also part of engineering applications, such as high-end CAD/CAM systems.

Compilers

A host of compilers including Apple C++, Bloodshed Dev-C++, Clang C++ and MINGW make use of C++ language. C and its successor C++ are leveraged for diverse software and platform development requirements, from operating systems to graphic designing applications. Further, these languages have assisted in the development of new languages for special purposes like C#, Java, PHP, Verilog etc.

Java

Java programming language was originally developed by Sun Microsystems which was initiated by James Gosling and released in 1995 as core component of Sun Microsystems' Java platform (Java 1.0 [J2SE]).

The latest release of the Java Standard Edition is Java SE 8. With the advancement of Java and its widespread popularity, multiple configurations were built to suit various types of platforms. For example: J2EE for Enterprise Applications, J2ME for Mobile Applications.

The new J2 versions were renamed as Java SE, Java EE, and Java ME respectively. Java is guaranteed to be Write Once, Run Anywhere.

Java is:

- Object oriented – In Java, everything is an Object. Java can be easily extended since it is based on the Object model.

- Platform independent – Unlike many other programming languages including C and C++, when Java is compiled, it is not compiled into platform specific machine, rather into platform independent byte code. This byte code is distributed over the web and interpreted by the Virtual Machine (JVM) on whichever platform it is being run on.

- Simple – Java is designed to be easy to learn. If you understand the basic concept of OOP Java, it would be easy to master.

- Secure – With Java's secure feature it enables to develop virus-free, tamper-free systems. Authentication techniques are based on public-key encryption.

- Architecture-neutral – Java compiler generates an architecture-neutral object file format, which makes the compiled code executable on many processors, with the presence of Java runtime system.

- Portable – Being architecture-neutral and having no implementation dependent aspects of the specification makes Java portable. Compiler in Java is written in ANSI C with a clean portability boundary, which is a POSIX subset.

- Robust – Java makes an effort to eliminate error prone situations by emphasizing mainly on compile time error checking and runtime checking.

- Multithreaded – With Java's multithreaded feature it is possible to write programs that can perform many tasks simultaneously. This design feature allows the developers to construct interactive applications that can run smoothly.

- Interpreted – Java byte code is translated on the fly to native machine instructions and is not stored anywhere. The development process is more rapid and analytical since the linking is an incremental and light-weight process.

- High performance – With the use of Just-In-Time compilers, Java enables high performance.

- Distributed – Java is designed for the distributed environment of the internet.

- Dynamic – Java is considered to be more dynamic than C or C++ since it is designed to adapt to an evolving environment. Java programs can carry extensive amount of run-time information that can be used to verify and resolve accesses to objects on run-time.

Tools you will Need

For performing the examples discussed in this tutorial, you will need a Pentium 200-MHz computer with a minimum of 64 MB of RAM (128 MB of RAM recommended).

You will also need the following softwares:

- Linux 7.1 or Windows xp/7/8 operating system.

- Java JDK 8.

- Microsoft Notepad or any other text editor.

Local Environment Setup

If you are still willing to set up your environment for Java programming language, then this section guides you on how to download and set up Java on your machine. Following are the steps to set up the environment.

Follow the instructions to download Java and run the .exe to install Java on your machine. Once you installed Java on your machine, you will need to set environment variables to point to correct installation directories.

Setting up the Path for Windows

Assuming you have installed Java in *c:\Program Files\java\jdk* directory:

- Right-click on 'My Computer' and select 'Properties'.

- Click the 'Environment variables' button under the 'Advanced' tab.

- Now, alter the 'Path' variable so that it also contains the path to the Java executable. Example, if the path is currently set to 'C:\WINDOWS\SYSTEM32', then change your path to read 'C:\WINDOWS\SYSTEM32;c:\Program Files\java\jdk\bin'.

Setting up the Path for Linux, UNIX, Solaris, FreeBSD

Environment variable PATH should be set to point to where the Java binaries have been installed. Refer to your shell documentation, if you have trouble doing this.

Example, if you use *bash* as your shell, then you would add the following line to the end of your '.bashrc: export PATH = /path/to/java:$PATH'

Popular Java Editors

To write your Java programs, you will need a text editor. There are even more sophisticated IDEs available in the market. But for now, you can consider one of the following:

- Notepad – On Windows machine, you can use any simple text editor like Notepad (Recommended for this tutorial), TextPad.

- Netbeans – A Java IDE that is open-source and free.

- Eclipse – A Java IDE developed by the eclipse open-source community.

When we consider a Java program, it can be defined as a collection of objects that communicate via invoking each other's methods. Let us now briefly look into what do class, object, methods, and instance variables mean.

- Object – Objects have states and behaviors. Example: A dog has states - color, name, breed as well as behavior such as wagging their tail, barking, eating. An object is an instance of a class.

- Class – A class can be defined as a template/blueprint that describes the behavior/state that the object of its type supports.

- Methods – A method is basically a behavior. A class can contain many methods. It is in methods where the logics are written, data is manipulated and all the actions are executed.

- Instance Variables – Each object has its unique set of instance variables. An object's state is created by the values assigned to these instance variables.

First Java Program

Let us look at a simple code that will print the words *Hello World.*

Example:

```
public class MyFirstJavaProgram {


  /* This is my first java program.
   * This will print 'Hello World' as the output
   */



  public static void main(String []args) {
    System.out.println("Hello World"); // prints Hello World
  }

}
```

Let's look at how to save the file, compile, and run the program. Please follow the subsequent steps:

- Open notepad and add the code as above.
- Save the file as: MyFirstJavaProgram.java.
- Open a command prompt window and go to the directory where you saved the class. Assume it's C:\.
- Type 'javac MyFirstJavaProgram.java' and press enter to compile your code. If there are no errors in your code, the command prompt will take you to the next line (Assumption : The path variable is set).
- Now, type ' java MyFirstJavaProgram ' to run your program.
- You will be able to see ' Hello World ' printed on the window.

Output

```
C:\> javac MyFirstJavaProgram.java

C:\> java MyFirstJavaProgram

Hello World
```

Basic Syntax

About Java programs, it is very important to keep in mind the following points.

- Case Sensitivity – Java is case sensitive, which means identifier Hello and hello would have different meaning in Java.
- Class Names – For all class names the first letter should be in Upper Case. If several words are used to form a name of the class, each inner word's first letter should be in Upper Case.

Example: *class MyFirstJavaClass.*

- Method Names – All method names should start with a Lower Case letter. If several words are used to form the name of the method, then each inner word's first letter should be in Upper Case.

  Example: *public void myMethodName().*

- Program File Name – Name of the program file should exactly match the class name.

  When saving the file, you should save it using the class name (Remember Java is case sensitive) and append '.java' to the end of the name (if the file name and the class name do not match, your program will not compile).

  Example: Assume 'MyFirstJavaProgram' is the class name. Then the file should be saved as *'MyFirstJavaProgram.java'.*

- Public static void main(String args[]) – Java program processing starts from the main() method which is a mandatory part of every Java program.

Java Identifiers

All Java components require names. Names used for classes, variables, and methods are called identifiers.

In Java, there are several points to remember about identifiers. They are as follows:

- All identifiers should begin with a letter (A to Z or a to z), currency character ($) or an underscore (_).
- After the first character, identifiers can have any combination of characters.
- A key word cannot be used as an identifier.
- Most importantly, identifiers are case sensitive.
- Examples of legal identifiers: age, $salary, _value, ___1_value.
- Examples of illegal identifiers: 123abc, -salary.

Java Modifiers

Like other languages, it is possible to modify classes, methods, etc., by using modifiers. There are two categories of modifiers:

- Access Modifiers – default, public , protected, private.
- Non-access Modifiers – final, abstract, strictfp.

Java Variables

Following are the types of variables in Java:

- Local Variables.

- Class Variables (Static Variables).

- Instance Variables (Non-static Variables).

Java Arrays

Arrays are objects that store multiple variables of the same type. However, an array itself is an object on the heap. We will look into how to declare, construct, and initialize in the upcoming chapters.

Java Enums

Enums were introduced in Java 5.0. Enums restrict a variable to have one of only a few predefined values. The values in this enumerated list are called enums.

With the use of enums it is possible to reduce the number of bugs in your code.

For example, if we consider an application for a fresh juice shop, it would be possible to restrict the glass size to small, medium, and large. This would make sure that it would not allow anyone to order any size other than small, medium, or large.

Example:

```
class FreshJuice {

  enum FreshJuiceSize{ SMALL, MEDIUM, LARGE }

  FreshJuiceSize size;

}


public class FreshJuiceTest {


  public static void main(String args[]) {

   FreshJuice juice = new FreshJuice();

   juice.size = FreshJuice.FreshJuiceSize.MEDIUM ;

   System.out.println("Size: " + juice.size);

  }

}
```

The above example will produce the following result:

Output:

```
Size: MEDIUM
```

Note – Enums can be declared as their own or inside a class. Methods, variables, constructors can be defined inside enums as well.

Java Keywords

The following list shows the reserved words in Java. These reserved words may not be used as constant or variable or any other identifier names.

abstract	assert	boolean	break
byte	case	catch	char
class	const	continue	default
do	double	else	enum
extends	final	finally	float
for	goto	if	implements
import	instanceof	int	interface
long	native	new	package
private	protected	public	return
short	static	strictfp	super
switch	synchronized	this	throw
throws	transient	try	void
volatile	while		

Comments in Java

Java supports single-line and multi-line comments very similar to C and C++. All characters available inside any comment are ignored by Java compiler.

Example

```
public class MyFirstJavaProgram {


    /* This is my first java program.

    * This will print 'Hello World' as the output

    * This is an example of multi-line comments.

    */


    public static void main(String []args) {

        // This is an example of single line comment
```

```
        /* This is also an example of single line comment. */

        System.out.println("Hello World");

    }

}
```

Output:

```
    Hello World
```

Using Blank Lines

A line containing only white space, possibly with a comment, is known as a blank line, and Java totally ignores it.

Inheritance

In Java, classes can be derived from classes. Basically, if you need to create a new class and here is already a class that has some of the code you require, then it is possible to derive your new class from the already existing code.

This concept allows you to reuse the fields and methods of the existing class without having to rewrite the code in a new class. In this scenario, the existing class is called the superclass and the derived class is called the subclass.

Interfaces

In Java language, an interface can be defined as a contract between objects on how to communicate with each other. Interfaces play a vital role when it comes to the concept of inheritance.

An interface defines the methods, a deriving class (subclass) should use. But the implementation of the methods is totally up to the subclass.

Applications of Java

Every enterprise uses Java in one way or other. As per Oracle, more than 3 billion devices run applications designed on the development platform. Java is used to design the following applications:

- Desktop GUI applications.

- Embedded systems.

- Web applications, including eCommerce applications, front and back office electronic trading systems, settlement and confirmation systems, data processing projects, and more.

- Web servers and application servers.

- Mobile applications including Android applications.

- Enterprise applications.

- Scientific applications.
- Middleware products.

Advantages of Java

- Java offers higher cross- functionality and portability as programs written in one platform can run across desktops, mobiles, embedded systems.
- Java is free, simple, object-oriented, distributed, supports multithreading and offers multimedia and network support.
- Java is a mature language, therefore more stable and predictable. The Java Class Library enables cross-platform development.
- Being highly popular at enterprise, embedded and network level, Java has a large active user community and support available.
- Unlike C and C++, Java programs are compiled independent of platform in *byte-code*language which allows the same program to run on any machine that has a JVM installed.
- Java has powerful development tools like Eclipse SDK and NetBeans which have debugging capability and offer integrated development environment.
- Increasing language diversity, evidenced by compatibility of Java with Scala, Groovy, JRuby, and Clojure.
- Relatively seamless forward compatibility from one version to the next.

Disadvantages of Java

- Performance: SIgnificantly slower and more memory-consuming than natively compiled languages such as C or C++.
- Look and feel: The default look and feel of GUI applications written in Java using the Swing toolkit is very different from native applications.
- Single-paradigm language: The addition of static imports in Java 5.0 the procedural paradigm is better accommodated than in earlier versions of Java.

Python

Python is a general-purpose language. It has wide range of applications from Web development (like: Django and Bottle), scientific and mathematical computing (Orange, SymPy, NumPy) to desktop graphical user Interfaces (Pygame, Panda3D).

The syntax of the language is clean and length of the code is relatively short. It's fun to work in Python because it allows you to think about the problem rather than focusing on the syntax.

Features of Python Programming

1. A simple language which is easier to learn:

    Python has a very simple and elegant syntax. It's much easier to read and write Python programs compared to other languages like: C++, Java, C#. Python makes programming fun and allows you to focus on the solution rather than syntax.

    If you are a newbie, it's a great choice to start your journey with Python.

2. Free and open-source:

    You can freely use and distribute Python, even for commercial use. Not only can you use and distribute softwares written in it, you can even make changes to the Python's source code.

    Python has a large community constantly improving it in each iteration.

3. Portability:

    You can move Python programs from one platform to another, and run it without any changes. It runs seamlessly on almost all platforms including Windows, Mac OS X and Linux.

4. Extensible and Embeddable:

    Suppose an application requires high performance. You can easily combine pieces of C/C++ or other languages with Python code.

    This will give your application high performance as well as scripting capabilities which other languages may not provide out of the box.

5. A high-level, interpreted language:

    Unlike C/C++, you don't have to worry about daunting tasks like memory management, garbage collection and so on.

    Likewise, when you run Python code, it automatically converts your code to the language your computer understands. You don't need to worry about any lower-level operations.

6. Large standard libraries to solve common tasks:

    Python has a number of standard libraries which makes life of a programmer much easier since you don't have to write all the code yourself. For example: Need to connect MySQL database on a Web server? You can use MySQLdb library using `import MySQLdb`.

    Standard libraries in Python are well tested and used by hundreds of people. So you can be sure that it won't break your application.

7. Object-oriented:

    Everything in Python is an object. Object oriented programming (OOP) helps you solve a complex problem intuitively.

    With OOP, you are able to divide these complex problems into smaller sets by creating objects.

Applications of Python

Web Applications

You can create scalable Web Apps using frameworks and CMS (Content Management System) that are built on Python. Some of the popular platforms for creating Web Apps are: Django, Flask, Pyramid, Plone, Django CMS.

Sites like Mozilla, Reddit, Instagram and PBS are written in Python.

Scientific and Numeric Computing

There are numerous libraries available in Python for scientific and numeric computing. There are libraries like: SciPy and NumPy that are used in general purpose computing. And, there are specific libraries like: EarthPy for earth science, AstroPy for Astronomy and so on.

Also, the language is heavily used in machine learning, data mining and deep learning.

Creating Software Prototypes

Python is slow compared to compiled languages like C++ and Java. It might not be a good choice if resources are limited and efficiency is a must.

However, Python is a great language for creating prototypes. For example: You can use Pygame (library for creating games) to create your game's prototype first. If you like the prototype, you can use language like C++ to create the actual game.

Good Language to Teach Programming

Python is used by many companies to teach programming to kids and newbies.

It is a good language with a lot of features and capabilities. Yet, it's one of the easiest language to learn because of its simple easy-to-use syntax.

Reasons to Choose Python as First Language

Simple Elegant Syntax

Programming in Python is fun. It's easier to understand and write Python code. **Why?** The syntax feels natural. Take this source code for an example:

```
1. a = 2

2. b = 3

3. sum = a + b

print(sum)
```

Even if you have never programmed before, you can easily guess that this program adds two numbers and prints it.

Not Overly Strict

You don't need to define the type of a variable in Python. Also, it's not necessary to add semicolon at the end of the statement.

Python enforces you to follow good practices (like proper indentation). These small things can make learning much easier for beginners.

Expressiveness of the Language

Python allows you to write programs having greater functionality with fewer lines of code. Here's a link to the source code of Tic-tac-toe game with a graphical interface and a smart computer opponent in less than 500 lines of code. This is just an example.

References

- Benefits-of-java-over-other-programming-languages: invensis.net, Retrieved 29 May 2020
- Python-programming: programiz.com, Retrieved 16 March 2020
- Applications-of-c-c-plus-plus-in-the-real-world: invensis.net, Retrieved 20 April 2020
- Variables-scope-details: studytonight.com, Retrieved 19 April 2020
- Benefits-c-language-programming-languages: geeksforgeeks.org, Retrieved 22 May 2020
- What-are-advantages-and-disadvantages: thecrazyprogrammer.com, Retrieved 10 June 2020

Permissions

All chapters in this book are published with permission under the Creative Commons Attribution Share Alike License or equivalent. Every chapter published in this book has been scrutinized by our experts. Their significance has been extensively debated. The topics covered herein carry significant information for a comprehensive understanding. They may even be implemented as practical applications or may be referred to as a beginning point for further studies.

We would like to thank the editorial team for lending their expertise to make the book truly unique. They have played a crucial role in the development of this book. Without their invaluable contributions this book wouldn't have been possible. They have made vital efforts to compile up to date information on the varied aspects of this subject to make this book a valuable addition to the collection of many professionals and students.

This book was conceptualized with the vision of imparting up-to-date and integrated information in this field. To ensure the same, a matchless editorial board was set up. Every individual on the board went through rigorous rounds of assessment to prove their worth. After which they invested a large part of their time researching and compiling the most relevant data for our readers.

The editorial board has been involved in producing this book since its inception. They have spent rigorous hours researching and exploring the diverse topics which have resulted in the successful publishing of this book. They have passed on their knowledge of decades through this book. To expedite this challenging task, the publisher supported the team at every step. A small team of assistant editors was also appointed to further simplify the editing procedure and attain best results for the readers.

Apart from the editorial board, the designing team has also invested a significant amount of their time in understanding the subject and creating the most relevant covers. They scrutinized every image to scout for the most suitable representation of the subject and create an appropriate cover for the book.

The publishing team has been an ardent support to the editorial, designing and production team. Their endless efforts to recruit the best for this project, has resulted in the accomplishment of this book. They are a veteran in the field of academics and their pool of knowledge is as vast as their experience in printing. Their expertise and guidance has proved useful at every step. Their uncompromising quality standards have made this book an exceptional effort. Their encouragement from time to time has been an inspiration for everyone.

The publisher and the editorial board hope that this book will prove to be a valuable piece of knowledge for students, practitioners and scholars across the globe.

Index

Printed in the USA
CPSIA information can be obtained
at www.ICGtesting.com
JSHW051417221024
72173JS00006B/1373